Cold War Asia

This innovative, interdisciplinary, and international collection of essays offers fresh perspectives on the history of global diplomacy. Experts in history, international relations, art history, and performance art have come together to examine a series of visual sources relating to Asia's role in global diplomacy during the Cold War. They explore how leaders, including Indonesia's Sukarno, the Philippines' Imelda Marcos, and Thailand's King Bhumibol, exploited the symbolic value of diplomacy to emphasise their agency in relationships with Great Powers. These case studies demonstrate the significance of Asian diplomacy in understanding the Cold War, shifting away from the use of 'war' as the dominant criterion for analysis of the region. *Cold War Asia* sheds critical light onto how culture shapes international relations, widening the lens of analysis to embed the role of gender, religion, and ethnicity, as well as the material world, into our understanding of diplomacy.

MATTHEW PHILLIPS is a Research Analyst at the Foriegn Commonwealth and Development Office (FCDO) and a Research Associate at the School of Oriental and African Studies (SOAS).

NAOKO SHIMAZU is a global historian of Asia and Professor at Tokyo College, International Institute for Advanced Study, University of Tokyo.

Cold War Asia

A Visual History of Global Diplomacy

Edited by

Matthew Phillips

*Research Analyst at the Foreign Commonwealth and Development Office (FCDO)
and Research Associate at the School of Oriental and African Studies (SOAS)*

Naoko Shimazu

Tokyo College, International Institute for Advanced Study, University of Tokyo

CAMBRIDGE
UNIVERSITY PRESS

Shaftesbury Road, Cambridge CB2 8EA, United Kingdom

One Liberty Plaza, 20th Floor, New York, NY 10006, USA

477 Williamstown Road, Port Melbourne, VIC 3207, Australia

314–321, 3rd Floor, Plot 3, Splendor Forum, Jasola District Centre,
New Delhi – 110025, India

103 Penang Road, #05-06/07, Visioncrest Commercial, Singapore 238467

Cambridge University Press is part of Cambridge University Press & Assessment,
a department of the University of Cambridge.

We share the University's mission to contribute to society through the pursuit of
education, learning and research at the highest international levels of excellence.

www.cambridge.org
Information on this title: www.cambridge.org/9781009379618

DOI: 10.1017/9781009379649

First published 2024

A catalogue record for this publication is available from the British Library.

Library of Congress Cataloging-in-Publication Data
Names: Phillips, Matthew (Historian), editor. | Shimazu, Naoko, 1964- editor.
Title: Cold War Asia : a visual history of global diplomacy / edited by Matthew
    Phillips, Foreign, Commonwealth and Development Office, UK, Naoko
    Shimazu, Tokyo College, International Institute for Advanced Study, University
    of Tokyo.
Description: Cambridge ; New York, NY : Cambridge University Press, 2024. |
    Includes bibliographical references and index.
Identifiers: LCCN 2024015827 (print) | LCCN 2024015828 (ebook) | ISBN
    9781009379618 (hardback) | ISBN 9781009379601 (paperback) | ISBN
    9781009379649 (epub)
Subjects: LCSH: Cold War. | Asia–Foreign relations–1945-
Classification: LCC DS33.3 .C555 2024 (print) | LCC DS33.3 (ebook) | DDC
    909.82/5–dc23/eng/20240606
LC record available at https://lccn.loc.gov/2024015827
LC ebook record available at https://lccn.loc.gov/2024015828

ISBN 978-1-009-37961-8 Hardback

Contents

Illustrations

Contributors

DEJAN DJOKIĆ is Professor of History at the National University of Ireland, Maynooth. He has previously been Professor of Modern and Contemporary History at Goldsmiths, University of London, and is, since 2020, Guest Professor in South-East European History at Humboldt University of Berlin. Djokić's publications include *Beyond the Curtain: Britain, Labour Party and the Left in Cold War Europe* (special issue of *European History Quarterly*, 36:3, 2006, guest-editor and contributor), *Elusive Compromise: A History of Interwar Yugoslavia* (2007), *Pašić and Trumbić: The Kingdom of Serbs, Croats and Slovenes* (2010), and *A Concise History of Serbia* (2023). His current project, 'Tito's Last Soldiers', has been funded by the British Academy and the Leverhulme Trust.

PATRICK FLORES is Professor of Art Studies at the Department of Art Studies at the University of the Philippines and Deputy Director of National Gallery Singapore. He is the Director of the Philippine Contemporary Art Network. He was a Visiting Fellow at the National Gallery of Art in Washington, DC, in 1999. Among his publications are *Painting History: Revisions in Philippine Colonial Art* (1999), *Past Peripheral: Curation in Southeast Asia* (2008), *Art after War: 1948–1969* (2015), and *Raymundo Albano: Texts* (2017). He was a Guest Scholar of the Getty Research Institute in Los Angeles in 2014. He was the Artistic Director of Singapore Biennale 2019 and was the Curator of the Taiwan Pavilion for the Venice Biennale in 2022.

CHRISTIAN GOESCHEL is a Professor in Modern European History at the University of Manchester. He has taught at Birkbeck College, University of London, and the Australian National University and has been a Fernand Braudel Senior Fellow at the European University Institute in Florence and a JSPS Invitational Fellow at the Graduate Faculty of Law, Kyoto University. Among his publications are *Suicide in Nazi Germany* (2009) and *Mussolini and Hitler: The Forging of the Fascist Alliance* (2018).

DEEPAK NAIR is a senior lecturer in international relations (IR) at Australian National University. He is a scholar of International Relations with substantive interests in the study of diplomacy and international bureaucracy. Nair's research appraises international politics with a micro-political and micro-sociological sensibility, which means an interest in the forms and effects of 'small' phenomena like everyday practices, face-to-face interactions, and emotions in shaping international processes and outcomes. He empirically interrogates the microworld of IR with immersive fieldwork, historical print media analysis, and in-depth interviews, especially in circuitries of ASEAN diplomacy in Southeast Asia. His research has been published in *International Studies Quarterly, European Journal of International Relations, International Studies Review,* and *International Political Sociology,* among other venues.

MATTHEW PHILLIPS is a senior research analyst on Southeast Asia at the UK Foreign, Commonwealth and Development Office (FCDO) and a Research Associate at the Centre of South East Asian Studies, the School of Oriental and African Studies (SOAS). Prior to that he taught modern Asian History at Aberystwyth University. He completed his PhD at SOAS in 2013 on the culture of the Cold War in Thailand. Phillips has published widely on Thai history and politics, including his book *Thailand in the Cold War* (2016). He has also contributed to various media, including the *New York Times.* Previously, he worked as a broadcast journalist for the BBC World Service.

PAUL RAE is Professor of Theatre Studies and Head of the School of Culture and Communication at the University of Melbourne. He is the author of *Theatre & Human Rights* (2009) and *Real Theatre: Essays in Experience* (2019). He is a former senior editor of the journal *Theatre Research International* and has published widely on theatre and performance in the Asia-Pacific region. He is currently writing two books: *Performing Islands* and *Mousetraps: Adventures in Theatrical Capture.*

GERARD SASGES is a historian of modern Vietnam and Associate Professor in the Department of Southeast Asian Studies at the National University of Singapore. His research uses non-Western histories of technology and work to reshape understandings of development under capitalist and socialist regimes. His books have been published in English with the University of Hawaii Press and the NUS Press, and in Vietnamese with the Thai Ha Press and the Ho Chi Minh General Publishing House. His articles have appeared in the *American Historical Review, Journal of Asian Studies, Modern Asian Studies,* and the *Journal of Southeast Asian Studies.* His current research traces flows of water and electricity to write energy-centred accounts of Vietnam's economic, social, political, and environmental transformation since 1975.

NAOKO SHIMAZU is Professor at Tokyo College, University of Tokyo. She was formerly at Yale-NUS College and Asia Research Institute, National University of Singapore. She is working extensively on the cultural history of global diplomacy, including a monograph on 'diplomacy as theatre' focusing on the Bandung Conference of 1955, and publications in *Diplomatica: Journal of Diplomacy and Society*, *Modern Asian Studies*, and *Political Geography*. She is the editor (with Christian Goeschel) of the *Oxford Handbook of Cultural History of Global Diplomacy, c. 1750–2000* (forthcoming 2025). Her other book publications include *The Russian Revolution in Asia: From Baku to Batavia* (co-editor, 2022), *Postcard Impressions from Early 20th Century Singapore* (co-author, 2020), *Japanese Society at War: Death, Memory and the Russo-Japanese War* (2009), and *Japan, Race and Equality: Racial Equality Proposal of 1919* (1998).

JIRAYUDH SINTHUPHAN is the Director of South Asia Research Center and a Lecturer in Communication Arts at Chulalongkorn University. He received his BA in Communication Arts from Chulalongkorn University, and a PhD in Drama and Performance Practice from the University of Exeter. His research interests include creative communications, media practice, communications and transculturalism, media adaptation and translation, South Asian studies, as well as puppet theatre. He is an editor of *Mapping Migration: Culture and Identity in the Indian Diasporas in Southeast Asia and the UK* (2018). He is currently leading a research consortium on 'Social Innovation for Sustainable and Livable ASEAN Cities' at Chulalongkorn University and on 'Extremism in South and Southeast Asia'. He has also taken part in the 'Media Literacy for Social Change' project for the ERASMUS+ University Network and in the 'Mindful Communication Curriculum' for the International Programme for the Development Communication (IPDC) of UNESCO.

TOM WHITE is originally from Yorkshire in the north of England. Between 2015 and 2022 he taught documentary and photojournalism at Yale-NUS College and has previously taught at Columbia University's Graduate School of Journalism and at the International Center of Photography in New York. As a photojournalist, his work has been published and exhibited internationally. White has also worked on a variety of photography-based projects and is interested in all aspects of visual literacy and communication, particularly regarding socially engaged art, journalism, and the intersection of environmental issues, political economy, media, technology, and society. His current research is focused on interactive documentary methods and community resilience.

Acknowledgements

Not unlike many other edited volumes, this volume has been a highly rewarding experimental project, which enabled us to try out an original idea of writing a history of global diplomacy using visual sources as our starting point. For that, 'Cold War Asia' was an obvious choice for the book title, especially in the light of the strong line-up of contributors, many of whose regional expertise rested in Asia, and especially Southeast Asia. Research funding from Yale-NUS College has enabled two workshops of the interdisciplinary team of scholars from Australia, Philippines, Singapore, Thailand, and the United Kingdom to take place at the College in 2017 and 2018. Without these foundational workshops, it would have been much more difficult to achieve the level of quality and the unity of purpose evident in this volume. We would like to express our collective gratitude to Yale-NUS College for the funding that made it all possible. Lucy Rhymer at the Cambridge University Press must be thanked for her firm belief in our project and for making it happen, and we would also like to thank the reviewers who provided particularly thoughtful comments. Special thanks go to Maurizio Peleggi and Priya Jaradi for their invaluable contributions to the workshops. As editors, a big 'thank you' to our contributors for their unstinting belief in this project, which resulted in their inspirational and ground-breaking essays that make up this volume – our collective intellectual journey.

Introduction
Visual Sources and Diplomacy

Matthew Phillips and Naoko Shimazu

At first glance, Fig. I.1 reveals a moment of spontaneity. Inconsequential fun shared among three leaders of newly independent nations: Burma (modern-day Myanmar), India, and Egypt. Yet elements of the scene are staged. All three are wearing the same iteration of Burmese national dress, and Burmese Prime Minister U Nu stands in the middle with a container of what looks like water. He seems poised to throw the contents into Egyptian Prime Minister Gamal Abdel Nasser's face as Indian Prime Minister Nehru looks on, but diplomatic convention suggests this won't happen. However relaxed they appear in each other's company, they stand on a stage: performing their moment of fun for their respective audiences. They might radiate friendship, but that does not necessarily make them friends. They might appear to occupy an equal standing, but that does not mean there is not rivalry. While the scene appears spontaneous, its diplomatic character paves the way for multiple readings and narratives. This volume, by taking the image as a starting point, explores how visual sources of diplomacy unlock a multiplicity of perspectives and positions otherwise obscured from the historical record.

The photograph was taken on the way to the Asian-African Conference, held in Bandung, Indonesia, between 18 and 24 April 1955. It thus resides at the intersection of two critical historical developments. The first was the wave of anti-colonial struggle and the politics of decolonisation that followed independence. The second was the emergence of a fresh global schism between the communist and capitalist blocs, associated primarily with the United States and the Soviet Union. Over the decades that followed, events connected to these transformative movements had an inexorable impact on the formation of state-to-state relations across the world, but particularly in Asia.

In the immediate aftermath of the Second World War, the Allied occupation of Japan (dominated by the United States) focused on 'correcting' those responsible for the war and restructuring Japanese society into a democratic post-war nation-state. However, by 1948, US policymakers became convinced that the more pressing concern was rising tension with the Soviet Union, and the potential spread of communism. In China, the communists were gaining the upper hand against the pro-West nationalists, and in Southeast Asia the

Figure I.1 Prime Minister Colonel Gamal Abdel Nasser (Egypt), Prime Minister Jawaharlal Nehru (India), and Prime Minister U Nu (Burma) celebrate the Burmese New Year water festival, Rangoon, 16 April 1955. Pan Asia Photo, Getty Images.

rapid collapse of the Japanese wartime occupation and the return of European imperial powers had ignited a wave of anti-colonial struggle, much drawing heavily from communist ideology but also from nationalist movements that predated the Second World War in Asia. In an effort to halt developments, the United States 'reversed course' on Japan (known as the 'reverse course debate') – focusing instead on establishing the country as a stalwart ally in the new era. In October 1949, the Chinese Communist Party finally took control of the Chinese mainland, forcing the nationalists to flee to Taiwan. Months later, the communist-backed Democratic People's Republic of Korea (DPRK) invaded the south of the Korean Peninsula, provoking the establishment of the Unified Command under the United Nations to effect an international intervention principally led by the United States. In Southeast Asia, meanwhile, the First Indochina War continued to escalate after the Vietnamese communists won support from the newly installed Chinese regime and the Soviet Union. In response to the dramatically shifting situation, the United States opted to shore up the French-backed Vietnamese regime of Emperor Bao Dai and renewed commitments to pay for French military operations. Now focused on containing communism globally, Vietnam became the primary focus of US officials who feared that if Vietnam was 'lost' to the communists, the dominoes (what became known as the 'domino theory') would keep falling throughout the region, and so they opted to violently halt the spread. The First Indochina War was concluded in 1954, but communist insurgencies continued to bubble, and by the end of the decade the Vietnamese communists reopened the conflict with the Republic of Vietnam in the South, ultimately leading to the US military escalation known in the West as the Vietnam War. Incisively, Wallerstein pointed out that talking about a Cold War is Eurocentric. In Europe the United States and the Soviet Union never exchanged gunfire directly, while in Asia the conflict was hot and sustained.[1]

The threat of conflict, whether from insurgency within or intervention from outside, was an ever-present reality in Asia. Yet for political elites in the region, the reports of war that occupied newspaper front pages were also peripheral to the day-to-day domestic challenges of governing, linked primarily to decolonisation and nation building. Most leaders ruled over countries with underdeveloped agrarian economies, poor standards in health and education, and deep ethnic and class differences.[2] Leaders who had emerged in an era of anti-colonial struggle now faced radical choices on matters such as land distribution, economic planning, and national security. They also had to compete with a multitude of distinct national visions proposed by rival elites who each came with their own constituency.[3] War was something to avoid, not court, and it is unsurprising that enormous energy went into achieving that end. Whether such leaders opted to align with one bloc or another, or whether they

---

[1] Immanuel Wallerstein, 'What Cold War in Asia? An Interpretative Essay', in Yangwen Zheng, Hong Liu, and Michael Szonyi (eds.), *The Cold War in Asia: The Battle for Hearts and Minds* (Leiden: Brill, 2010), pp. 15–24.

[2] Tuong Vu and Sean Fear, *The Republic of Vietnam, 1955–1975: Vietnamese Perspectives on Nation Building* (Ithaca, NY: Cornell University Press, 2019), p. 3.

[3] Ibid.

sought to balance their relations with rival centres, their principal struggle was fought through diplomacy.

Diplomacy depends on at least the semblance of a level playing field. As such, it provided a unique opportunity for Asian leaders to assert their agency. In a world of collapsing empires, emerging superpowers, and global ideological struggle, the mere presence of some Asian leaders in diplomatic fora could feel like a provocation, and therefore have a far greater impact than the size of their respective countries' influence would automatically suggest. When Sukarno visited the United States on a diplomatic tour in May 1956, for example, he was invited to talk to a Joint Session of Congress, and his speech was subsequently reprinted on two full pages in the *New York Times*.[4] Simply by attending the Asian-African Conference in Bandung in 1955, Zhou Enlai was able to provoke a fundamental rethink in the American approach to the Cold War globally.[5] As the struggle in Asia intensified and the contours of the so-called Cold War became more defined, the art of hosting a president, secretary of state, business leader, or diplomat carried ever-increasing weight. In such fora, Thailand's King Bhumibol, the Philippines' Imelda Marcos, or Burma's U Nu were not peripheral actors. They took centre stage. While no doubt charismatic, their confidence and authority in diplomatic events was heightened because what they said mattered, and they spoke in the knowledge that their words carried historic significance.

Westad argues that both Soviet and US discourse during the Cold War was underpinned by criticism of European imperialism, and that propagated a deep and genuine belief in their respective visions.[6] Interventions such as that of the United States in Vietnam, he goes on, make sense only when one recognises the genuine feeling of solidarity Americans felt with the people they sought to defend. This belief no doubt furnished decision makers in Washington or Moscow with the confidence necessary to take unilateral action, but it also raised the stakes of diplomatic encounter, where an interaction offered a rare but clear opportunity for Asian leaders to challenge, or even flip, the asymmetrical nature of the exchange. Young nations, unable to wield the threat of war, could use such fora to elicit security guarantees, financial or military aid, or technical support, or simply to assert national sovereignty to bolster their own credentials at home. Given the significance of Asia as a focus of the global conflict, political elites across the region mobilised whole

---

[4] 'Text of President Sukarno's Address before Congress on the Aims of Indonesia', *New York Times*, 18 May 1956, p. 4.

[5] Jason Parker, 'Cold War II: The Eisenhower Administration, the Bandung Conference, and the Reperiodization of the Postwar Era', *Diplomatic History* 30:5 (2006).

[6] Odd Arne Westad, *The Global Cold War: Third World Interventions and the Making of Our Times* (Cambridge: Cambridge University Press, 2005).

bureaucracies, and in some cases populations, into transforming what was perceived outside as a theatre of war into a theatre of diplomacy. This effort has left with it a vast, yet to date largely unexplored visual record that provides the subject matter of this book.

The recent re-emergence of great power competition globally has drawn attention to the importance of understanding Asian perspectives during the Cold War and fuelled a new scholarship that explores how Asian actors managed complex and, at times, contradictory local and international prior-ities.[7] By focusing on diplomatic activity, it is therefore critical to de-emphasise Western-centric interpretations and restore the memory of how Asian leaders shaped the conflict globally. Through a unique focus on diplo-macy, all the chapters in this volume add to this trend. Collectively, they demonstrate how, by harnessing the power and importance of diplomatic exchange, Asian actors were able to actively engage and shape the international system.

Visual Sources and Diplomatic History

The substantive work of diplomatic historians is to get behind the scenes, to better understand the complex tensions, power dynamics, personal rivalries, and geopolitical developments that ultimately determine state-to-state rela-tions. Speeches, communiqués, and joint declarations are routinely presented as pre-prepared moments of resolution within, or disjuncture from, the unfolding of world events. The diplomatic image, meanwhile, tends to be used as shorthand for such moments, evidence that the encounter took place and a means to locate the exchange within a particular series of events. On closer reflection, however, such images provide further insights that are not only connected to but also independent of the textual record. Many of these insights derive from the inherently ambiguous character of the image. As Berger explains in reference to the photograph, the image 'isolates the appearance of a disconnected instant' and must therefore be lent a past and a future by a viewer who is disconnected from the captured instant itself.[8]

---

[7] Notable contributions include Albert Lau, *Southeast Asia and the Cold War* (Abington: Routledge, 2012); Malcolm H. Murfett, *Cold War Southeast Asia* (Singapore: Marshall Cavendish Publications, 2012); Cheng Guan Ang, *Southeast Asia's Cold War: An Interpretative History* (Honolulu: University of Hawai'i Press, 2018); Wen-Qing Ngoei and Anne Foster, 'Re-thinking Region: US-Southeast Asian Relations in the Twentieth Century', *Diplomatic History*, 45:2 (2021), 219–222; Wen-Qing Ngoei, *Arc of Containment: Britain, the United States, and Anti-Communism in Southeast Asia* (Ithaca, NY: Cornell University Press, 2019); and Tuong Vu and Wasana Wonsurawat (eds.), *Dynamics of the Cold War in Asia: Ideology, Identity, and Culture* (New York: Palgrave Macmillan, 2009).

[8] John Berger, *Understanding a Photograph* (London: Penguin Classics, 2013), p. 64.

Practitioners of diplomacy, as well as those who capture and publish diplomatic images, are intimately aware of this ambiguous character, overcoming the potential for subjective readings by denoting a set of prescribed meanings. Think of the ceaseless flow of analogous images that emanate out of the various summits and meetings, in which representatives perform the same benign gestures, handshakes, and smiles to a set of cameras, whose expectant operators pass on the images to expectant editors who select and frame the image to suit their respective narratives. What is often missed is that the photograph has a specific historical and cultural context – that is, as Barthes explains, the image will have been worked on, chosen, composed, constructed, and treated according to aesthetic and ideological norms. It will have been perceived, received, and read by a public that 'consumes it to a traditional stock of signs'.[9] The diplomatic image, in other words, has its own story or stories to tell.

The collection of essays in this book aims to expand the range of source material in the study of global diplomacy by working with visual sources. In recent years others have done something similar. Proponents of the 'aesthetic turn' in international relations studies, for example, assert that images can offer alternative insights and include people and perspectives excluded from existing accounts.[10] They have identified how images encourage or even force us to see what may otherwise be absent from scholarly view, challenging normative approaches and supporting efforts to decolonise our respective interpretations.[11] From the start, however, this study has been guided primarily by methodological rather than theoretical concerns: about *how* we can use visual sources to enrich our understanding of diplomacy. Step one involves choosing an image, broadly defined. Contributors considered not only photographs, but also posters, paintings, sculptures, gifts, souvenirs, as well as representational productions such as documentaries, newsreels, feature films, or theatre productions. Most contributors spent time observing the selected visual source, applying a level of scrutiny and critical engagement that had not necessarily come instinctively. Over a series of workshops, we then established a set of questions to frame the study: What do we see in the image? Who is in the image, and what are they doing? What is the significance of the 'place' in which this diplomatic image is situated? How is the event staged and framed? Does the image fit within a series of images, or does it stand alone?

---

[9] Roland Barthes, *Music Image Text* (London: Fontana Press, 1977), p. 19.
[10] Roland Bleiker, 'The Aesthetic Turn in International Political Theory', *Millennium – Journal of International Studies*, 20 (2001), p. 512. Also, Roland Bleiker, *Aesthetics and World Politics* (New York: Palgrave, 2009).
[11] Sophie Harman pays particular attention to how the visual aids efforts to bring female voices, in particular, to the fore: Sophie Harman, *Seeing Politics: Film, Visual Method, and International Relations* (Montreal: McGill-Queen's University Press, 2019).

Next, contributors conducted a 'deep reading' of the image, akin to Geertz's 'thick description',[12] peeling off layers of interpretation. They began thinking about what might be the surface-level reading – the most basic interpretation, and arguably the most widespread. Then, what about an intermediate level of reading – one that is perhaps more accessible to those who are literate in a common language of culture and politics? Finally, are there deeper embedded symbols that can only be unlocked by those who know their meanings? Are there potentially contested narratives, and what are the reasons for these? Overall, we read the source 'expansively', considering the connective narrative(s) to the diplomatic event and how it relates to the broader account of international diplomacy taking place.

One further guiding principle is the desire to situate global diplomacy in the everyday,[13] locating it within political, but also social and cultural terms of enquiry, and not only in the realm of high politics as has traditionally been the case. On the one hand, visual sources of global diplomacy can reveal the role of the crowd, including women and children, in the creation of a diplomatic scene. On the other, situating global diplomacy in the everyday means that visual records of global diplomatic events are consumed by the people at large.

Authors have learned to acknowledge, and even embrace, the ambiguous nature of the visual source drawn from a range of disciplines, including history, art history, cultural studies, geography, theatre studies, international relations, and photojournalism. As editors, we have not sought to bind contributions under a unified theoretical frame. Instead, by applying their distinct interpretative lens, each author demonstrates how visuals provide an opportunity to bring in individuals who are otherwise missing from the written record.[14] They have also applied their own knowledge and expertise, serving to further internationalise the collection and convey unique insights. As a result, the volume does *not* present an off-the-shelf methodology, but promotes a rich diversity of approaches and interpretations with strong historical contextualisation.

As already discussed, the backdrop to diplomacy in Southeast Asia during the Cold War charged such exchanges with potentially existential implications. For those leaders who sought entrance into the communist or capitalist bloc, journeys to and from Moscow or Washington, Beijing or New York became essential, presenting further challenge to those focused on securing legitimacy

---

[12] Clifford Geertz, 'Thick Description: Toward an Interpretive Theory of Culture', in *The Interpretation of Cultures: Selected Essays by Clifford Geertz* (New York: Basic Books, 1973), pp. 3–30.

[13] For instance, Magnus Marsden, Diana Ibañez-Tirado, and David Henig, 'Everyday Diplomacy: Introduction to the Special Issue', *Cambridge Journal of Anthropology*, 34:2 (2016), 2–22.

[14] William A. Callahan, *Sensible Politics: Visualizing International Relations* (Oxford: Oxford University Press, 2020), p. 1.

at home. Practically, the need to balance the receipt of foreign aid and technical support from international patrons had to be paired with the often-contradictory effort to defend sovereignty and act independently on the world stage. Asian leaders often had to harness imported universal ideologies, while projecting a strong and relevant local identity, invariably drawing from religious and cultural themes to assert their distinctive status. Underpinned domestically by potential insurgencies and fractious elite-level tensions, the fear of military intervention, whether from the United States, the communist bloc, or a historic regional foe, raised the stakes. We therefore situate our study alongside those that have elevated new voices and experiences in Cold War Asia, recognising the diverse raft of actors who shaped the period.[15] By taking the image as our starting point, we seek to re-contextualise diplomatic space as a dynamic site, into which complex and at times competing narratives intertwine and new voices emerge.

Locating Diplomacy

During the colonial period, diplomacy in Asia was linked inexorably to legitimising the supremacy of Europe in the minds of colonial regimes. As such, diplomatic encounters took place within a system of thought and practice dominated by the effort of Europeans to 'take charge' of the world.[16] In practice, this led to encounters that emphasised Europe as the origin of a 'standard of civilisation', realised through the juxtaposition of European material culture, etiquette, and technology to those of 'the Orient', in turn cast either as 'barbarian' or merely aspirant to European norms.[17] The collapse of the European empires from the end of the Second World War transformed the geopolitical context, but diplomacy in the era that followed remained tied to discourses of civilisation.

---

[15] In addition to texts already mentioned, others that have been critical in expanding the range of actors who participated in the Cold War include Tony Day and Maya H. T. Liem (eds.), *Cultures at War: The Cold War and Cultural Expression in Southeast Asia* (Ithaca, NY: Cornell University Press, Southeast Asia Program Publications, 2010); Tuong Vu and Sean Fear (eds.), *The Republic of Vietnam, 1955–1975: Vietnamese Perspectives on Nation Building* (Ithaca, NY: Cornell University, Southeast Asia Program Publications, 2019); Jeremy E. Taylor and Lanjun Xu (eds.), *Chineseness and the Cold War: Contested Cultures and Diaspora in Southeast Asia and Hong Kong* (Abingdon: Routledge, 2022); Eugene Ford, *Cold War Monks: Buddhism and America's Secret Strategy in Southeast Asia* (New Haven, CT: Yale University Press, 2017); Taomo Zhou, *Migration in the Time of Revolution: China, Indonesia, and the Cold War* (Ithaca, NY: Cornell University Press, 2019); and Matthew Phillips, *Thailand in the Cold War* (Abingdon: Routledge, 2016).

[16] John Agnew, *Geopolitics: Revisioning World Politics* (London: Routledge, 1998), p. 8.

[17] Andrew Linklater, 'The "Standard of Civilisation" in World Politics', *Social Character, Historical Process*, 5:2 (2016).

Across the region, therefore, officials responsible for hosting VIPs from abroad focused on sites of diplomatic exchange that gave the right message, often having to overcome or obscure the material indicators of a developmental lag with the West. Motorcades depended on good roads; formal dinners required an appropriate cuisine; anthems demanded trained musicians; and summits needed hotels, plush foyers, and suitable meeting rooms. During the early 1950s, the Thai capital Bangkok hosted a rapid expansion of diplomatic activity, after key United Nations agencies, and later the Southeast Asia Treaty Organization (SEATO), were based in the city. As a result, Thai bureaucrats, trained to worry deeply about conforming to 'universal' (*Sakon*), 'civilised' (*Siwili*), or 'modern' (*Than samai*) standards of hospitality, put enormous energy into the construction of a 'five-star' hotel to cope with the influx.[18] Similarly, in anticipation of the Bandung Conference, the Local Committee of the conference made sure the West Javanese city was renovated to send out the right messages to foreign delegates, local populations, and the global media.[19] In this context, colonial-era architecture may have provided spectacular backdrops, but they also showcased contradiction in an era of independence. Alternatively, once maligned sites of traditional power such as temples or palaces were reconfigured into post-colonial sources of national pride and identity. Overall, post-colonial politics imbued national spaces with new meanings that contested the European-derived order, and could be activated through diplomatic exchange.

As a site of vanguard post-colonial politics, scripted diplomatic activities in Southeast Asia raised questions about existing hierarchies and drew attention to the status of guests from the 'old' world. In Chapter 5, Christian Goeschel reflects on the anxieties of the West German leader President Lübke, who in 1963 opted to visit Indonesia on his tour of the region, but remained tied to an outdated, asymmetrical view of the encounter. By focusing on a particularly remarkable image, of the president paying respect at the Kalibata Heroes Cemetery just outside Jakarta, Goeschel raises a host of questions about the power dynamics on display. The heat of the sun, beating down onto a black-clad, white-skinned leader, becomes an active part of the scene, as does the unremarkable wall he stands in front of. Adding to the complexity, Goeschel points out how the West Germans had a particular sensitivity about the Nazi past in their post-war diplomacy, but one in which the Indonesians had little or no interest, adding another element of asymmetricality to our interpretation of

---

[18] Matthew Phillips, 'Making a "Free World" City: Urban Space and Social Order in Cold War Bangkok', in Richard Brook, Martin Dodge, and Jonathan Hogg (eds.), *Cold War Cities: Politics, Culture and Atomic Urbanism, 1945–1965* (London: Routledge, 2020), pp. 281–300.

[19] Naoko Shimazu, 'Diplomacy as Theatre: Staging the Bandung Conference of 1955', *Modern Asian Studies,* 48:1 (January 2014), 238–239.

the image. Through Goeschel's sensitive eye, a seemingly unremarkable stock image of a state visit begins to produce discomfort and ambivalence, revealing a web of underlying emotions about West Germany's position vis-à-vis Indonesia.

In most cases, capital cities and other urban centres remained ubiquitous, but diplomatic activity was also forced to attend to new locations of international importance. As local governments and global powers struggled to win the hearts and minds of Southeast Asian populations, rural areas were a particular priority. The rice field loomed large as a potential site of insurgency, and thus became a charged ideological space, within which new technologies, social practices, or political actions could help integrate whole communities into a respective vision for the future. In Chapter 2, Patrick Flores demonstrates how the Filipina first lady, Imelda Marcos, skilfully embodied historical and contemporary themes to assert herself in the diplomatic space. His image, of a pastoral scene, shows Imelda inspecting rice field in Los Banos with President Lyndon Johnson and Lady Bird Johnson. The site was home of the International Rice Research Institute, where 'miracle rice' had been cultivated. Portrayed as a key tool in the struggle to mollify the villages of Southeast Asia, the field thus formed a key part of the American presidential visit to the Philippines in 1966.

At first sight, we are struck by the incongruity of the composition, centred on the elegantly clad Imelda with the distinguished presidential party. Yet the president looks visibly flustered with heat and humidity, standing on an elevated plank. Under Flores' richly poetic deep reading of the image, he juxtaposes multiple narratives. Specifically, he demonstrates how Imelda was able to present a coherent overarching narrative associated to being the Philippine First Lady, exploiting American anxieties about race and gender relations at home to carve out a form of 'liberal recognition' for her distinctive aesthetic and character. Charming and disarming leaders abroad, Imelda and her husband also cultivated a domestic image that evoked the Filipino cosmogonic legend that tells the story of the first woman and first man to walk on earth. In other words, Flores shows that the many public images of Imelda in circulation in the Cold War years is a composite narrative site of its own. At the risk of stating the obvious, her beauty was a sine qua non constituent of her charismatic power, which she used adroitly in politics and the 'not quite official' sites of 'surrogate' diplomacy.

Narrating Diplomacy

At the heart of the diplomatic encounter lies the relationship between states, leaders, and people. Images can be successfully used to capture such dynamics, particularly the non-verbal forms of communication not easily grasped in textual sources. In the cauldron of the Cold War, nations invariably framed their sense of relationship through the prism of distinct ideological positions. State-to-state ties within the communist, free, or non-aligned worlds were generally expressed through the language of friendship or shared brotherly bonds. Yet this did not mean they did not mask more problematic associations. In all diplomatic encounters, closeness can mean historic enmity, competition, and contestation – regardless of the smiles, toasts, and gift-giving. Distance, on the other hand, can be overcome through attention to key details and carefully crafted performances. One persistent observation, therefore, is how the ambiguity of diplomatic images can be used to indicate a specific narrative interpretation, transplanting new, unspoken meanings, often laced with ideological significance, onto otherwise highly formalised exchanges.[20] In Chapter 1, on diplomatic encounters between Tito and Sukarno, key figures in the non-aligned movement, Dejan Djokić shows how both used the meetings to successfully boost their respective charismatic status. Despite representing nations on opposite sides of the world, images of the two betray a genuine sense of commonality and mutual respect. Some reveal such a symmetrical synchronicity that we observe a near 'mimicry' of dress and gesture between them. Djokić concludes that these bonds of comradeship helped activate a sense of common purpose, furnishing the non-aligned movement with character and appeal. In so doing, he demonstrates how the performative value of this friendship between state officials can be interpreted as a barometer for the health of the diplomatic relationship between those states.[21]

In Chapter 8, Gerard Sasges explores how a unique set of actors emerged as diplomats in his study of Soyuz 37, the 1980 Soviet mission to space that doubled as an example of Soviet friendship with Vietnam – five years out from having won the Second Indochina War. For his images, Sasges explores a panel of photographs intended for popular dissemination in Vietnam, each of which illustrates a distinct set of messages. Phạm Tuân was the first Asian man in space, and as a citizen of a developing nation, his trip demonstrated a degree of dependency on Soviet engineers and officials, contributing to the celebration of Soviet technological prowess. At the same time, the images of Phạm Tuân evoke Vietnamese envoys who, in previous centuries, were glorified at home in view of their forthcoming journeys to pay tribute to China. Just as they were bestowed with high ranks and provided with lavish gifts, so Phạm Tuân was elevated to a model citizen and national hero before travelling into

---

[20] Mieke Bal notes the importance of reflexivity in the interpretation of images, emphasising how the act of interpretating images itself requires a necessary process of narrativisation, whereby the space between the image and interpretation is 'filled in'. Mieke Bal, *Double Exposure: The Subject of Cultural Analysis* (New York: Routledge, 1996), pp. 1–12.

[21] Christian Goeschel, *Hitler and Mussolini: The Forging of the Fascist Alliance* (New Haven, CT: Yale University Press, 2018).

space – a journey itself imbued with transformative power. In all, the images reveal 'poetically' the Soviet use of soft power to foster the sense of a socialist future for the Vietnamese people, through a familiar trope of Confucian social dynamics. Such examples identify how diplomatic images tend to serve as vehicles for several narratives, ones that align with the well-established flow of international events, but also carry special and precise meanings for local audiences.

Chapter 6, by Naoko Shimazu, challenges the conventional understanding of a 'diplomatic image' by de-centring the gaze away from state leaders, and instead situating it in the everyday. Her choice of photograph is of the local Chinese women in Bandung during the Asian-African Conference of 1955 (commonly known as the Bandung Conference), who break out into rapturous smiles as they excitedly point at some leader (most likely the Chinese premier Zhou Enlai). She finds this image 'charismatic' because it is imbued with powerful emotions, giving centre-stage to these local women who would otherwise be marginalised figures in the history of the conference, as well as in post-war Indonesian history. Shimazu uses the photo as a starting point to explore how the photographer, Lisa Larson, propels these neglected subjects into a new set of narratives onto the pages of *LIFE* magazine. In this way, these women play an integral role as audience in the theatre of Asian-African diplomacy unfolding in front of their eyes on the streets of Bandung, just as much as their demonstrable 'Chineseness' reminds us of the history of the overseas Chinese communities in Indonesia and elsewhere in Southeast Asia. Above all, her essay is a reflection on how women can have greater agency in diplomacy, as both protagonists and image-makers, using visual representations.

In Chapter 4, on King Bhumibol and Queen Sirikit's 1960 trip to Burma, Matthew Phillips explores how a Thai public relations film presented the monarch as a superior world conqueror in the Buddhist tradition. By drawing subtle associations between images from the tour and well-known cosmological tropes, the film suggests the king's ability to subdue the leadership of a weaker regional rival. His chapter reads like a scroll painting unfolding with the journey, replete with Buddhist symbolisms, powerfully resonant to those who appreciate their significance. Phillips' unpeeling of the complex layers awakens our senses to the possibilities of visual symbols, ranging from the choice of colours to material culture, and the overall choreography. At the same time, his skilful rendering through a 'thick description' reading of the film reminds us of how ambiguous visual symbols can be, as the astonishing insights that unravel before our eyes are only made visible and meaningful to those in the know and, in this case, are only possible through an interlocutor like himself. Like Imelda Marcos, Queen Sirikit plays a central role, transforming herself into a globally recognisable 'First Lady' while simultaneously evoking the mythical Gem Queen of Buddhism. Once again, his chapter underlines the importance of visual sources in enabling the visibility of women in diplomacy. In all, Phillips' reading demonstrates a superabundance of rich visual material, yet to be tapped into, that will inevitably deepen our understanding of the symbolic in Buddhist diplomacy.

Afterlife of Images

While many images in this volume restore lost moments or perspectives, others caught the attention of the authors due to their assumed ubiquity. In Chapter 3, for example, Jirayudh Sinthupan explores a famous image, also of Queen Sirikit and King Bhumibol, meeting with Elvis Presley, popularly known as the 'King' (of rock and roll), in Hollywood's Paramount Studios. The couple met Elvis there in 1960 during their world tour, when he was filming the movie *G.I. Blues*. Sinthupan's account offers a rare insight into the tour, through his access to royal sources and insights. But he also notes how the image, by Nat Dallinger, has grown in importance within Thailand and is now widely displayed across the kingdom. In fact, the meeting was far from unique. As part of Hollywood's own cultural diplomacy, Elvis met many prominent figures, including the Danish and Nepalese royal families, while on set. Moreover, at the time of the meeting, domestic audiences in Thailand were unsure how to respond to the meeting. In 1960, Elvis remained morally ambiguous in Thailand, associated with a rebellious youth culture rather than a new world aristocracy. All this would change over the following decade, as Thailand became more integrated into the American-centred world and Elvis grew in the Thai public consciousness. Over time, this appealing photograph of the 'two Kings' acquired new meanings and significance, giving it a successful afterlife as visual documentation and artefact.

Similarly, in his study of the signing of the Association for Southeast Asian Nations (ASEAN) declaration in 1967, Deepak Nair in Chapter 9 shows how a relatively mundane photograph of the moment has since become emblematic of the ASEAN story.[22] Nair traces the process by which the non-descript 1967 photograph became the blueprint for the 'ASEAN mural' – a specially commissioned painting of the image that formed the central plank of the fiftieth anniversary event of ASEAN in 2017. Unveiled with great fanfare as leaders gathered in Manila, the painting was later transferred to the ASEAN Secretariat in Jakarta, where it remains today. What becomes clear is that the original black and white photograph gains potency as the preferred representation of the moment, not so much because it is a great image, but as a visual mnemonic – a site of multiple narratives. The image 'bided its time', Nair

---

[22] ASEAN currently has ten member states: Brunei, Cambodia, Indonesia, Laos, Malaysia, Myanmar, Philippines, Singapore, Thailand, and Vietnam. The secretariat is in Jakarta.

explains, 'waiting for ASEAN as a body to consolidate during the Cold War', before re-emerging as the stock image of ASEAN in the era of social media. Notwithstanding the irony of men in grey suits 'giving birth', the artist Peter Paul Blanco undertook a whole year of research into the 1967 photograph, only for his painting to acquire a distinct 'aura' of authenticity as *the* legitimate depiction of that founding moment.

In Chapter 7, Paul Rae directs our attention to an unlikely diplomatic image, a 'Madam Tussauds of sorts' waxwork depiction of the Japanese surrender to British officials in Singapore in 1945. In 1974, the said waxwork was displayed in the City Hall Chambers in Singapore, and was later transferred to Fort Siloso on Sentosa Island where it currently sits in the Surrender Chambers. As a theatre studies specialist and a performance artist, Rae sees a performative potential in the waxwork and extrapolates on several hidden stories that its making entailed. By focusing on the materiality of wax, Rae's story questions the surrender as having a more ambivalent afterlife, ex post facto, as embodied in the waxwork itself. His historical research further traces the contemporary diplomatic concerns in Singapore-Japan relations in the mid-1970s, when Japan had become Singapore's most important trading partner. Intriguingly, the waxwork was supposedly created as a tourist attraction to cater to increased Japanese visitors to Singapore, though part of the intention was possibly to remind the Japanese of their shameful past. Exploring how the waxwork was researched, crafted, and ultimately displayed in different ways over time, Rae reminds us that the meaning of images is in constant flux. While a representation of the surrender meant one thing in 1945, it came to mean quite another once Singapore was an independent state. Placing the material culture frontstage invites us to explore alternative scenarios, sparking curiosity into the potential insights non-textual sources can help illuminate.

We end our volume with Chapter 10, by the photojournalist Tom White, whose insights have been invaluable to our collective intellectual endeavour. White's astute observations as a practitioner provide an account into how images are made and used – exposing the fascinating goings-on 'behind the scenes' – in Goffman's sense of 'front stage' and 'back stage'. White does this through three stories that each illustrate the behind-the-scenes workings of diplomatic reporting as a photojournalist on the diplomatic media circuit, and in so doing, he unpicks the meticulous staging and choreographing involved in making famous pictures. He finishes with what became one of the most iconic Cold War encounters between the United States and the USSR, Erwin Elliot's famous photograph of Nixon and Khrushchev at the American Exhibition in Moscow in 1959. By tracing contact sheets, White explores how the picture was selected, revealing in the process how the image was constructed to retell a distorted but nevertheless powerful 'reality'.

Separately, White explores the media circus surrounding the much-hyped summit between former President Donald Trump and North Korean Chairman Kim Jong-Un in Singapore in 2018, a staged performance of the most outlandish kind – but one that, told from the perspective of a journalist chasing for an image from behind the scenes, afforded him enticing insights into how the event was staged. The cover image of the volume of the Trump and Kim impersonators is one such striking photograph taken by White on the summit circuit. The funeral of Lee Kwan Yew (the founding father of Singapore) in 2015, on the other hand, was an event of a different order. White's photo of the Padang (the large open green space in the Central Business District) where Singaporeans queued, drenched in a tropical downpour to pay their final respects, struck an unexpected chord with *New York Times* editors, capturing the mood of the occasion in a way unforeseen by the photographer himself. Finally, White takes us behind the lens to his experience of capturing two images of Aung San Suu Kyi, one of which was not selected for publication by any editor, but which for him is particularly poignant, considering later events. Overall, White's photojournalistic experiences reveal insights into not only how diplomatic moments are staged, but how such stages might be subverted or re-imagined at any moment. White's chapter is about the reflections of a practitioner on the afterlife of the diplomatic moments that he was partly responsible for creating.

Conclusion

By embracing both the ambiguous nature of images along with their respective subjectivities, the contributors to this book have not sought to provide a definitive take on a given moment or diplomatic encounter. Rather, they have expanded the view. In this regard, context remains key. While the styles and approaches of the individual contributors are all unique, each contribution is equally concerned with matters of substantiation, although not always in the same way. At times it has meant returning to well-perused national collections with new eyes, or efforts to seek out new materials from private collections or cultural organisations. At others it has meant talking with family or revisiting galleries or museums with a fresh perspective. By opening such terrains, our volume aims to enliven the study of diplomacy, to welcome new scholars into the field, and to shed new light onto historical moments in all their full dramatic complexity.

Even this cursory introduction to the chapters has given rise to several prominent thematic insights that demonstrate how visual sources enrich the field. For one, visual sources contribute to a more sophisticated understanding of the power dynamics in play during diplomacy events. Goeschel's discussion of Lübke in Indonesia, like Flores' image of Imelda serenely observing the rice fields alongside a sweltering Johnson, reminds us that power is not always where the diplomatic record might suggest. On the other hand, the near-comical symmetricality evident in the dress and gesture of Tito and Sukarno betray a charismatic competition between autocratic leaders, while Nair's discussion of the painting symbolising the birth of ASEAN emphasises the, albeit contrived, symmetricality of relations within ASEAN. The waxwork depicting the Japanese surrender in 1945 in Rae's chapter appears at least in part to be about Singapore retaining some power over an ascendent Japan in the bilateral relationship. Sasges' discussion of the Vietnamese cosmonaut situates asymmetrical power dynamics vis-à-vis the Soviet Union, while Phillips' chapter shows how the Thais used Buddhist cosmological symbolism to affect the narrative of the Thai conquest over a traditional regional rival, Burma.

The images in this volume also expose the complex racial politics that dominated diplomatic encounters at the time. Asian leaders often were able to actively exploit the racial politics to further assert their position, particularly when engaging with white Western representatives. At other times, the reference to race was more subtle. Shimazu's essay, focusing on the image of ethnic Chinese women at the Bandung conference and taken by a white American female photographer, identifies how gender links photographer and subject. Yet this moment of intersection is transient and contingent. The female photographer's background links her directly to the influential *LIFE* magazine, while her image alludes to a community with a rich and complex back-story from across a vast social, political – and critically racial – divide. Elsewhere, the images in this volume also reveal, or allude to, the at times fraught nature of intra-regional racial dynamics, or indeed the effort to overcome or flatten differences or inherited hierarchies. Perhaps most notable here is the revelation in Nair's chapter that the artist who portrayed ASEAN's five founding fathers actively chose to give all those depicted the same tone of skin colour, empha-sising racial unity as a way to signpost the common political agenda. By situating diplomatic settings in Asia, Asian diplomatic actors are operating in their more familiar milieu. Instead, it is the 'foreignness' of the non-Asian actors that stands out through the simple visible cue of race.

Another pertinent theme to have emerged is the central importance of visual sources in understanding the role and impact of gender in diplomacy, particu-larly as it pertains to the role of women. Shimazu's chapter highlights the place of women both as the subject of photography and as the image-creator. Flores', Phillips', and Sinthupan's chapters would not have the same impact without visual evidence of the charismatic women leaders they portray. Elsewhere, contributors have drawn attention to the role played by masculinity in diplo-macy. King Bhumibol, Tito, Sukarno, and Elvis Presley in different ways display their masculinity through the images. Even the non-charismatic painting of the birth of ASEAN retells a foundation myth that co-opts gender in its rendition of men giving birth. Images thus reveal the subtext of gender power dynamics that cannot be expressed explicitly in words, though are silently visible. More broadly, there is no denying that visual sources do give more agency to women in diplomacy, far more than traditional textual sources.

Another fascinating outcome is that images reveal emotions effortlessly, and critically, without the beholder having to understand the social, cultural, or political context of the situation. Examples of how an outburst of emotions can encapsulate the mood of the diplomatic moment can be found in the delightful expressions of Queen Sirikit in meeting Elvis Presley, the confidence exuded by the two dictators pictured in Djokić's chapter, or the seething emotions under the midday sun in the image in Goeschel's chapter. Even in the stillness that dominates Goeschel's photograph of the West German president, there is evident oppressiveness from the heat and discomfort. Finally, images draw greater attention to the enduring role played by symbols and symbolism in diplomacy, features that have not tended to be embraced in scholarly accounts of modern and contemporary diplomacy. This is less true of medieval and early modern historians, who have been better attuned to the importance of cultural symbols in their work on diplomacy and are generally more used to fully exploiting the value of images in their analysis.

Overall, the chapters in this volume challenge scholars of diplomacy to consider more seriously the use of visual sources because they enable us to appreciate the myriad layers of meaning, new voices, and fresh perspectives that may be better understood visually. In all, our understanding of global diplomacy will be richer for it. The volume forms part of the burgeoning field of the cultural history of global diplomacy. In so doing, we hope it encourages further interdisciplinary collaborations and spurs new creative endeavours.[23]

---

[23] Some of the contributors to this volume are involved in the *Oxford Handbook on the Cultural History of Global Diplomacy, c1750 to present (Oxford: Oxford University Press, forthcoming)*, edited by Christian Goeschel and Naoko Shimazu.

1   Reframing Non-alignment
Tito, Sukarno and the 1961 Belgrade Conference

Dejan Djokić

The Image

In this chapter, I use the black and white photograph shown in Fig. 1.1 as a departure point for analysis.[1] Historians have long ago moved beyond approaching written documents as mere sources of facts, but do we treat photographs with the same degree of scrutiny and imagination? Photographs, more so than texts, have the capacity to inspire confidence that what is presented before us is what had actually happened, even though the manipulation of, and through, images is perhaps as old as image production itself. Manipulated or not, photographs can often provide additional insights and new meanings to textual sources. When we also consider similarities between the methods of a photographer and a historian – both, for example, choose angle, focus and frame – then it might be argued that photographs represent potentially a highly rewarding, though perhaps not fully exploited, source material for the historian.[2]

Taken by a photographer employed by TANJUG, the official news agency of socialist Yugoslavia, the photograph shows presidents Sukarno of Indonesia and Josip Broz Tito of Yugoslavia driven in an open-roofed car through central Belgrade in late August 1961. The car is driving past the Yugoslav parliament building, the venue of the first summit of what would become the Non-aligned Movement (NAM). The Belgrade Conference, as the event is usually known,

---

[1] The photograph was almost certainly taken on 29 August 1961, when Sukarno arrived in Belgrade. Arhiv Jugoslavije, 837 Kabinet predsednika republike (hereafter AJ, 837 KPR), I-4-a/2, box 201, 'Official Welcome of H.E. Dr Sukarno, President of the Republic of Indonesia, Batajnica airport', [Belgrade], 29 August 1961. I should like to thank Naoko Shimazu, Matthew Phillips and other participants of two 'Diplomatic Images' workshops (Yale-NUS, Singapore, 2017, 2018) for their feedback on earlier drafts; Budimir Lončar, one of the organisers of the 1961 Belgrade Conference and also, as Yugoslavia's last foreign minister, of the Ninth Summit of the Non-Aligned Movement in Belgrade, 1989; Ivana Božović and Marko Radovanović (Arhiv Jugoslavije/Archives of Yugoslavia, Belgrade); Radovan Cukić (Muzej Jugoslavije/ Museum of Yugoslavia, Belgrade); staff of the Politisches Archiv des Auswärtigen Amts/The Political Archive of the Federal Foreign Office, Berlin; and Jonna Rock, who read the final draft.

[2] Ludmilla Jordanova, *The Look of the Past: Visual and Material Evidence in Historical Practice* (Cambridge: Cambridge University Press, 2012), pp. 130–32.

Figure 1.1 'The Belgrade Conference: Citizens of Belgrade Warmly Greet
President of the Republic Josip Broz Tito and President of the Republic of
Indonesia Dr Ahmet [*sic*] Sukarno, outside the Federal People's Assembly'.
Muzej Jugoslavije, Foto-arhiv Josipa Broza Tita (hereafter MJ, Tito's Photo Archive),
Belgrade, 1–5 September 1961, 1961_179_0027.

took place between 1 and 6 September 1961; it opened with speeches by Tito and Sukarno.

The motorcade is secured by uniformed guards on motorcycles and is observed by citizens, standing still in the background. The image allows us to imagine the scene captured by camera – as well as the forthcoming conference that it announces – as a piece of diplomatic theatre, with principal actors, stage, audience, and security personnel all featuring within a single frame.[3] It also invites us to 'peek' through, look beyond the obvious, 'zoom out' and expand the frame, in order to understand and contextualize a seemingly frozen moment in history caught by the unknown Yugoslav photographer.[4]

The photograph serves as a vehicle through which I address performative aspects of non-aligned diplomacy and the importance of the public image projected by non-aligned leaders. My analysis focuses on Tito, and Yugoslavia, but I introduce preliminary points of comparison between Tito and Sukarno, two key figures in the movement – something not done previously, to the best of my knowledge. I also discuss the symbolism of the conference venue, seen in the photograph, and explain the ideological and historical context in which the image was created. The Belgrade Conference took place just days after the erection of the Berlin Wall had begun, a development that prompted a partial mobilization in the United States, which in turn led to the resumption of nuclear testing by the Soviet Union. Humanity was, it seemed, on the brink of a Third World War, as Tito and Yugoslavia hosted African and Asian leaders in Belgrade in a quest for global peace.

The origins of the non-alignment may be traced back to the 1955 Asian-African Conference in Bandung, Indonesia, and a number of subsequent meetings between 'Third World' leaders, including Prime Minister Nehru of India and presidents Gamal Abdel Nasser of the United Arab Republic/Egypt, Kwame Nkrumah of Ghana, Sukarno of Indonesia and Tito of Yugoslavia. A sole European among the founders of the non-alignment movement (not counting Archbishop Makarios III, president of Cyprus who attended the Belgrade Conference), Tito was particularly proactive. He travelled to Asia and Africa in the years preceding the Belgrade Conference (and continued to do so after 1961) and also regularly hosted foreign dignitaries – Eastern and Western – in Yugoslavia.[5]

---

[3] Naoko Shimazu, 'Diplomacy as Theatre: Staging the Bandung Conference of 1955', *Modern Asian Studies*, 48:1 (January 2014), 225–52.
[4] John Berger, *Understanding a Photograph* (London: Penguin, 2013), pp. 62–63, and his *Ways of Seeing* (London: Penguin, 2008).
[5] For the official Yugoslav view of the NAM, see Josip Broz Tito, *The Historical Mission of Non-alignment* (Belgrade: Socialist Thought and Practice, 1979); Edvard Kardelj, *The Historical Roots of Non-alignment* (Belgrade: STP, 1979); Leo Mates, *Nesvrstanost: Teorija i savremena praksa* (Belgrade: Institut za medjunarodnu politiku i privredu, 1970); Ranko Petković,

Countless photographs were taken during the Belgrade Conference, which brought a hitherto unprecedented number of world leaders to this part of Europe. Twenty-five heads of state or government of non-aligned countries, mostly from Africa and Asia, convened in the capital of Yugoslavia. In total, around 3,000 statesmen, delegates, guests, observers and journalists from all over the world gathered in Belgrade in late August and early September 1961.[6] Only Tito's funeral in 1980, attended by leaders of nearly 130 states and liberation movements, and the Ninth Summit of the NAM (1989 – sometimes known as the Second Belgrade Conference), would exceed the 1961 Belgrade summit in size.

The arrival at and departure from Belgrade of the conference participants was broadcast on Yugoslav state television and radio and reported in the country's print media. In Tito's photo archive alone there are hundreds of images, some possibly never seen by public. They include a group of photographs documenting Sukarno's arrival and his procession, together with Tito, from a military airport just outside Belgrade to the city centre (Fig 2.1). The photograph captures a moment in the early history of non-alignment particularly effectively. It shows the hosts of the Bandung[7] and Belgrade conferences driven in an open-roofed car outside the Yugoslav parliament, the main venue of the first summit of non-aligned states.

Despite the hot weather, both men are fully dressed for the occasion, and in spite of the seriousness of the moment, both appear calm and relaxed. Sukarno wears a uniform, his medals on full display, and a *peci* cap, 'invented' as a revolutionary accessory in Indonesia. He is waving at Yugoslav citizens who are greeting the motorcade. Seated next to him is Tito, dressed in a dark suit, white shirt and a tie. (A colour image taken earlier that day shows that Tito

---

Non-aligned Yugoslavia and the Contemporary World: The Foreign Policy of Yugoslavia, 1945–1985 (Belgrade: Review of International Affairs, 1986). Alvin Z. Rubinstein's pioneering *Yugoslavia and the Non-aligned World* (Princeton, NJ: Princeton University Press, 1970) is joined by a number of more recent scholarly works, including Dragan Bogetić and Ljubodrag Dimić, *Beogradska konferencija Nesvrstanih zemalja 1–6. septembra 1961: Prilog istoriji Trećeg sveta* (Belgrade: Zavod za udžbenike i nastavna sredstva, 2013); Jürgen Dinkel, *The Non-aligned Movement: Genesis, Organization and Politics (1927–1992)* (Leiden: Brill, 2019); Tvrtko Jakovina, *Treća strana Hladnog rata* (Zaprešić: Fraktura, 2011); Nataša Mišković, Harald Fischer-Tiné and Nada Boškovska (eds.), *The Non-aligned Movement and the Cold War: Delhi-Bandung-Belgrade* (London: Routledge, 2014); Svetozar Rajak, 'No Bargaining Chips, No Spheres of Interest: The Yugoslav Origins of Cold War Non-Alignment', *Journal of Cold War Studies*, 16:1 (Winter 2014), 146–79; and special issues of *International History Review*, 37:5 (2015), guest-edited by Janick Marina Schaufelbuehl, Sandra Bott, Jussi Hanhimäki and Marco Wyss, and *Nationalities Papers*, 49:3 (May 2021), guest-edited by Ljubica Spaskovska, James Mark and Florian Bieber.

[6] 'Organizational and Technical Preparations', *Belgrade Conference* (Belgrade), 1 (August 1961), 16.

[7] Indonesia provided the venue, but the Bandung Conference was co-sponsored by the so-called Colombo Powers: Burma, Ceylon, India, Indonesia and Pakistan.

wore a navy-blue suit, white shirt and a red tie – the colours of the Yugoslav flag.) Both presidents wear sunglasses, which serve as protection from the late summer Belgrade sun, but that also create an impression of mystery, celebrity and glamour. For someone whose attractive, penetrating and almost hypnotic eye-stare was noted by contemporaries,[8] Tito wore sunglasses rather frequently, often indoors – as did Sukarno. The uniformed security officers riding motorcycles on both sides of the luxury car, decorated with the national flags of the two countries, only add to a sense of the significance of the occasion and obvious power and importance of the two men at the centre of the image.

The Actors

The car procession enables us to imagine movement. The vehicle is most probably driving the two leaders from the Batajnica Air Base, near Belgrade, where earlier that day Tito and other high-ranked Yugoslav officials had greeted the Indonesian president and his delegation upon their arrival. The car's destination is likely the Hotel Metropole. Prior to the conference, Sukarno had requested to stay at Belgrade's most luxurious hotel, rather than in one of official residences made available by the host country to the heads of state or government attending the conference. This fuelled rumours about Sukarno's fondness for late-night partying, usually in the company of attractive women.[9] During an earlier visit to Yugoslavia, Sukarno had reserved a whole floor of the Metropole and asked that he be introduced to local female singers and dancers. Tito made suitable arrangements regarding the accommodation, but as for the second request he replied with a characteristic wit and a sense of humour: 'I agree, but on the condition that the singers and dancers are the same age as President Sukarno!'[10]

Tito was no stranger to Sukarno's partying ways. A New Year's celebration in 1958 on the island of Bali hosted by Sukarno and attended by visiting Tito and his wife Jovanka was a lavish and decadent event of which Roman emperors might have been proud. According to *Time* magazine:

---

[8] Including British actor Richard Burton, Croatian writer Miroslav Krleža, Tito's fellow revolutionary and later dissident Milovan Djilas, British World War II envoy with the Partisans Fitzroy Maclean and US Secretary of State Henry Kissinger, as helpfully summarised by Jože Pirjevec, *Tito and His Comrades* (Madison: University of Wisconsin Press, 2018), pp. 3–5. Zvonimir Vučković, a Yugoslav Army officer who saw Tito in the autumn of 1941 during failed negotiations between royalist officers and Communist-led Partisans over a common resistance action, also noted Tito's 'sharp gaze, not evil looking, but rather confident and perceptive, in *Sećanja iz rata*' (London: Naše delo, 1980), p. 141.

[9] Author's interview with Budimir Lončar, Zagreb, 22 June 2018; Ivan Ivanji, *Titov prevodilac* (Belgrade: Laguna, 2014) pp. 181–82.

[10] Ivanji, *Titov prevodilac*, p. 181.

100 barefoot maidens in sarongs swivelled up and offered silver bowls filled with flowers to Yugoslavia's President Tito, 66, and Indonesia's President Sukarno, 57. Then host and his guest retired to the new palace at Tampaksiring, where at sunset maidens splash naked in Roman-style baths beneath Sukarno's windows. With food and music furnished by Sukarno, champagne and slivovitz [Yugoslav plum brandy] brought in off Tito's ocean-going yacht Caleb [*sic* – the name of the yacht was Galeb/ Seagull], the two Presidents and their wives rang in the New Year in memorable fashion.[11]

Time magazine's descriptions of Tito and Sukarno's public appearances carried an implicit homosocial message, revealing perhaps a homophobic undertone to the US media reporting. According to one scholar, the coverage of the obvious camaraderie between the Indonesian and Yugoslav presidents was meant 'to elicit the disapproval of the interpellated white, middle-class, heterosexual-male, US "citizen-reader" of the 1950s.'[12] However, it was not just the conservative American public that found Sukarno's extravagance objectionable. Soviet leader Nikita Khrushchev felt similarly uneasy with what he described as 'Sukarno's theatricality' during a visit to Indonesia just over a year later, in February 1960. Khrushchev caused a small diplomatic incident by walking out half-way through a performance of Balinese dance performed in his honour.[13]

Tito had no such qualms, and he was obviously impressed with his reception in Indonesia. During the Yugoslav leader's visit in late 1958, Sukarno presented him with a 'Guerrilla Star', Indonesia's highest military medal normally not awarded to foreigners. The medal was awarded in recognition of Tito's contribution to anti-colonial struggle (see Fig. 1.2). The Yugoslav president also received an honorary doctorate in law at the Padjadjaran University in Bandung. During the visit to Bandung, Tito was taken on a tour of the building where the Asian-African conference had taken place.[14] In retrospect, this was an act of a high symbolic value.

---

[11] 'Tito's Travels', *Time*, 19 January 1959; see also Bernard Kalb, 'Sukarno Shows Tito Bali Sights: Yugoslav Leader Showered with Flowers on His Last Full Day in Indonesia', *New York Times*, 1 January 1959.

[12] Konstantin Kilibarda, 'Non-aligned Geographies in the Balkans: Space, Race and Image in the Construction of New "European" Foreign Policies', in Abhinava Kumar and Derek Maisonville (eds.), *Security beyond Discipline: Emerging Dialogues on Global Politics* (Toronto: York Centre for International and Security Studies, 2010), pp. 27–57, 32. Matthew Isaac Cohen makes a similar point in 'Three Eras of Indonesian Arts Diplomacy', *Bijdragen tot de Taal-, Land- en Volkenkunde* (Leiden), 175:2–3 (July 2019), 253–83, 260.

[13] Cohen, 'Three Eras of Indonesian Arts Diplomacy', p. 261.

[14] MJ, Tito's Photo Archive, 1958_1959_100_0018, 'Visit to Indonesia: Return to Bandung and Visit to the Building Where the Asian-African Conference Took Place', Bandung, 26 December 1958; cf. Ljubodrag Dimić, Aleksandar Raković and Miladin Milošević, *Jugoslavija-Indonezija, 1945–1967: Istraživanja i dokumenti* (Belgrade: Arhiv Jugoslavije, 2014), pp. 49–50.

Figure 1.2 Tito receiving the 'Guerilla [Star] Medal' from President Sukarno,
Jakarta, 28 December 1958. Tito's typically grand posture and a stern look is
met with Sukarno's seeming nonchalance as he decorates the
Yugoslav leader.
MJ, Tito's Photo Archive, 1958_1959_100_0081.

Several images convey a certain symmetry between Tito and Sukarno,
suggesting a number of parallels that may be drawn between them (while
keeping in mind important differences). Although from different parts of the
world, of different social backgrounds, and separated in age by almost a
decade, they were both born in late nineteenth-century imperial peripheries:
Tito (born Josip Broz in 1892) in a small village in Habsburg Croatia, and
Sukarno (b. 1901) in Surabaya, a cosmopolitan port city in the Dutch East
Indies. They grew up in complex, multi-cultural societies with parents of
different ethnicities. Tito, whose father was Croatian and mother Slovenian,
was raised in a large peasant, Roman Catholic household on the modern
Croatian-Slovenian border. He became a communist in Russia where the
1917 Revolution found him as a Habsburg army prisoner-of-war. Sukarno's
father was a Muslim Javanese teacher, while his mother was of Hindu Balinese
background. This could possibly explain Sukarno's later ideological potpourri,
which mixed religion with socialism and nationalism. Indeed, the two men's
family backgrounds may explain their success as leaders of ethnically, reli-
giously and culturally diverse societies such as Indonesia and Yugoslavia.

In both countries the official ideology was closely associated with the national leader. A complex mix of socialism, nationalism, religion and authoritarian was known as Sukarnism. Yugoslavia's socialism, based on brotherhood and unity, ethnic federalism forged in the war, workers' self-management, and non-aligned foreign policy, developed after 1948, is usually referred to as Titoism.[15]

Both leaders believed in personal diplomacy and travelled frequently. Intensifying his diplomatic activities following the Bandung Conference, Sukarno visited China, Soviet Union, the United States and Yugoslavia in 1956 alone. Fig. 1.1 captures a scene from what was already Sukarno's fifth trip to Yugoslavia (he had previously visited in September 1956, January 1958, April 1960 and June 1961). In 1970 Tito was already described as the most travelled non-aligned leader of all time. During his long period in power (1945–1980), he held 450 meetings with heads of state, prime ministers and leaders of communist parties and liberation movements, including Soviet leaders and US presidents.[16]

Tito and Sukarno had a penchant for uniforms and tailor-made suits (see Figs. 1.3 and 1.4). As revolutionaries and leaders of national liberation movements they personified their nations' freedom achieved after years of domination by foreign powers. Tito was the leader of a Yugoslav resistance against the Second World War occupation by Nazi Germany, Fascist Italy and their regional allies and other local rivals. Similarly, Sukarno led the Indonesian independence struggle against the Dutch. While most leaders at the Bandung conference wore a national costume or a Western-style suit, Sukarno, together with Nasser, appeared in military uniform.[17]

Tito and Sukarno fashioned themselves as political *and* military leaders of their countries, which probably explains why they continued to wear uniforms long after the war was over. Moreover, Indonesia and Yugoslavia were among a handful of countries (together with Brazil, Canada, Colombia, Denmark, Finland, India, Norway and Sweden) that provided troops for the first United

---

[15] Sukarno: Bernhard Damm, *Sukarno and the Struggle for Indonesian Independence*, trans. Mary F. Somers Heidhues (Ithaca, NY: Cornell University Press, 1969); J. D. Legge, *Sukarno: A Political Biography* (London: Penguin, 1984); *Sukarno: An Autobiography, as Told to Cindy Adams* (Hong Kong: Gunung Agung, 1966); Donald E. Weatherbee, *Ideology in Indonesia: Sukarno's Indonesian Revolution* (New Haven, CT: Yale University Press, 1966). Tito: Vladimir Dedijer, *Novi prilozi za biografiju Josipa Broza Tita*, 3 vols. (Zagreb: Mladost, 1980–84); Milovan Djilas, *Tito: The Story from Inside* (San Diego, CA: Harcourt Brace Jovanovich, 1980); Fitzroy Maclean, *Tito: A Pictorial Biography* (London: Macmillan, 1980); Stevan K. Pavlowitch, *Tito, Yugoslavia's Great Dictator: A Reassessment* (London: Hurst, 1992); Richard West, *Tito and the Rise and Fall of Yugoslavia* (London: Sinclair-Stevenson, 1994).

[16] Bogetić and Dimić, *Beogradska konferencija Nesvrstanih zemalja*, p. 187.

[17] Shimazu, 'Diplomacy as Theatre', pp. 20–24.

Figure 1.3 Tito's visit to Indonesia, Tanjung Priok, 23 December 1958.
MJ, Tito's Photo Archive, 1958_99_0019.

Nations peacekeeping mission, deployed between 1956 and 1967 on the Egypt-Israel border. As commanders-in-chief of armies that contributed to the UN Emergency Force, Tito and Sukarno simultaneously projected images of militant revolutionaries and peace-keepers of global significance. (Incidentally, the conflict in the Middle East brought together the future key founders of the NAM: Nehru, Sukarno and Tito as leaders of countries that provided the peace-keepers, and Nasser of Egypt; during the 1970s Ghana, too, would contribute to the UNEF peace-keepers, albeit during the presidency of General Joseph Arthur Ankrah, Nkrumah's successor.)[18]

The uniform therefore represented both a political and a fashion statement, not merely a garment designed to be practical. Even during the war, most of which he spent in the mountains of Yugoslavia, Tito was usually dressed smartly in a specially tailored marshal's uniform. Before his death in May 1980, Tito's wardrobe included over seventy uniforms and numerous

[18] Vojni arhiv, fond JNA (the Military Archive, the Yugoslav People's Army Papers, Belgrade), boxes 550–81, contain documents relevant to the Yugoslav UNEF mission, an under-researched topic. Aleksandar Životić's *Forsiranje peska: Odred JNA na Sinaju* (Belgrade: Medija Centar 'Odbrana', 2011) is informative but reads like an official, army-commissioned account.

Figure 1.4 Tito and Sukarno are seen wearing nearly identical white navy
uniforms on the occasion of Tito's arrival at the Indonesian port city.
MJ, Tito's Photo Archive, 1958_99_0031.

military coats, shirts and hats, as well as a large quantity of the finest, unused
cloth.[19]

Headwear was important too. Sukarno often wore the *peci* cap (as seen in
Fig. 1.1). Similarly, Tito was associated with a 'revolutionary resistance' cap,
titovka, worn by him and Yugoslav partisans during the Second World War.
Soldiers and officers of the Yugoslav People's Army, originally formed out of
Partisan units at the end of the Second World War, wore the *titovka* cap until
the demise of the army, and Yugoslavia, in the early 1990s. The obvious feel
for the visual was also reflected in Sukarno's and Tito's fondness for staged
performance. Tito was a filmophile with a personal projectionist who screened
films for him almost every night for thirty-two years. He liked to watch
Yugoslav Partisan films, which combined the aesthetic and ideology of the
Tito-led armed resistance with the American Western and Italian 'spaghetti
Western'.[20] Such a seemingly contradictory mix reflected Yugoslavia's

---

[19] MJ, Permanent exhibition, Maršalska uniforma, registration no. 362 (VI/c).
[20] See *Cinema Komunisto* (dir. Mila Turajlić, 2012). Some Yugoslav Partisan movies were co-
produced with Soviet and US film studios, for example, *Hell River* (in Yugoslavia released as

international position following the 1948 conflict with the Soviet Union: a relatively liberal communist country that was receptive to Western cultural influences (and financial and military aid), but nevertheless a one-party state where the cult of the leader was promoted and dissent forbidden and punished. Sukarno was similarly fascinated by Hollywood and the film industry, and had a keen interest in *wayang*, the Indonesian puppet theatre, and *legong*, the traditional Balinese dance mentioned previously.

Both leaders were known by a single name. While in Indonesia it is not unusual to use only one name, and Tito was certainly not the only communist leader to be better known by his *nomme de guerre*, this gave them, in my view, a certain celebrity and royal aura. Indonesians and Yugoslavs also referred to Sukarno and Tito by various nicknames. Thus Sukarno was Bung Karno (brother/comrade Karno) and Pak Karno (Mr Karno), while Tito was variously, and fondly, called Drug Tito (comrade Tito), Drug Stari (comrade Old Man), or simply Maršal (the Marshal). This informality was meant, I believe, to give the impression of a certain familiarity between the Leader and his People (or rather Peoples in the case of both Indonesia and Yugoslavia). The Leader was at once the embodiment of the nation and its values, and also 'one of us'.

Tito and Sukarno were charismatic *bons vivants* who married more than once, although Sukarno probably led a more extravagant life. They both enjoyed the company of international celebrities; in fact, they were celebrities themselves. While Sukarno famously posed with Marilyn Monroe at a Hollywood party during his 1956 visit to the United States (Fig. 1.5), Tito's photo archive includes numerous images of the Yugoslav president posing for cameras with international film stars such as Richard Burton, Elizabeth Taylor and Sophia Loren (Fig. 1.6). The audience witnessing the procession shown in Fig. 1.1 are therefore witnessing not just two international statesmen in a motorcade; they are also loyal and curious fans waiting for hours to catch a glimpse of two political celebrities, or their idols.

The Stage

As already mentioned, the opening image (Fig. 1.1) captures the moment when the two leaders are driven past the Yugoslav People's Assembly. Positioned in the background, in the top left-hand corner, the building is the other dominant image within image. It provides a sense of balance, a static contrast to the

---

Partizani, dir. Stole Janković, 1974), with Rod Taylor in the lead role. A clip from this film is briefly shown in Quentin Tarantino's *Once upon a Time in Hollywood* (2019), itself inspired by the Western and 'spaghetti Western' genres – and perhaps also the Yugoslav Partisan film? (I am grateful to Sanja Petrović Todosijević of the Institute for Recent History of Serbia for the information about the *Hell River* clip).

Figure 1.5 Sukarno and Marilyn Monroe, Beverly Hills Hotel, June 1956. Getty Images, www.gettyimages.co.uk/detail/news-photo/indonesias-president-sukarno-is-shown-chatting-with-actress-news-photo/517257514? adppopup=true.

obvious dynamic movement of the leading men (and their driver and security), who occupy the front of the photograph and are 'moving' towards the bottom right-hand corner and eventually out of the frame. It was inside the assembly building where the summit would open a few days later, so it is thus possible to read another implicit message here: the stage is ready for the main perform-ance, while two lead actors rehearse in front of an audience.

Figure 1.6 Elizabeth Taylor and Tito walk the red carpet, Pula Film Festival, Croatia/Yugoslavia, 1 August 1971.
MJ, Tito's Photo Archive, 1971_468_102.

Although most Belgraders and visitors to the city today would not necessarily associate the parliament building with the first summit of the non-aligned countries, the visual presence of the venue in contemporary sources was striking. It featured on commemorative stamps and coins issued for the occasion and on the cover of the conference daily bulletin. The latter was published 'during the conference of the uncommitted countries' by the official *Review of International Affairs*, which appeared in English, French, German, Russian, Serbo-Croatian and Spanish.[21]

The parliament building is the sole immovable object in the photograph, if the trees and lamp-posts are excluded. The building thus may be said to represent one constant in this story: the host city. Leaders come and go, countries and governments form and disappear, but the uninterrupted human settlement on the confluence of the Danube and Sava Rivers, where the largely

---

[21] MJ, Tito's Photo Archive, 1961_176_0001, 'Beogradska Konferencija: Beograd za vreme Konferencije', http://foto.mij.rs/site/gallery/4636/photo/1 (accessed 10 October 2022), and *Belgrade Conference*, 1–5 (August–September 1961).

imagined borders of the Balkans and Central Europe lie, and past empires meet, remains. The city's long history goes back to Celtic, Roman and Slav settlements, followed by long periods of Hungarian, Austrian and Ottoman rule, during which Belgrade was repeatedly exposed to siege and destruction and its inhabitants forced to migration and murder. It was thus perhaps appropriate that only fifteen years after the Second World War, during which it was heavily bombarded, the capital of Yugoslavia hosted the founding event of a movement designed to contribute to world peace at the time of a dangerous confrontation between the two ideological blocs. In his opening address, Tito indeed referred to Belgrade's turbulent past, expressing hope that a new era was beginning for the Yugoslav capital as it welcomed 'for the first time in its history ... the highest representatives of 27 countries, ... the champions of peace'.[22]

The parliament building and the surrounding area witnessed major political and social changes, radical ruptures and forced departures, as well as some important continuities. For the projected new legislature of Serbia, the construction of the building had begun in the early twentieth century. The central Belgrade location that was chosen for the new seat of the parliament was at or near the site of a sixteenth-century mosque, one of at least eighty Muslim shrines that existed in the city during the Ottoman era (between the early sixteenth and early nineteenth centuries, not counting several periods of Habsburg occupation in the eighteenth century).[23] It was also near a place where a revolutionary assembly proclaimed Serbia's autonomy from the Ottoman Empire in 1830. Due to lack of funding and the outbreak of the Balkan and First World Wars of 1912–18, work on the building was not completed until 1936.

In the meantime, Belgrade had become the capital of Yugoslavia, formed in 1918 as the Kingdom of Serbs, Croats and Slovenes. In 1929, the country became a royal dictatorship, albeit an increasingly relaxed one following the assassination of King Aleksandar in 1934. Interwar Yugoslavia followed a general European trend of abandoning democracy in favour of a non-parliamentary, authoritarian form of rule, but by the mid-1930s – as the neighbouring states of Bulgaria, Greece and Romania turned into

---

[22] AJ, 837 KPR, I-4-a/2, box 203, 'Govor njegove ekscelencije Josipa Broza Tita, predsednika Federativne narodne republike Jugoslavije prilikom otvaranja konferencije šefova država i vlada vanblokovskih zemalja', Belgrade, 1 September 1961. In addition to twenty-four non-aligned countries, three South American states – Bolivia, Brazil and Ecuador – had observer status at the conference.

[23] Hazim Šabanović, 'Urbani razvitak Beograda od 1521. do 1688.', *Godišnjak grada Beograda* (Belgrade), 17 (1970), 5–41. Only one mosque remains in Belgrade today. The official *History and Heritage of the National Assembly* fails to mention that the building served as the Belgrade Conference venue (www.parlament.gov.rs/upload/documents/activities/Istorijat%20Dom%20NS%20ENG.pdf, accessed 10 October 2022).

dictatorships – the Yugoslavs restored the parliament as a partial renewal of political life and as quasi-democratic elections took place.[24] In the late 1930s, Tito returned to the country from Moscow, tasked by Stalin with reorganizing the Yugoslav Communist party, nearly extinguished by the government oppression, internal 'factionalism' and Stalinist purges. During the Nazi occupation of Serbia (1941–44), the parliament building had been turned into the headquarters of German occupation authorities. After the war it became the Yugoslav assembly once again, albeit in a communist, one-party state now firmly ruled by Tito and the party.

The parliament's House of the Republics and Provinces and the Federal House symbolized socialist Yugoslavia's complex arrangement, which collapsed in the early 1990s, as the South Slav federation broke up and descended into a brutal war a decade after Tito's death. Images of the siege and partial destruction of the assembly building during protests, which in October 2000 brought down Slobodan Milošević, the Serbian authoritarian leader, are still fresh in memory of many Belgraders. The building finally became Serbia's parliament, a century later than planned, when in 2006 Montenegro declared independence and the last remnants of Yugoslavia ceased to exist.

Audience

It is unlikely that Yugoslavs observing the procession shown in Fig. 1.1 could have envisaged such a violent demise of their country, due to internal conflict, only three decades later. At the beginning of the 1960s Yugoslavia was entering its 'golden age', serious political crises of the late 1960s and early 1970s notwithstanding. The country's, and Tito's, international prestige was enhanced by the hosting of the Belgrade Conference. Anonymity of comrades-citizens witnessing the motorcade in Fig. 1.1 is accentuated by their blurred faces (due to the camera's focus on the car procession), and is in stark contrast to world-wide fame of the two statesmen driven in a car along one of Belgrade's main boulevards.

The citizens are standing along the pavement in front of the assembly building as the car drives by. Some are seen clapping while others are simply standing still, providing a background image that sends the message of hospitality to the foreign guest and acts as evidence of their support for the leader. However, they are not mere eyewitnesses to the event. They represent an audience, historically considered by the state as an important part of diplomatic theatre. Those who turned up may have done so out of genuine curiosity, opportunism, as plain clothes security, or as part of a compulsory exercise

---

[24] I elaborate this in 'A Very Yugoslav Paradox? The Strange Afterlife of Interwar Democracy (and Authoritarianism)', *Journal of Modern European History*, 17:1 (February 2019), 28–36.

staged by the authorities, as was common in socialist Yugoslavia and throughout Eastern Europe (and as remains common in parts of former Yugoslavia).
'[A]ll these socialist regimes, including our own, were new, relishing official
parades and the external symbols of nationhood,' recalled Milovan Djilas, a
member of the Central Committee of the League of Communists of Yugoslavia
and the Party's chief ideologue, until his purging in 1954. 'So began an
exchange of state visits full of pomp and ceremony. It was as if the new power
brokers and the people, too, craved these demonstrations.'[25]

The frequency of Yugoslav media reports, including published images and
daily radio and TV broadcasts, practically made the whole Yugoslav public
spectators of the late summer diplomatic spectacle in Belgrade. One can only
speculate what went through the minds of Yugoslavs observing the car
procession in person or via media, but they had become used to such scenes.
As already mentioned, this was Sukarno's fifth trip to Yugoslavia, and ordinary Yugoslavs had become used to his public appearances, sometimes without
Tito. When in Belgrade, the Indonesian president would prefer to stay in a
hotel rather than in an official residence, and he sometimes walked the city
streets, visiting shops and posing for cameras with local children. Sukarno was
probably not merely courteous when during the opening session of the
Belgrade Conference he said he felt at home in Yugoslavia.[26]

Tito's frequent departures abroad and hosting of foreign officials in
Yugoslavia were accompanied by mass rituals of 'sending-offs' and 'welcom-
ings' of the leader and his guests by Yugoslav citizens.[27] The visit to London
in March 1953, Tito's first trip abroad after the conflict with Stalin, was highly
significant in this respect.[28] It brought the Yugoslav communist leader to the
attention of the Western public, but it also showed him, I believe, in a new
light back home. Previously, he was visualized with or in opposition to Stalin.
With the Soviet leader on his deathbed in the spring of 1953, scenes of Tito
mingling with and not looking out of place alongside Churchill and members
of the British royal family symbolized a new era and must have left quite an
impression on the Yugoslav public. According to (possibly exaggerated)
Yugoslav sources, some 200,000 people greeted Tito at the Belgrade train

---

[25] Djilas, *Rise and Fall* (London: Macmillan, 1985), p. 114; Ivanji, *Titov prevodilac*, p. 136;
Predrag J. Marković, *Beograd izmedju Istoka i Zapada, 1948–1968* (Belgrade: Službeni list,
1996) pp. 101–6.

[26] AJ, 837 KPR, I-4-a/2, box 203, 'Address by H.E. Dr. Sukarno, President of the Republic of
Indonesia before the Conference of Heads of State or Government of Non-aligned Countries',
Belgrade, 1 September 1961.

[27] Kilibarda, 'Non-aligned Geographies in the Balkans', p. 33; Marković, *Beograd*, pp. 101–6.

[28] Katarina Spehnjak, 'Posjet Josipa Broza Tita Velikoj Britaniji 1953. godine', *Časopis za
suvremenu povijest* (Zagreb), 33:3 (December 2001), 597–631.

station upon his return from London.[29] Those gathered witnessed an unusual scene: Tito, dressed in marshal's uniform, addressed the crowd outside the train station, outlining the main direction of Yugoslavia's independent foreign policy. This was a political street theatre par excellence, which turned thousands of Belgrade citizens into an audience, and not for the last time. The scene represented an early example of Tito bypassing the party and the state to engage directly with the people, something he would repeat later on several occasions (for example, in 1962, when he addressed a crowd in Split, Croatia, and criticised the party, and in 1968, when he joined Belgrade University student demonstrators and danced with them).

Tito's cult was fostered by the party, which had a monopoly over historical production and public memory, and exercised near-complete media control. Streets, squares and even towns across Yugoslavia were named after Tito – in the case of Montenegro, the republic's capital city, Podgorica, was renamed Titograd, just weeks after Tito's conflict with Stalin. The Yugoslav leader's portrait hung on school walls, factory halls, at post offices and at military parades. Daily news usually started with reports on Tito's activities, as increasingly affordable television sets (which Yugoslavia started mass-producing in 1959) brought the nation's leader into many a Yugoslav home. He exuded authority, no doubt was feared by many, but also was almost universally admired, even loved. Tito's charisma and photogenic appearance helped his popularity, which sometimes turned into adulation. His personality cult initially resembled that of Lenin and Stalin, but Tito's public appearances gained additional layers of glamour and luxury more associated with stereotypical central European royals (or perhaps James Bond villains).[30]

The Yugoslav leader's increasing engagement with Asia and Africa enhanced his growing reputation as a world statesman. If the 1953 London trip created a 'royal' Tito, the visit to India and Burma the following year introduced to the Yugoslav public and the world a 'post-colonial', 'non-aligned' Tito.

---

[29] Marković, *Beograd*, pp. 101–2. Tito travelled to London by sea, but used the presidential 'Blue Train' for the inland journey. His favourite vehicles survive him, and Yugoslavia. The Blue Train is now a 'museum train' in Belgrade, available for commercial bookings. The 'Galeb' trans-oceanic yacht – manufactured in Mussolini's Italy, turned into a warship by the German navy, sunk by the Allies and restored by the Yugoslavs after the war – is moored, and left abandoned for the time being, in the Croatian port city of Rijeka. A luxury model of a US-manufactured DC-6B airplane that the Yugoslav state purchased for Tito in the late 1950s, and later sold to President Kaunda of Zambia, is now owned by an Austrian billionaire. Tito also drove, and was driven in, a number of luxury cars (one of which is shown in Fig. 1.1) manufactured by Chrysler, Mercedes and Rolls-Royce. Some of these have been allegedly auctioned by Yugoslav successor states following the country's break-up.

[30] Stanislav Sretenović and Artan Puto, 'The Leader Cults in the Western Balkans, 1945–1990: Josip Broz Tito and Enver Hoxha', in Balázs Apor et al. (eds.), *The Leader Cults in Communist Dictatorships* (London: PalgraveMacmillan, 2004), pp. 208–23; cf. West, *Tito and the Rise and Fall of Yugoslavia*, pp. 331–32, 339.

The trans-oceanic journey on the 'Galeb' also showcased the luxury that surrounded the president and those who travelled with him, and introduced to the wider public the president's new wife. Thirty-two years his junior, Jovanka Broz was a striking-looking Croatian Serb who served as a lieutenant colonel in the Yugoslav People's Army and had served as Tito's nurse and secretary before they begun a relationship after the war. Following her marriage to Tito, Jovanka would transform into a US-style 'first lady' and a fashion icon of socialist Yugoslavia.[31] She was the Yugoslav equivalent of Jacqueline Kennedy, one might say.

The luxury and wealth that surrounded Tito and Jovanka did not seem to bother ordinary Yugoslavs, even though many of them lived in relative poverty. If anything, they seemed to be proud of their leader and of their country's predicament. While visiting Yugoslavia in the early 1950s, Hubert Butler, an Anglo-Irish writer with an intimate knowledge of the Balkan country, was told that the world was divided into 'East, West and Yugo-Slavia'. This was an expression of pride and defiance, following the Tito-Stalin split. Gradually, the Yugoslavs began to enjoy relative freedom and, largely thanks to Western aid, an improvement in the standard of living.[32]

Khrushchev's historic visit to Belgrade in late May 1955 – just days after the formation of the Warsaw Pact – was significant above all because it represented a thaw in relations between the Soviet Union and Yugoslavia. The Soviet leader's acknowledgement that Stalin was wrong in 1948 was a major boost to Tito's and Yugoslavia's international standing and represented a modern version of the Humiliation of Canossa (in which the Pope went to the Emperor to seek forgiveness). The British ambassador to Belgrade noted the Yugoslavs' superior dress sense, especially in comparison to tired members of the Soviet delegation, who wore creased, ill-fitted suits.[33] The Yugoslav public could not have failed to observe the same: Tito, in his sharp uniforms and smart, bespoke suits, looked more glamorous and authoritative than Khrushchev, who was shorter and appeared older than his Yugoslav host (even though he was Tito's junior by two years).

A year later – '[r]esplendent in a panama white linen suit, white shoes and black pocket handkerchief', in words of a *Time* correspondent – Tito hosted Nasser and Nehru at his luxury summer residence on the Yugoslav Adriatic coast. A 'peasant's son' who 'now lives in a palace, drinks the finest wines,

---

[31] Danijela Velimirović, 'Moda, ideologija i politika: Odevanje Jovanke Broz', *Antropologija* (Belgrade), 1 (2006), 50–60.

[32] Hubert Butler, 'In Europe's Debatable Lands', in Chris Agee and Jacob Agee (eds.), *Balkan Essays* (Belfast: Irish Pages Press, 2016), pp. 411–42, 411; Patrick Hayder Patterson, *Bought and Sold: Living and Losing the Good Life in Socialist Yugoslavia* (Ithaca, NY: Cornell University Press, 2011).

[33] Predrag J. Marković, *Tito i njegovo doba* (Belgrade: Službeni glasnik, 2012), p. 180.

hunts boar and drives a bulletproof car' seemed to have fascinated inter-national media.[34] While Djilas (until 1954) and Edvard Kardelj provided the ideological and theoretical foundations and Aleksandar Ranković, another leading communist, was in charge of the secret police, Tito was responsible for the performative aspects of Titoism. His 'post-revolutionary dandyism'[35] arguably became the dominant image of socialist Yugoslavia, at home and abroad.

Did Yugoslav citizens observing the scene shown in Fig. 1.1 and in numer-ous other photographs of Tito and non-aligned leaders consciously or subcon-sciously think about race? Just looking at the photographs of Tito and other non-aligned leaders, Tito's whiteness is hard to ignore. This is especially true of images of Tito in sub-Saharan Africa, sometimes dressed in attire resem-bling that of former colonial rulers.[36] In other words, how did the Yugoslavs see their African and Asian allies, and how did they read images of Tito alongside his non-aligned counterparts? Scholars of Yugoslavia have only recently begun to point out examples of the Yugoslavs' Eurocentric thinking, introducing the previously largely absent question of race into the analysis.[37]

There is no evidence that Sukarno and other frequent non-aligned visitors to Yugoslavia were not welcomed genuinely by the Yugoslav public. Displays of the welcome Tito received in Asia and Africa were even more impressive. The authorities – ever engaged in monitoring the citizens, lest they show any sign of dissent – were notified of some criticism of the large spending involved in organizing and hosting the Belgrade Conference, when benefit for the country was likely to be insignificant considering the 'poverty' of Asian and African states. A few racist jokes were also reported by the police. However, these were rare incidents and do not appear to have reflected the mainstream sentiment among the population.[38]

The history of non-alignment offers an exciting opportunity to introduce race into Yugoslav studies, but this requires careful analysis and nuance. If to a non-European eye former Yugoslavia seems unquestionably European and

---

[34] 'Yugoslavia: Come Back Little Tito', *Time*, 6 June 1955, pp. 20–23 (Tito was on the cover of this issue, published shortly after Khrushchev's visit to Belgrade); 'Diplomacy: Accentuating the Negative', *Time*, 30 July, 1956, pp. 19–23.
[35] Kilibarda, 'Non-aligned Geographies in the Balkans', pp. 28–30.
[36] See Radina Vučetić and Paul Betts (eds.), *Tito in Africa: Picturing Solidarity* (Belgrade: Muzej Jugoslavije, 2017).
[37] Catherine Baker, *Race and the Yugoslav Region: Postsocialist, Post-conflict, Postcolonial?* (Manchester: Manchester University Press, 2018); Kilibarda, 'Non-aligned Geographies in the Balkans'; Jelena Subotić and Srdjan Vučetić, 'Performing Solidarity: Whiteness and Status-Seeking in the Non-aligned World', *Journal of International Relations and Development*, 22:3 (September 2019), 722–43.
[38] Marković, *Beograd*, p. 106.

white, in the Western imagination it usually represents an 'Other', at once European and non-European, because of its Ottoman, Byzantine and, more recently, communist legacies and an alleged disposition to perennial violence, as exemplified by the Yugoslav wars of the 1990s.[39] While almost all former Yugoslavs may be categorized as white, their whiteness is often conditional from a north-western European perspective; in other words, they are 'white, but not quite'.[40] Similar stereotypes exist within the former Yugoslav space, whereby north-western regions are allegedly more European (or at least Central European), in contrast to the less developed, south-eastern, Balkan periphery of Europe.[41]

Yugoslav attitudes towards the outside world were defined by their own self-perception, but this was not necessarily linked to race. Milovan Djilas recalled his and his comrades' superiority complex in relation to other East European regimes as well as West European communist parties. 'We conceded to Stalin historical supremacy on a world-wide scale', Djilas wrote, 'but in Yugoslavia Tito was lauded right along with him.'[42] It is easy to forget now that prior to the Tito-Stalin split, this is also how Moscow and its satellites viewed Belgrade, chosen as the seat of the Communist Information Bureau after it was founded in 1947. Hosting the inaugural event of the Non-aligned Movement in 1961 only added to the Yugoslavs' sense of importance and served as proof that the country was fully recovered from the conflict with the Soviet bloc in the late 1940s. Furthermore, if the Yugoslav communists understood the world in terms of 'less and more developed' binaries, this may have been shaped by their own experience at home. The party classified Yugoslavia's peoples according to level of national consciousness, and additional hierarchies and labels were introduced to distinguish main ethnic groups from minorities. Moreover, the country's resources were distributed in line with the regional level of development. Consciously or not, these internal hierarchies could have been easily projected onto the outside world.

---

[39] A whole body of literature inspired by and critically engaged with Edward Said's *Orientalism* (1978) has emerged in relation to the West's negative stereotypes about the Balkans. See especially Vesna Goldsworthy, *Inventing Ruritania: Imperialism of the Imagination* (New Haven, CT: Yale University Press, 1998), and Maria N. Todorova, *Imagining the Balkans* (New York: Oxford University Press, 1997).

[40] Baker, *Race and the Yugoslav Region*, p. 108; cf. Linda Alcoff, 'What Should White People Do?', *Hypatia*, 13:3 (August 1998), 6–26.

[41] Milica Bakić-Hayden, 'Nesting Orientalisms: The Case of Former Yugoslavia', *Slavic Review*, 54:4 (Winter 1995), 917–31.

[42] Djilas, *Rise and Fall*, 90; cf. Stevan K. Pavlowitch, 'La crise Yougoslave et ses conséquences sur L'Europe orientale', in Coll.[ectiff], *L'Europe de l'Est et de l'Ouest dans la guerre froide, 1948–1953* (Paris, 2002), pp. 83–97.

The Conference

Although visually a still moment from the past, the scene captured in Fig. 1.1 represents part of a longer history. Communist Yugoslavia's interest in Asia preceded the 1948 conflict with the Soviet Union, an event traditionally seen as a turning point in Belgrade's domestic and foreign policies. Contacts with Chinese, Indian and Burmese communists were established in 1947, initially with Soviet blessing.[43] A more sustained engagement with South and South-East Asia would begin in the early 1950s. The escalation of the Korean War in 1950 – which Belgrade feared might have anticipated a Soviet intervention against Yugoslavia – was a turning point. Strong opposition to the war by India, Indonesia and Burma did not go unnoticed in Belgrade.

In January 1953, a high-level delegation headed by Djilas attended the Conference of Asian Socialists in Rangoon, Burma (today Yangon, Myanmar).[44] The interest was mutual. Burma had, like Yugoslavia, pursued a neutral foreign policy. The Burmese were intrigued by Yugoslavia's type of socialism and admired the Yugoslavs for defeating Hitler and Mussolini and for having the courage and political skill to survive a conflict with Stalin.[45] Yugoslavia's prestige among Asian socialists was evident in the publicity its small delegation received during the conference, and it is likely that the Yugoslav representatives further enhanced their country's reputation. Despite (at the time) his modest command of English, the language of the conference, Djilas' speeches and participation in conference debates and in seminars he hosted outside the main conference sessions were regularly reported in the local press.[46]

---

[43] Jovan Čavoški, 'Overstepping the Balkan Boundaries: The Lesser Known History of Yugoslavia's Early Relations with Asian Countries (New Evidence from Yugoslav/Serbian Archives)', *Cold War History*, 11:4 (November 2011), 557–77; Nataša Mišković, 'The Pre-history of the Non-aligned Movement: India's First Contacts with the Communist Yugoslavia, 1948–50', *India Quarterly*, 65:2 (April 2009), 185–200.

[44] In addition to the host country, delegates of socialist parties from the following countries took part in the Rangoon conference: Egypt, India, Indonesia, Israel, Japan, Lebanon, the Malayan Federation and Pakistan. The Yugoslavs and representatives of the Socialist International, headed by former British Prime Minister Clement Atlee, at the time leader of the opposition Labour Party, attended as 'fraternal delegates'. *Report of the First Asian Socialist Conference* (Rangoon: Asian Socialist Publication, 1953); Djilas, *Rise and Fall*, pp. 310–18; Saul Rose, *Socialism in Southern Asia* (New York: Octagon Books, 1959), pp. 4–13.

[45] Djilas, *Rise and Fall*; Rubinstein, *Yugoslavia and the Non-aligned World*, p. 54. The British Left was in awe of Tito and the Yugoslavs for the same reasons (as the Burmese), as Michael Foot told me when I interviewed him in 2005. Dejan Djokić, 'Britain and Dissent in Tito's Yugoslavia: The Djilas Affair, ca 1956', *European History Quarterly*, 36:3 (July 2006), 371–95, 373.

[46] Su Lin Lewis, 'Asian Socialism and the Forgotten Architects of Post-colonial Freedom, 1952–1956', *Journal of World History*, 30:1–2 (June 2019), 55–88, 68.

If Rangoon paved the way for Bandung Conference, and thus indirectly for the Belgrade Conference as well, in the short term, and as far as the Yugoslavs were concerned, it also served as preparation for the aforementioned visit by Tito to India and Burma in late 1954. The previously mentioned public displays of luxury notwithstanding, Tito spent the journey in working mode. It was during the trip that the principles of active peaceful coexistence and non-commitment as a global initiative crystalized in his mind.[47] The Yugoslav president laid out his vision of a new international order during a speech in India's parliament in December 1954: 'What I have in mind is not a sort of passive coexistence, but an active cooperation and a peaceful and agreed settlement of different problems, as well as the removal of all elements liable to impede a broad cooperation between States, large and small.' His message was warmly received in both India and Burma, where he was compared to Aung San, the leader of the Burmese national revolution.[48]

Yugoslavia's interest in anti-colonialism was both pragmatic and genuine. The Tito-Stalin split forced the Yugoslav leadership to develop a new set of policies and seek fresh alliances. These were shaped by the notions of self-management of the proletariat at home and active coexistence and non-alignment abroad. The emergence of independent states out of former Western colonies in Asia and Africa offered an opportunity for an isolated Yugoslavia to establish new relations and in the process extend its influence globally.[49] As already mentioned, the Yugoslavs felt confident enough to send peace-keeping troops to the Middle East in the 1950s and '60s. The UNEF offered an opportunity to sell not only the Titoist version of socialism but also Yugoslavia's military expertise and weapons. Indeed, economic interests played an important part, with emerging markets, unexploited resources and surplus manpower to be found in the post-colonial world, as a 1956 Yugoslav government report noted.[50]

Had Yugoslavia remained part of the Soviet bloc, it is likely that it would have engaged with the 'Third World' anyway, albeit in a less independent role. Moscow saw in the former Western colonies in Africa, Asia and Latin America an opportunity to export both ideology and goods. Yugoslavia, together with

---

[47] Bogetić and Dimić, *Beogradska konferencija Nesvrstanih zemalja*, pp. 141–42; Rajak, 'No Bargaining Chips', p. 147.

[48] Ljubodrag Dimić, *Jugoslavija i Hladni rat: Ogledi o spoljnoj politici Josipa Broza Tita (1944–1974)*, (Belgrade: Arhipelag, 2014), p. 123; Rubinstein, *Yugoslavia and the Non-aligned World*, pp. 54–58 (Tito's speech: 57–58).

[49] Rajak, 'No Bargaining Chips', pp. 146–79.

[50] Rubinstein, *Yugoslavia and the Non-aligned World*, pp. 75–76.

China, offered competition, and a complex rivalry developed between the three communist states, which sometimes involved India.[51]

A bona fide sense of solidarity and sympathy with the Third World influenced Yugoslavia's non-alignment also. Anti-colonialism was not fundamentally different from anti-imperialism, and '[f]or us ... there has never been any question of whether non-aligned policy is anti-imperialistic or not', wrote Kardelj, Yugoslavia's key theoretician and foreign minister between 1948 and 1953.[52] Rather than 'simply ... a reaction to the bloc division of the world and the dominant role of the blocs', non-alignment was 'the reflection of a much longer socio-historical tendency of contemporary mankind, one that dates before the Second World War', he argued.[53] Just like nineteenth-century South Slav nationalism developed in opposition to Ottoman, Habsburg and Venetian rule, Yugoslav communists in the 1940s fought the Nazi, fascist and eventually Soviet 'empires'. It was in this context that one should understand the rehabilitation in the 1950s Yugoslavia of the Black Hand and the Young Bosnians, responsible for the assassination of the heir to the Habsburg throne in Sarajevo on 28 June 1914.[54]

As a Yugoslav delegate in Rangoon told the Asian Socialists' conference, Yugoslavia viewed the Asian peoples' struggle for independence with sympathy because the Yugoslavs too had fought for freedom and survival, paying a high price in the process. 'Yugoslavs arose from the horrible Fascist invasion only to face the shadow of Soviet imperialism,' the delegate stated.[55] In a speech delivered at the Belgrade Conference, Tito identified colonialism as perhaps the main reason for the global crisis and issued strong support to anti-colonial movements.[56] '[T]ogether with Nehru, Nasser, Sukarno and Nkrumah, at the fifteenth anniversary session of the General Assembly in 1960 [see Fig. 1.7], we took the initiative to have the two big powers engage not in confrontation but in negotiations in the interest of reducing tensions,' Tito recalled in Havana in September 1979, his last appearance at a non-aligned summit. 'We pointed out that the United Nations is the place

---

[51] Jovan Čavoški, *Jugoslavija i kinesko-indijski konflikt: 1959–1962* (Belgrade: INIS, 2009); Jeremy Friedman, 'Soviet Policy in the Developing World and the Chinese Challenge in the 1960s', *Cold War History*, 10:2 (May 2010), 247–72; Alessandro Iandolo, 'The Rise and Fall of the "Soviet Model of Development" in West Africa, 1957–64', *Cold War History*, 12:4 (November 2012), 683–704; Tobias Rupprecht, *Soviet Internationalism after Stalin: Interaction and Exchange between the USSR and Latin America during the Cold War* (Cambridge: Cambridge University Press, 2015).
[52] Kardelj, *Historical Roots of Non-alignment*, p. 19.   [53] Ibid., pp. 5–6.
[54] See Dejan Djokić, *A Concise History of Serbia* (Cambridge: Cambridge University Press, 2023), pp. 392–403, 507–8.
[55] *Report of the First Asian Socialist Conference*, p. 21.
[56] AJ, KPR 837, I-4-a, box 202, 'Govor predsednika Tita u generalnoj debati', Belgrade, 3 September 1961.

Figure 1.7 Left to right: 'Founding fathers of the NAM': Prime Minister
Jawaharlal Nehru of India and Presidents Nkrumah of Ghana, Nasser of the
United Arab Republic/Egypt, Sukarno of Indonesia and Tito of Yugoslavia,
New York, 29 September 1960.
MJ, Tito's Photo Archive, 1960_143_127.

where all key problems of the world should be discussed. This still holds
true today.'[57]

Diplomatic activities intensified in the months leading up to the Belgrade
Conference. Between February and April 1961 Tito visited north and west
Africa, while Sukarno and President Keita of Mali came to Belgrade in June,
shortly before another preparatory meeting in Cairo, hosted by Nasser. This
was followed by a visit to Yugoslavia by President Nkrumah of Ghana in early
August.[58] Belgrade was chosen as a neutral venue, to avoid rivalry between
Africa and Asia. Since both world wars had broken out in Europe (and the
spark for the First World War was lit by Yugoslav nationalism), it was, it

[57] Tito, *The Historical Mission*, pp. 12–13.
[58] Vladimir Petrović, 'Josip Broz Tito's Summit Diplomacy in the International Relations of
Socialist Yugoslavia, 1944–1961', *Annales/Annals for Istrian and Mediterranean Studies,
Series Historia et Sociologia* (Koper/Slovenia), 24:4 (2014), 577–92, offers a useful summary
of Tito's trips during this period.

might be said, symbolic that foundations of a new movement seeking to contribute to world peace should be laid at this continent. Today associated with the Yugoslav wars of the 1990s and at that time the worst violence in Europe since the Second World War, Belgrade played host to a global initiative to prevent another world war only three decades earlier.

In preparation for the conference, the hosts took care of every detail, from accommodation, security and food to a rich and truly international programme of cultural events organized for the guests. These included ballet (featuring, among other performances, *Evgeniy Onegin* and *Swan Lake* by Tchaikovsky and *Giselle* by Adolphe Adam), opera (Charles Gounod's *Faust*, Verdi's *Don Carlos* and Borodin's *Prince Igor*), and plays by Harold Pinter and George Bernard Shaw. Works by leading contemporary Yugoslav authors (such as Serb Dobrica Ćosić and Croat Miroslav Krleža) were also featured, as were folk dance performances representative of all parts of Yugoslavia. The guests were taken to sports events, including basketball and football games involving Yugoslavia's leading clubs Partizan and Red Star (both from Belgrade) and Hajduk Split. The cost of hosting the conference was estimated at over 5.5 billion Yugoslav dinars (close to US$7.4 million at the time).[59]

It was the first time such a large number of African and Asian leaders attended an international summit in Europe to discuss the main global issues and offer their views and recommendations, rather than merely watch the powers decide their destiny. Similarly, Belgrade had never before hosted an event of that magnitude. The Yugoslavs must have felt empowered that for once they were not mere spectators or marginal players at international congresses that had profoundly shaped their destinies. For example, it was in Berlin in 1878 that the Great Powers convened to decide on the destiny of the Balkans; the independence of Serbia and Montenegro (and Romania) was recognized, but Bosnia-Herzegovina was occupied by Austria-Hungary (a decision directly linked with the outbreak of the First World War in 1914), while Bulgaria remained an Ottoman province. Four decades later, the 1919–20 Paris Peace Conference recognized, albeit reluctantly, Serbia's unification with Montenegro, Croatia, Bosnia and Slovenia to form Yugoslavia.

President Tito probably echoed a predominant view at the conference when he pointed out during the opening session that no longer would the few most powerful states determine the course of international relations: small

---

[59] AJ, 837 KPR, I-4-a/2, box 201, 'Izveštaj o organizaciji kulturnih, zabavnih i sportskih priredaba za vreme Beogradske konferencije', [Belgrade] 25 August–10 September 1961. The official Yugoslav exchange rate in 1961 was 750 dinars for 1 US dollar. Biljana Stojanović, 'Exchange Rates of the Dinar, 1945–1990: An Assessment of Appropriateness and Efficiency', in *Experience of Exchange Rate Regimes in Southeastern Europe in a Historical and Comparative Perspective (Proceedings of the Österreischische Nationalbank Workshop)*, 13, 2008, pp. 198–243, 207.

and non-aligned nations were now seizing an opportunity to make their voices heard, too.[60] The south-east Asian origins of non-alignment were acknowledged. 'The Bandung Conference and the principles proclaimed there were, after the adoption of the Charter of the U.N. [in June 1945], the first powerful display of this contemporary view [based on non-bloc politics] of international relations,' Tito said in his opening address.[61] The next speaker was Sukarno – the speaking order acknowledged Indonesia's place in the emerging movement – who described his country as one of the pioneers of non-alignment, promoting 'independence, abiding peace, social justice, [and] the freedom to be free'. Non-alignment, however, should not be confused with neutrality, he argued, but instead ought to become a 'coordinated moral force'.[62] This last part revealed a 'hawkish' approach, in contrast to that of Prime Minister Jawaharlal Nehru, whose position was more genuinely neutral.

Nehru's participation in the conference, and his leading role in the nascent movement, was a coup for the non-aligned countries. India had begun to regard itself as an emerging power capable of influencing international affairs on its own, unlike the smaller states represented in Belgrade, which looked to increase their influence through the new movement. These included Indonesia, whose President Sukarno openly sided with the Soviets at the conference, calling, for example, for the recognition of East Germany. They also included Yugoslavia, the only country at the conference that had recognized the German Democratic Republic (in 1957, leading West Germany to suspend diplomatic relations with Belgrade). The West German foreign ministry threatened the conference participants with suspension of aid if they recognized Berlin. Bonn viewed the division of Germany as 'artificial and temporary', demanding free elections and reunification.[63]

Tito believed that India's prime minister was too cautious and admired Sukarno's 'action-oriented' foreign policy, although he also thought that unlike Nehru, the Indonesian president could be at times reckless and unrealistic.[64] Yet it was Tito's failure to condemn the Soviets for their role in East

---

[60] AJ, 837 KPR, I-4-a/2, box 203, 'Govor njegove ekscelencije Josipa Broza Tita, predsednika Federativne narodne republike Jugoslavije prilikom otvaranja konferencije šefova država i vlada vanblokovskih zemalja', Belgrade 1 September 1961.

[61] Ibid.

[62] AJ, 837 KPR, I-4-a/2, box 203, 'Address by H.E. Dr. Sukarno, President of the Republic of Indonesia before the conference of heads of state or government of Non-aligned countries', Belgrade, 1 September 1961.

[63] AJ, 112 TANJUG, 434, Dnevni informativni bilten, 7:00am, 7 September 1961; Politisches Archiv des Auswärtigen Amts, Berlin, B42–19-2 (reports from Belgrade), September 1961.

[64] Author's interview with Budimir Lončar, Zagreb, 22 June 2018. For tensions between Indonesia and Yugoslavia, over the direction of the movement during the time of the second conference of the non-aligned countries held in Cairo in September 1964 (which coincided with Khrushchev's fall), see Tvrtko Jakovina, *Budimir Lončar: Od Preka do vrha svijeta* (Belgrade: Službeni glasnik, 2021), pp. 164–70, 184–94.

Germany and for the resumption of nuclear testing that infuriated the United States.[65] Yugoslavia may have been non-aligned, but it was not necessarily neutral.

Conference discussions focused on the global political crisis that seemed to have brought the world to the brink of a Third World War. The Suez Crisis and the Hungarian Revolution had barely ended when the building of the Berlin Wall began in August 1961. This triggered a partial mobilization of the US army, which in turn was followed by the resumption of Soviet nuclear testing, announced on the eve of the Belgrade summit. If Belgrade was confronted with a 'moment of truth', as a historian of the non-alignment noted,[66] then Fig. 1.1 captured a key symbolic moment within the moment. The fragile world peace would be once again seriously challenged a year after Belgrade, during the Cuban Missile Crisis.

At its conclusion, the conference adopted a 'Statement on the Danger of War and Appeal for Peace', drafted by Nehru. Identical copies of the declaration were delivered personally to US President John F. Kennedy by Sukarno and to Khrushchev by Nehru and Nkrumah. It called for the end of nuclear testing and armament and of colonialism. It condemned violence in Angola and Congo, supported Indonesia's claims over West Irian (Western New Guinea) and demanded social and economic emancipation of underdeveloped countries.[67]

Where Did the Car Go To?

Although the scene in the opening image (Fig. 1.1) is still, the car invites us to imagine movement. As the vehicle drove away, eventually out of the camera's reach, the most immediate next stop was probably the Metropole Hotel, where Sukarno was staying. More symbolically, the journey took Tito and Sukarno to the central stage of an emerging global movement, which advocated for the freedom and independence of small nations and the end of the division of the world into mutually hostile blocs. A Third World War was avoided, but to what extent this was down to Tito, Sukarno and the other non-aligned leaders is not easy to say. In retrospect, their role was probably fairly modest, but even small contributions matter at times when international tensions threaten global peace. The Cold War eventually ended (or it seemed so) in 1989–91, thirty years after the Belgrade Conference, ironically just as Yugoslavia began to break up.

---

[65] Frederick P. Bunnell, *American Reactions to Indonesia's Role in the Belgrade Conference* (Ithaca, NY: Cornell University Press, 1964), pp. 74–75.
[66] Rubinstein, *Yugoslavia and the Non-aligned World*, p. 107.
[67] AJ, 837 KPR, I-4-a/2, box 204, 'Deklaracija Konferencije šefova država i vlada neangažovanih zemalja sa apelom o opasnosti od rata i apel za mir', Belgrade, 6 September 1961.

If the immediate international impact of Belgrade was largely symbolic, like Bandung before it,[68] its real value became obvious in the mid- to long run, when the NAM properly took shape in the 1970s. The Belgrade Conference represented a landmark in the evolution of non-alignment as a factor in international relations. Bandung may have anticipated Belgrade, but it was a one-off. The Belgrade Conference, on the other hand, was the first in a series of summits that reintroduced the traditional diplomatic practice of discussing difficult issues and recommending solutions in a world dominated by the confrontation between the two main ideological blocs.

In the short term, the non-aligned countries succeeded in bringing about the enlargement of the UN Disarmament Committee in 1962, which included non-nuclear, non-engaged nations, making a small, but significant step towards easing the arms race between the blocs. They also contributed to the rejection of Khrushchev's proposal for a collective, three-member general secretariat of the UN following the death of Dag Hammarskjöld in a plane crash in Congo, just days after the Belgrade Conference. The conference represented a diplomatic triumph for Tito and Yugoslavia, justifying the Yugoslav leader's fondness for international summitry and cementing his emerging reputation as an important world statesman. He was accepted and trusted by new nations who remained mistrustful of Western leaders. By contrast, Tito did not seem to aspire to interfere in their internal affairs or to dominate and exploit them.[69] Starting out as a group of countries independent of the US-led Western and Soviet-dominated Eastern bloc, and brought together by a commitment to global peace, decolonization, and economic and social emancipation of the underdeveloped world, the NAM came to enjoy considerable prestige and influence. It eventually grew into an organization with over 100 members. Its significance has diminished to the point of irrelevance since the fall of the Berlin Wall; the rise and decline of the NAM therefore coincided with the erection and destruction of the wall. Nevertheless, the fact that the NAM continues to exist, with headquarters in Jakarta and offices in New York, means that it is possible to say that the legacy of the Belgrade Conference remains alive.

The summit was not equally significant for all the participants. For example, main works on Indonesia[70] rarely refer to the NAM, let alone the movement's founding event. On the other hand, non-alignment provides a key to

---

[68] Christopher J. Lee, 'The Rise of Third World Diplomacy: Success and Its Meanings at the 1955 Asian-African Conference in Bandung, Indonesia', in Robert Hutchings and Jeremi Suri (eds.), *Foreign Policy Breakthrough: Cases in Successful Diplomacy* (Oxford: Oxford University Press, 2015), pp. 47–71, 49.

[69] Rubinstein, *Yugoslavia and the Non-aligned World*, pp. 110–12.

[70] For example, Michael Leifer, *Indonesia's Foreign Policy* (London: George Allen & Unwin, 1983); Legge, *Sukarno*; Adrian Vickers, *A History of Modern Indonesia* (Cambridge: Cambridge University Press 2005).

understanding Tito's Yugoslavia. Belgrade represented a pivotal moment in Tito's career, putting him firmly on the global stage. From the mid-1960s – by coincidence around the time Sukarno lost power – Tito increasingly focused on international affairs. At the same time, he used a carefully built image of a world statesman, independent from and mediating between the blocs, in order to help maintain Yugoslavia's sensitive ethnic and religious balance and suppress dissent at home. Milovan Djilas, who was once seen as Tito's likely successor, was purged and imprisoned for challenging party dogma in the mid-1950s. Living in de facto house arrest in a flat just around the corner from the parliament building, he was kept under close surveillance during the Belgrade Conference.

Frequent and well-publicized meetings with Sukarno and Nasser as well as Belgrade's open support for the Algerian independence movement did not harm Tito's doctrine of 'brotherhood and unity' of the Yugoslavs, many of whom were Muslim. Tito continued to visit non-aligned countries almost until his death in May 1980. His last international performance was at the sixth non-aligned summit in Havana in September 1979, when he played an important role in neutralizing Castro's pro-Soviet line.

Tito's international prestige inspired a mix of admiration, pride and fear among Yugoslavs. Their charismatic leader, always looking authoritative and smartly dressed, was respected worldwide and given prominence greater than a president of a country of Yugoslavia's size would normally merit. These individual and collective memories, preserved in part by photographs such as the ones reproduced here, are in stark contrast to images of post-Yugoslav leaders whose international roles are largely insignificant, especially when compared with Tito's. This partly helps explain a nostalgia for socialism, for Tito and for Yugoslavia, across the former Yugoslav space.[71]

As John Berger has argued, photographs send a message of discontinuity because they have the ability to arrest 'the flow of time in which the event photographed once existed . . . so that, unlike a lived past, it can never lead to the present'.[72] The sense of discontinuity projected by Fig. 1.1 is only enhanced by the fact that Yugoslavia is no more, that Tito and Sukarno are both long dead and that the movement they had helped inaugurate in Belgrade is almost forgotten. Yet is it not the historian's task to contextualize a historical source and to try to bridge the abyss that exists between the past and the present, to point at ruptures and identify continuities? By 'defrosting' a seemingly frozen moment from history shown in Fig. 1.1, I have tried to make sense of it, through discussing both that which is seen and that which is not necessarily obvious to a non-historian – or at least to someone other than this historian.

---

[71] Mitja Velikonja, *Titostalgia: A Study of Nostalgia for Josip Broz* (Ljubljana: Mirovni inštitut, 2008).

[72] Berger, *Understanding a Photograph*, pp. 62–63.

2   In the Image of Imelda

The Surrogate Diplomacy of the First Lady

Patrick Flores

In October 1966, almost at high noon and amid a drizzle, the American President Lyndon B. Johnson descended on humid Los Baños in the Philippines to visit the International Rice Research Institute (IRRI), a facility that was producing 'miracle rice' (Fig. 2.1). In his speech, Johnson said that 'the war on hunger is the only war we seek to escalate'.[1] The region was at war and the United States was complicit, even though Johnson's predecessor, the immensely charismatic John F. Kennedy, had expressed interest in the plight and struggle of post-independence nation-states. The latter may have been described as by turns anti-colonial, anti-communist, and non-aligned, and Third World as a way to signal the 'Cold War's emerging multipolarity ... and the ensuing diffusion of political power'.[2] In 1965, Johnson sent troops to support South Vietnam, and in the same political season, a communist purge plunged Indonesia into a bloodbath.[3] Surely, war was the theatre of this moment, and alongside it were rehearsed the narratives of international development and global food security.

It is for this reason that the landscape was the milieu par excellence on which to choreograph the battle of images between those of terror and plenty in the Cold War. As the 'representative anecdote'[4] of the pastoral or the idyll, the Los Baños landscape of the tropics proved to be the proper vista for the political economy of the miracle of rice to come to light as scenography. And, in this instance, the image is pivotal in the way it supports the witnessing of the conversion. As a politician would sketch out the shift from the village to

[1] Lyndon Johnson, 'Remarks at the International Rice Research Institute, Los Banos, the Philippines, October 26, 1966', in *Public Papers of the Presidents of the United States: Lyndon B. Johnson* (Washington, DC: United States Government Printing Office, 1967), p. 550.

[2] Robert B. Rakove, *Kennedy, Johnson, and the Non-aligned World* (Cambridge: Cambridge University Press, 2014), p. xxviii.

[3] See Jonathan Colman, *The Foreign Policy of Lyndon B. Johnson: The United States and the World, 1963–1969* (Edinburgh: Edinburgh University Press, 2010), and Vincent Bevins, *The Jakarta Method: Washington's Anticommunist Crusade and the Mass Murder Program the Shaped Our World* (New York: Public Affairs, 2020).

[4] Paul Alpers, 'What Is Pastoral?', *Critical Inquiry*, 8:3 (1982), 451.

Figure 2.1 Left to right: Imelda Marcos, Lady Bird Johnson, President
Lyndon Johnson, President Ferdinand Marcos, and Robert Chandler touring
the Los Baños rice fields near Manila, Philippines.
Getty Images.

the plantation by pointing to two diametric opposites: 'Here is the bullock cart.
Here is the nineteenth century ... here is the jumbo jet! The twentieth
century.'[5] The visit of Johnson would ratify this tangibility: '"It's something
you can see"... You can say, "well, go out and look at it." It did happen.'[6] The
scholar Nick Cullather would further dramatize this as a 'parable of seeds':
'IRRI served as a convenient backdrop. Striding onto the experimental rice
field beside Ferdinand and Imelda Marcos, Johnson crouched and sampled the
soil with his fingers.'[7]

On this landscape was composed another performance. Atop a makeshift
wooden walkway, slightly raised from the rice paddy, stand Johnson, his wife
Lady Bird, Institute director Robert Chandler, Philippine President Ferdinand
Marcos, and the First Lady Imelda Marcos, who leads the way. Dressed in the
national formal attire for women, Imelda features prominently in the picture,
one that may embody the relationship between diplomacy and the image as
mediated by the presence, and the beauty, of Imelda, who withstands the

[5] Nick Cullather, 'Miracles of Modernization: The Green Revolution and the Apotheosis of
Technology', *Diplomatic History,* 28:2 (2004), 227.
[6] Ibid.   [7] Ibid.

weather in the sultry environs of the Philippine wetlands. It is Imelda's flexible rhetoric as a First Lady and as a woman that coordinates the people in space, as well as the nature encompassing it. Such a coordination of figure and ground in the production of the image subtends the bonds between nature and culture along with the political function of diplomacy and the material allure of beauty. All condense in the image, or more specifically, the tropic and the tropical image, because it turns and it precipitates.

The aesthetic labour of First Lady Imelda for the Manila Summit on the Vietnam War in 1966 (Fig. 2.1) is an instructive index of the 'diplomatic image'. It exemplifies Imelda's transformative project to translate, or calibrate, the political power of her husband, and later his regime, in terms of 'sensuous particularities'. The latter largely pertain to the production of a theatre commensurate with, or proper to, the statecraft of a post-colonial developing nation-state in the Southeast Asian region. 'For four hundred years we were a subject people', said Imelda, in a *Vanity Fair* interview.[8] 'When Marcos became president, we had been independent for only twenty years. We were a mixture of races. We had to identify who we are. We helped our people to understand what it meant to be Filipino.'[9] Part of this aestheticization of identity as a way to mystify political ascendancy was to incrementally build up the sensible language of the spectacle and the aesthetic education of the self, of which the image was primordial and diplomacy was a trajectory into a worldly presence. Ferdinand became president in 1965; Imelda was thirty-six when she became the 'chatelaine of Malacañang Palace'.[10] The close relationship between Imelda and the image, her persona, and the diplomatic rhetoric it has engendered is a knot hard to untie. Thus, the discussion of the photograph is inextricably a discussion of the persona of Imelda, which informs the salience of the picture.

According to Imelda's biographer, Kerima Polotan, the Summit 'would go down in memory as a brilliant triumph of Imelda Marcos' to achieve the theatre that the government had put up to be part of an emerging international order in which the Third World was asserting its place.[11] Polotan elaborates on this stratagem: 'She headed a committee that called on everyone … to give Manila a new face. Multicolored bulbs for the great trees in the Palace grounds. Coconut leaf matting to camouflage the fishermen's hovels on Roxas Boulevard. Banana trees planted overnight by the roadside to give the foreign ladies something rustic to see on the way to Cavite.… She even

---

[8] Dominic Dunne, 'Imelda in Exile', *Vanity Fair*, 15 September 2008, accessed 26 April 2020, www.vanityfair.com/magazine/1986/08/dunne198608.
[9] Ibid.   [10] Ibid.
[11] Kerima Polotan, *Imelda Romualdez Marcos: A Biography of the First Lady of the Philippines* (Cleveland: World Publishing, 1969), p. 222.

remembered the pickpockets who were rounded up by the police and kept on board a ship just offshore for the duration of the Summit.'[12] The Summit was held in October and culminated in a dinner, hyped as a fiesta, at the Presidential Palace, which was turned into

a fairyland of light and color ... There were fireworks, tilburies, a fluvial parade, ceaseless music, folk dancers – and where the main driveway curved, Imelda Marcos stood.... When she moved, the sequins parted to reveal a shimmering rainbow running from throat to hemline, but the face above the dress excelled any rainbow, and it turned to smile upon everyone, foreigner and political enemy alike.[13]

The aesthetic labour, therefore, coalesced with the contrivance of the locale and the aggrandizement of the self: Imelda restyled Manila in some kind of ethnographic surrealism where the various rituals of the Philippine folk life-cycle taking place across the seasons mingled into a singular pageant. It was at once Maytime and Christmas at the Palace in October.

It must be noted that a month before this event, the Marcoses were in Washington, DC, for a state visit on the invitation of President Johnson, and Imelda, this early in the reign of Ferdinand, had verisimilarly staged their foray into American media and politics with keen attention to the details of appearances. *LIFE* dedicated pages on the visit, characterizing a 'First Lady's lilting diplomacy'.[14] The word 'lilt' is significant, because it subtly references an inflection or an intricacy. It is in many ways a supplement not in the sense that it is supernumerary but in its capacity to address a lack or an imperfection in the typical male presidency, or the routine diplomatic project. Furthermore, the attitude towards Imelda's aesthetic work as a work of gender ('a woman's knowing eye') and culture, of being a woman and being Filipino, discloses a production of 'talent' premised on colonial and persistent discriminations based on gender and culture. After all, this was the time of feminist ferment, systemic racism, and the alacrity of American global power. Imelda would rework the Philippine or the Filipino through these maligned, hegemonic, and incendiary categories to realize an identity-effect, a form of liberal recognition for the achievement of being different amid the exceptional exclusions. The writer Polotan rightly discerns here excess, or 'unabashed immoderation',[15] but one that she deems fitting, in fact perfect, to the degree that it is realizable and yoked to some extent to the dominant apparatus.

Perhaps it is on this desire for perfection, or the prospects of perfectibility, that Imelda's role as a diplomatic agent may hinge: how the office of the First Lady invested in the ornament of governmentality. Ornament here is

[12] Ibid., p. 223.   [13] Ibid., p. 224.
[14] 'Visit: Mutual Admiration Alliance', *Life*, 30 September 1966, p. 134.
[15] Nicole CuUnjieng, 'Ferdinand Marcos: Apotheosis of the Philippine Historical Tradition', unpublished AB thesis, University of Pennsylvania, 2009, p. 9.

conceptualized as an elaboration of basic form, on the one hand, and of the very basis itself of a political aesthetic, on the other. This becomes the problematic of the image of a tenuous, tempting Imelda, embedded in diplomatic practice; and Imelda itself as image, the trope of embodied power. In this scheme, the ornament is situated within what anthropologist Alfred Gell frames as a 'technology of enchantment' and 'enchantment of technology'. Gell contends that 'technology is enchanted because the ordinary technical means employed ... point inexorably towards magic, and also towards art, in that art is the idealized form of production'.[16] Attractiveness and attraction are the dynamics at play here: 'we are fascinated because we are essentially at a loss to explain how such an object comes to exist in the world'.[17] The makers of the object similarly 'express the fascination ... with the efficacy of their actual technology which, converging towards the magical ideal, adumbrates this ideal in the real world'.[18] Locating an enchanting Imelda in the world through the technology of diplomacy suspends easy reductions of her image between idealizations borne in gender and culture. It is the aesthetic, this fabulation of the self through the devices of ornament, that lets Imelda elude the overdeterminations of, let us say, masculine and western political formation. The idealization collects at the stem of woman and gender, but it does not settle there.

Adjacent to this idea of ornamentation, which lets the self extend to others in open-ended variations, is the concept of comparativity that bedevils, as seen in what Jose Rizal, the polymath patriot who became the National Hero of the Philippines, intuits as the 'demonio de las comparaciones', or 'specter of comparisons' in Benedict Anderson's translation, or the 'temptation of affinities' in the mind of the Tagalog writer Patricio Mariano.[19] Affinity is regarded here not as the self-consciousness of the enlightened early modern subject but as the folklore of relations. In Spanish, the word *relación* is at once ties and tales; in Filipino, the word *engkanto* from the lexicon of Spanish colonial lower mythology clusters around enchantment. It points as well to the spirit that plays tricks on the eye, leads people astray, and transforms itself 'into the likenesses of mortal friends and relatives'.[20] The *engkanto* at once expresses strangeness and explicates estrangement as it conjures the 'tangibility of the

---

[16] Alfred Gell, 'The Technology of Enchantment and the Enchantment of Technology', in Jeremy Coote and Anthony Shelton (eds.), *Anthropology, Art and Aesthetics* (Oxford: Clarendon Press, 1992), pp. 61–62.

[17] Ibid.   [18] Ibid.

[19] See Patrick D. Flores, 'Polytropic Philippine: Intimating the World in Pieces', in Michelle Antoinette and Caroline Turner (eds.), *Contemporary Asian Art and Exhibitions: Connectivities and World-Making* (Canberra: Australian National University Press, 2014), pp. 47–65.

[20] Filomeno V. Aguilar, Jr., *Clash of Spirits: The History of Power and Sugar Planter Hegemony on a Visayan Island* (Manila: Ateneo de Manila University Press, 1998), p. 33.

Spanish spirit-world, a force that had impinged upon the islands'.[21] Imelda would gravitate around these notions of the spell and the charm in the encounter between the foreign and the preternatural, in the national and the native. In the end, the accretion of her persona's traces in the neologism 'Imeldific' lays bare a subject and an aesthetic, the indigenous and the intruder. Dictionaries define the word in terms of ostentation, extravagance, and vulgarity.[22] Again, excess and perfection compete in the production of the disproportionate, if not immoderate, image. It must be stressed, however, that attendant to this devotion to image is the iconoclasm. When the Marcoses were deposed in 1986, throngs of protesters stormed the Palace and took down and disfigured their images. Indeed, this was a symptom of the structural condition that ensured Imelda's accumulation of capital through political power and the corresponding insurrection against it. Such accumulation – epitomized by her collection of shoes, dresses, jewellery, art, silver, and so on – would be laid bare as decadent in the days after the uprising, with the accumulation becoming the basis of an opportunity for the Palace to set up a museum for this plethora.

The Facture of the First Lady

My contribution to this volume is a discussion of the role of Imelda Marcos in the Marcos government's diplomatic practice and foreign policy. At the outset, I cast Imelda both as a First Lady and as a vital co-operator in running the affairs of the Philippine state from the 1960s through the 1980s, the other half of the so-called Marcos conjugal dictatorship, with Ferdinand assuming the role of either the sultan or the predatory boss.[23] At one point in time, in fact, she was simultaneously Governor of Metro Manila (1975), Minister of Human Settlements (1976), Member of the Interim Parliament (1978), and de facto Ambassador Plenipotentiary and Extraordinary. These positions meant that she had access to the appreciable resources of government and benefitted from the largesse, evidenced by the numerous charges of corruption against her. This being said, her status as First Lady and Patroness of the Arts was an altogether different, though not isolated, institution; and it is not to be dismissed as a mere appendage of whatever political privilege accrued to her station in the hierarchy. It was, initially and finally, as First Lady that Imelda evinced a compelling presence in the political narrative of the Marcos era. The combination of

---

[21] Ibid., p. 34.
[22] 'Imeldific', *Urban Dictionary*, accessed 26 April 2020, www.urbandictionary.com/define.php?term=Imeldific.
[23] CuUnjieng, 'Ferdinand Marcos'.

her beauty and charisma accumulated a particular aesthetic that inevitably evolved into a policy of culture and democracy so central in the formation of a post-independence nation-state in Southeast Asia. Also, it must be said that Imelda had a hand in Ferdinand's party nomination for president in 1965. Many accounts portray Imelda as a captivating figure whose physical attributes (height, complexion) and political skills may have enhanced or even exceeded those of her husband's. She would, for instance, remember the birthdays of the wives of politicians and work the crowd with her singing: she was a beauty queen, after all, and in a culture that cherishes the intimacy of voice and face, Imelda was a remarkable ensemble.[24] Ferdinand Marcos, Jr., the only son of Ferdinand and Imelda who was elected president in 2022, believes in fact that the most gifted politician in the family is his mother, describing her as 'intuitive'.[25] Such an observation is important as a foil to the rationality that supposedly governs the acumen of male politicians. Imelda plays with both the typification of gender and its contravention; she finds virtue in not being taken too 'seriously'.[26] This has in a way undermined Imelda's credibility, making her look frivolous, if not loony. Imelda herself encourages this impression in her interviews. To cite a case, she claims that when she kissed Mao Zedong's hand on her visit to China in 1974, Mao supposedly told her that in five minutes, she 'started the end of the Cold War'.[27] She also explains that on her diplomatic missions, she refused to be briefed on the people she would be meeting: 'I didn't want to read books about the leaders that I was going to meet because I had my own eyes, I had my own ears and senses. Many leaders were called monsters.... They were humane.'[28]

For this chapter, I chose the image of Imelda Marcos standing on a wooden walkway built across a rice paddy at the International Rice Research Institute (IRRI) in Los Baños in Laguna, a province south of the capital, Manila. Here, she is with a group that includes President Johnson, Lady Bird Johnson, Ferdinand Marcos, and Robert Chandler of the IRRI. The tableau is deep, completed by rice farmers on the left side, water buffaloes in the foreground, and lush flora in the background that surrounds the visiting dignitaries. The Johnson diaries describe Los Baños as a 'beautiful, but hot place ... The weather must have been in the 90 degree range, with intermittent – very sparse – drizzle. And the President and First Lady both showed the wear of the heat. The President was perspiring heavily, and Mrs Johnson's makeup

[24] See Fenella Cannell, *Power and Intimacy in the Christian Philippines* (Cambridge: Cambridge University Press, 1999).

[25] *The Kingmaker*, directed by Lauren Greenfield (New York: Showtime Documentary Films, 2019).

[26] Ibid.　　[27] Ibid.　　[28] Ibid.

needed freshening.'[29] The entire scene is exemplary of the Philippine pastoral or picturesque, which is both interior and frontier, that intersects with the spectacle of Cold War modernity, consisting of professions to peace and the conquest of hunger. The Johnson chronicle confirms this 'very picturesque sight – an umbrella being held over the President to protect him from the hot sun, palm trees in the background, and in the far far background, great mountains covered in deep green vegetation'.[30] Johnson was in Manila in October 1966 to attend the Manila Summit Conference hosted by Marcos and joined by Prime Minister Harold Holt of Australia, President Park Chung Hee of the Republic of Korea, Prime Minister Keith Holyoake of New Zealand, President Ferdinand E. Marcos of the Philippines, Prime Minister Thanom Kittikachorn of Thailand, and Chairman Nguyen Van Thieu and Prime Minister Nguyen Cao Ky of the Republic of Vietnam. Officially, the meeting sought to achieve 'freedom in Vietnam and in the Asian and Pacific areas': 'to be free from aggression; to conquer hunger, illiteracy, and disease; to build a region of security, order, and progress; to seek reconciliation and peace throughout Asia and the Pacific'.[31] After the conference, President Johnson went to Vietnam to visit the American troops. Before coming to Manila, he embarked on what had been projected as an 'Asian Odyssey' to usher in a 'new Asia'.[32] This began with a visit to Hawaii, American Samoa, New Zealand, and Australia, with the Pacific decisively lodged in this Asian axis.

I reference in this picture the role of rice research at this time through the IRRI, established in 1960 by the Philippine government and the Ford and Rockefeller Foundations, mainly as a response to global hunger and exponential population growth. Here, we glean how Imelda iterates the character of the First Lady as largely a consort and a hostess, reinforced by the earlier account of how she had fastidiously prepared, or perhaps facelifted, Manila for the visit of Johnson and how she angled for a particular image and look when she and her husband visited the United States prior. In both instances, Imelda played true to form, a form that she considerably enhanced by her investment in beauty. This iteration and this enhancement of the persona of the First Lady are quite clear. But Imelda more than just reproduced the existing model; she transformed it so that the institution became distinct and intelligible by way of

[29] 'The White House President Lyndon B. Johnson Daily Diary (October 26, 1966)', LBJ Presidential Library, accessed 26 April 2020, www.lbjlibrary.net/assets/lbj_tools/daily_diary/pdf/1966/19661026.pdf.

[30] Ibid.

[31] 'Joint Communique: Goals of Freedom,' *Philippine Official Gazette*, 25 October 1966, www.officialgazette.gov.ph/1966/10/25/joint-communique-goals-of-freedom.

[32] 'Asian Odyssey, October 1966. MP761,' LBJ Library, 24 July 2012, YouTube, 59:02, https://youtube.com/watch?v=Q6frLmliG0s.

her techniques.[33] Through the vehicle of the First Lady, Imelda emerged with a certain surplus that she parlayed into a signature stature to transcend the traditional expectations of the First Lady as exclusively consort, hostess, confidante, campaigner, or advocate.[34] With Imelda, the First Lady was all these, and the peer of leaders over and above. This is clear in the photograph as the personae are arrayed and not arranged in a hierarchy. Imelda was without equal, at the same time she was First Lady, a position that a man or a male president can never take on, but by the early 1970s there were already rumours that she would succeed her husband. Imelda, moreover, was not the only First Lady of her time to take on a larger political role. Precedents may be cited: Pat Nixon's solo trip to Africa in 1972 mixed ceremony with high-level discussions about her husband's visit to China. During a tour of Latin America, Rosalyn Carter trumpeted 'the dominant themes of Jimmy Carter's foreign policy' such as human rights and nuclear non-proliferation. Similarly, the beauty and grace of Eva Peron and Madame Chiang Kai-shek were utilized to gain sympathy for their national governments in the 1940s.[35]

In a paternalist context, the Marcoses conveyed their ascendancy as mythic and ancestral, cultivating a hybrid legend of the First Man and First Woman on earth as their analogues in the form of the Strong and the Beautiful (Malakas at Maganda). The First Lady discourse sustained this, only to be re-functioned and inevitably superseded by the incipient Imelda figure that would inaugurate a moment of sensuous particularity for an altogether singular aesthetic. But the emergence of this figure was not without its trauma. Two instances are germane. Early in the tenure of Ferdinand, Imelda was so strained by the duties of the First Lady that she suffered a nervous breakdown. She went to New York for psychiatric treatment. Doctors told Ferdinand that Imelda could not withstand the pressures of a hectic political life, whereupon he decided to leave politics if this was the only way for his wife to recover. It was at this point that Imelda reframed her mindset and reoriented that same political life to be no longer a burden but a privilege to help those who most needed it. The second instance was occasioned by Imelda's discovery of Ferdinand's affair with the American movie actress Dovie Beams in 1970. This created a scandal involving a sound recording of Ferdinand during one of his trysts with the

---

[33] See Kristine E. Corpuz, Yasmine B. Stones, Alexandra Cates, and Erika B. Suyo, 'Imelda Marcos' Diplomacy: The Transformation of the Role of a First Lady', unpublished paper, Manila Ateneo de Davao University, 2016.

[34] Robert P. Watson, 'The First Lady Reconsidered: Presidential Partner and Political Institution', *Presidential Studies Quarterly*, 27:4 (1997), 805–18; and Natalie Gonella-Platts and Katherine Fritz, *A Role without a Rulebook: The Influence and Leadership of Global First Ladies* (Dallas: George W. Bush Institute, 2017).

[35] Dean J. Kotlowski, 'The Possibilities and Limitations of First-Lady Diplomacy: Imelda Marcos and the Nixon Administration', *Diplomatic History*, 40:2 (2016), 328.

woman. Imelda was crushed and scorned. Crawling out of this sordid episode, Imelda henceforth flexed more political muscle and assumed a more dominant position across the spheres of governing the nation. In 1975, when Imelda had tea with First Lady Betty Ford at the White House, her dossier already read thus:

> Marcos recently created some controversy in her heavily Christian country (95%) when she publicly stated that she was not totally opposed to divorce and abortion. She reportedly said that she favored more positive (preventive) birth control measures over abortion, but would not totally rule out the latter in all cases. Mrs. Marcos has developed a considerable public role during the past year. In 1974, she traveled to Peking to promote better relations between the People's Republic of China and the Philippines. Her husband has just named her as governor (mayor) of metropolitan Manila, which encompasses the entire urban area of that capital city and includes a population of 5.4 million. Apparently she plans to involve herself in the day to day operations of the city.[36]

A study of technocracy in the Marcos cabinet reveals that Imelda consolidated her own base within the power elite through the political party and a faction in the military, and at some point became a formidable force in light of her perceived ambition to replace her husband: 'Mrs. Marcos, being the wife of the president, was deemed ... more powerful than Marcos's chief cronies. Mrs. Marcos's intervention in the country's development was also viewed as a form of patronage politics.'[37] But this politics was to be considerably mediated by another politics, the politics of beauty, which Imelda expressed with virtuosity and deployed with palpability through mostly brutalist infrastructure. The soft and the hard converge in Imelda's image, which can be traced to the primal scene, as it were, of her first encounter in 1954 with Ferdinand, who was then a promising legislator from the north of the Philippines. They met in Congress, where Imelda's uncle, a politician from the central islands, was the Speaker. She had political pedigree, but she did not belong to the traditional political elite. She built on this limited symbolic capital the capital of beauty. She was the Rose of Tacloban, a beauty title from her province of Leyte and the Muse of Manila in the big city. She was a 'beauty queen' of two cities, in other words.

This phrase 'beauty queen' is foundational in the discourse and structure of Imelda's politics and power. First, it assembles a history of image-making across the country's three successive colonialisms in the hands of Spain, the

---

[36] 'Talking Points for Visit of Mrs. Imelda Marcos, November 19, 1975,' Betty Ford White House Papers, 1973–1977, Ford Library Museum, accessed 26 April 2020, www.fordlibrarymuseum .gov/library/document/0018/4515782.pdf.

[37] Teresa S. Encarnacion Tadem, *Philippine Politics and the Marcos Technocrats: The Emergence and Evolution of a Power Elite* (Manila: Ateneo de Manila University Press, 2019), p. 191.

United States, and Japan. The potency of beauty is simultaneously religious and secular, as the word 'queen' can simultaneously describe Mary and a self-possessed woman. Beauty, therefore, derives attractiveness from a range of identifications between the religious and secular; Imelda prides on calling herself the 'star and slave' of her people, partaking of the religious and secular valences of being an icon. Second, the formulation of 'beauty queen' cites a civilizational pretension, a royal or a monarchical system within which Imelda wanted to site herself. Her penchant for regalia and other accoutrements such as the tiara and the sash testifies to this disposition. She had also claimed to have descended from ancient nobility, with citations of the Assyrian Semiramis, and cultivated friendships with heiresses and socialites linked to royalty. Portraits by modern-day court painters, such as Basuki Abdullah, Ralph Cowan, and Claudio Bravo, depicted Imelda and her family as monarchs, or monarch-like. In 1971, she was at the breath-taking commemoration of the founding of Persepolis, presided over by the Shah of Iran. She stood shoulder to shoulder with heads of state and royalty, and might have thought of herself to be both. She might have also admired and later emulated Empress Farah, the wife of the Shah who was a patroness of the arts and humanitarian projects. Moreover, it is reported that Imelda had bought the pearl and diamond tiara of Empress Maria Feodorovna, wife of Tsar Alexander III and mother of Nicholas II. In March 1986, *Newsweek* ran a cover with Imelda's image alongside the text 'Queen Imelda'. It is this queenship that transcodes Imelda's aspirations to ordain her own court, independent of Ferdinand, through a kind of 'divine' destiny held up by mythology, religion, folklore, and popular culture.

Finally, the idea of 'beauty queen', while immersed in the abstractions of the sublime, likewise crystallizes a level of modernity in the form of the modern woman in the artifice invented by Imelda: a deliberately crossbreed signifier of tradition and innovation to precisely overcome the constraints of this binarism, but which has only served to retain the normative commitments of patriarchy and post-colonial dependency on paradigms set by western democracies. As a US Embassy official appraised Imelda during her husband's campaign for the presidency in 1965: Imelda's success during the campaign lay in 'combining regal looks and bearing with the simplicity and directness of a successful young career woman in a more technically advanced society'.[38] Imelda's cultural vision derived from this repertoire: civilizing and modernizing art, on the one hand, and indigenous and local creativity, on the other. For Imelda, the Philippines, and she, were both.

---

[38] Katherine Ellison, *Imelda: Steel Butterfly of the Philippines* (Lincoln, NE: iUniverse, 1988), p. 70.

Vectors: Culture, Development, and the International

The ambiguity may have sustained interest in Imelda's viability as a political presence. As a scholar comments: 'Imelda Marcos was a unique case since no one, male or female, occupied a position comparable to hers in the Philippines. She was enough of a presidential insider to be able to undertake high-profile foreign trips and enough of a foreign policy outsider to employ non-traditional metaphors in making her points to American officials – language that drew criticism.'[39] It is within this framework that Imelda's diplomatic practice and image may be more productively grasped. As mentioned earlier, an identity for the post-colonial nation-state in Southeast Asia was avidly desired. This identity could be analyzed by looking at certain aspects that constitute it and that render any diplomatic project present and cogent for it to fully flourish.

First is the discourse of culture through which Imelda gains passage and symbolic capital. The cultural may be contrasted here with the political, with the First Lady promoting Philippine culture in her local and international sorties largely through her dress, which henceforth would become emblematic of her persona and the cultural polity it signified. The dress is called the *terno*. It is a formal attire worn largely by the Filipino elite and which Imelda appropriated to allude to a Philippine heritage for the world to know and acknowledge. It is most likely that the paradigm at work here was of Jacqueline Kennedy, who was likewise known for sharpening a profile for American culture in refurbishing the White House or endorsing modern art through the Museum of Modern Art of New York. Imelda renovated the Presidential Palace called Malacañang, too, and built up an infrastructure for cultural institutions in the Philippines, alongside hospitals. As one of what she preached as the 'basic needs of man', culture, therefore, became her currency through which to become present on the world stage as a representative of her husband and the Philippine government. This enabled Imelda to assert her coeval status in the political sphere and craft an identity distinguishable from Ferdinand. It was also convenient for Ferdinand to let Imelda carry out diplomatic endeavours with sufficient public attention, but without official imprimatur. Imelda's surrogate diplomacy was almost, but not quite, diplomatic in the orthodox sense, making her work as envoy attractive but not sanctioned, potent but not necessarily binding.

Culture in Imelda's mind was not only an abstraction. It had to be ensconced in public life and supported by infrastructure. She reclaimed land from the fabled Manila Bay to build the Cultural Center of the Philippines. The transformation of water into terra firma may serve as an allegory of Imelda's

---

[39] Kotlowski, 'The Possibilities and Limitations of First-Lady Diplomacy', p. 350.

transfiguration herself from First Lady to a co-producer of political power. She did it by instilling culture as a foundation to what Ferdinand contemplated as a revolution from the centre, with democracy and development propped up to countervail an earlier oligarchy and an emergent socialism. Without culture, there would be no tangible democratic ethos to be sensed, because the body politic would have no reason to fit in a Philippine collective. And without culture, the amelioration of the human would be bereft, merely instrumentalized by economic and political ideals.

Second is the objective of the Marcos government to embrace international presence. One way to concretize this was for Imelda to be visible in diplomatic affairs and to broaden the foreign policy as premised on Marcos' effort to cast the Philippines as relatively autonomous and not exclusively within the American matrix. It was Imelda who opened the Philippine diplomatic missions in Eastern Europe, paved the visit of Ferdinand to China, visited Cuba and met Fidel Castro, and persuaded Muammar Gaddafi of Libya to sign the Tripoli Agreement to stop the shipment of weapons to the south of the Philippines, among other activities that she undertook. With Imelda as the vector of this internationalism, to be consolidated at the heart of the initiative was an encompassing discourse that addressed the costs of economic progress and specified the aspect of the human as an indispensable element.

Philippine foreign policy began to take firm shape in 1972 after Marcos declared martial rule over the country. The vision was to give it a 'non-ideological character' and had led to the establishment of diplomatic relations with all socialist countries of Europe, except Albania. These included the USSR, Romania, Yugoslavia, Poland, Czechoslovakia, Bulgaria, Hungary, and the German Democratic Republic. The overarching goal was development diplomacy. In 1975, Imelda spoke at the United Nations General Assembly to represent the president, at which she said, 'We identified ourselves with other developing nations in the common search for a just distribution of the human heritage.'[40] Through Imelda, this agenda would assume a human dimension: 'The new international economic order confronts not only our instinct for survival, or our natural desire for material well-being, but also the deepest values of our civilization. The challenge, therefore, is ultimately addressed to the conscience of humanity. We are called upon to create a new moral image of man.'[41]

Layered around culture and internationalism is the concern for nature as a frontier of development, but at the same time as a defence against the

---

[40] Imelda Romualdez Marcos, 'Towards a New World Society', in Carlos P. Romulo (ed.), *The Diplomacy of Consent* (Manila: Department of Foreign Affairs, National Media Production Center, 1976), p. 10.

[41] Ibid., p. 15.

exploitation of the relentless engines of human progress. In this scenario, the presence of Imelda during the visit of President Johnson to IRRI in Los Baños is crucial, as she absorbs the energy of the natural in relation to her tilling of the cultural. That this transpires in an agrarian setting coordinates the natural and the cultural as impulses of rearing and refinement. The basis of her mythology as the beautiful, the maternal, and the goddess intertwined also resonates in this event as it bolsters the category of woman as being of nature and as the source of fertility. The IRRI was built specifically to solve the problems of hunger: its research focused on genetics and plant breeding, agronomy, plant pathology, entomology, plant physiology, chemistry, soil chemistry, soil microbiology, statistics, agricultural economics, and agricultural engineering.

Set against a rustic landscape in Los Baños, Imelda vivifies her diplomatic work, supported by the spectacle of a 'miracle rice'. According to IRRI, 'the successful breeding of the now famous high yielding varieties [started] with IR8, known as the "miracle rice", and [was] followed in succession by IR5, IR20, IR22, and more recently, IR24 ... The potential for service it holds for mankind gives the rice-eating peoples every reason to be optimistic in a world anxiously engrossed in the life-and-death race between food production and population growth.'[42] These ventures in rice research and production were part of the political economy of rice in the New Society regime of Ferdinand Marcos. It formed part of a succession of other projects like Masagana 99, launched in May 1973, in which the government supplied 'credit, fertilizer and other chemicals, and guidance from farm technicians'.[43] It must be stated that in the New Society, 'land reform shifted in earnest from rental reduction to land transfer'.[44] Another project was helmed by Imelda herself, the Palayan ng Bayan (Rice Field of the Nation), unveiled in July 1973, in which new land was opened up for rice.[45]

Cullather supports this trope of advancement and is invested in this process of visualization, investigating a particular technicity: 'the use of a technology – such as rice – to visualize a boundary between tradition and modernity ... an opportunity where irrigation, fertilizer, and peasant education can produce miracles in the sight of the beholder'.[46] The Cold War dualities of tradition and modernity, progress and stasis were part of this visual opportunity, and this was carried through the infrastructure of IRRI itself.[47]

---

[42] D. L. Umali, 'Rice Improvement through International Cooperation', in *Rice, Science & Man: Papers Presented at the Tenth Anniversary Celebration of the International Rice Research Institute, April 20–21, 1972* (Los Baños: International Rice Research Institute, 1972), p. 81.

[43] Mahar Mangahas, 'The Political Economy of Rice in the New Society', *Food Research Institute Studies,* 14:3 (1975), 300.

[44] Ibid., p. 303.   [45] Ibid., p. 307.   [46] Ibid., p. 229.   [47] Ibid., p. 233.

Imelda and the Paddy

I am drawn to the picture of Imelda at IRRI because it summons the early Marcos period, before the deification and demonization of the Marcoses that came in the 1970s. From the perspective of art history as it comes in contact with diplomatic history, this picture for me generates strata of possible theoretical concerns, and all these revolve around the figure, the being and the thing, that is Imelda. I remark on three moments of this figure.

First is Imelda's surface. It is indexed by a distinct dress, the *terno*, which at first was used to denote a suit for men and women and later described an outfit with matching details. In the array of political personages in the country or elsewhere, the dress sets Imelda apart, but with the careful mixture of so-called western details like jewellery and the fabled shoes, Imelda transforms into a cosmopolite, at once of a place and of an elsewhere, local and world-class, so to speak. The dress also shores up her maternal stature in Marcos' patrimonial and paternalist state; it has been argued that the dress was originally Marian in origin, with the sleeves eventually flaring into a scallop design over time and then finally tapering and clipped like the wings of the butterfly. This formal wear implies Filipino identity at a certain level and would be appropriated by Imelda as an iconic conflation of that identity and herself. Nation and self, therefore, congeal in the attire. This leads to a certain diminution of iconicity afforded by the dress, because Imelda wears it quite ubiquitously, with the formality of the apparel thinning out as it becomes commonplace through the very conspicuous Imelda. This leads us to ask if Imelda wears the dress as a 'costume' of sorts, to consciously signify a mélange of signs and makes those signs necessarily quotidian. This pursuit of the consequences of 'costuming' may be an expression of style and distinction, on one hand, and a popularization of the use of a highly coded dress, on the other.

The dress, however, has been modified by Imelda, again a testimony to her effort to make it au courant, or to modernize it, as it were. Previously, the zipper had been introduced to make it easier for women to wear it. According to an account,

She told couturier Ramon Valera to make the butterfly sleeves smaller and shorter – three inches above the elbow. Then the top of the sleeves was subtly beveled instead of upright. These techniques gave the illusion of a wider shoulder and drew attention to Marcos's waistline. Hence, the silhouette. The neckline circumference was adjusted to make her neck look longer.[48]

---

[48] Marge C. Enriquez, 'Ternocon – And How Imelda Marcos Changed the Terno', *Philippine Daily Inquirer*, 25 May 2018, https://lifestyle.inquirer.net/295345/ternocon-imelda-marcos-changed-terno.

In the occasion at Los Baños, Imelda wore a white *terno* of most likely crepe, with a black tulip design all over. The single-piece dress hangs from Imelda's broad shoulders from which the entire fabric falls, held by butterfly sleeves from the sides, cinched at the waist in an Empire cut, which allows for a drape all the way down to the hem. Imelda's typical *terno* was heavy, and she was said to have complained that the structure constrained her, making it hard to raise her hand, for instance. Again, the tedium and the suppleness merge in the dress itself.

In this particular image, the dress heightens the pastoral aesthetic, evoking the visual language of the first Philippine National Artist, Fernando Amorsolo, who helped define a Philippine identity in the popular imagination in the first half of the twentieth century, when the Philippines was under American colonialism. Amorsolo propagated the idyllic tableau of the countryside in which the rice paddy figured strongly and fascinated American officials and tourists. It is somewhat reprised here in the photography, with the foreground presenting the embellishments of the theatre: the water buffalo, the paddy, and the surrounding nature. Imelda was an exponent of projects related to agriculture as earlier mentioned, and so this was not a tangent in her inventory of roles. A recurring image in Amorsolo's paintings was the 'country maiden' who leisurely tended the fields. Imelda spoke to this iconography as well. She named Amorsolo the country's first National Artist for refracting a nuance of authentic, autochthonous light that is, according to the official citation, 'the light of optimism, the light of a world unsullied by technology and materialism'.[49]

In this silhouette captured by the butterfly sleeves, Imelda would earn the name 'Iron Butterfly' or 'Steel Butterfly', echoing perhaps the later label 'Iron Lady' for the British Prime Minister Margaret Thatcher. It cites the intersection between the 'natural' quality of the hovering butterfly and the industrial property of 'iron' and 'steel'. The tension between the words marks the fluidity and the conviction of the Imelda figure. It is this catachresis that defines the diplomatic image, an amalgam of First Lady and Steel Butterfly.

Alongside the dress delineating the image of Imelda is her coiffure that completes the silhouette. It is technically called a bouffant, which was popular in the 1950s and can be traced to the eighteenth century. It was 'an elaborate style in which large quantities of hair were back-combed or teased and frozen into place with aerosol spray'.[50] Imelda followed this basic procedure, only to augment the already voluminous hair with a hairpiece, which was fixed to the crown by hairpins, to effect more density. The bouffant demanded time and

---

[49] From the citation of Fernando Amorsolo as National Artist, 1972.
[50] Miriam Forman-Brunell (ed.), *Girlhood in America: An Encyclopedia* (Santa Barbara, CA: ABC-CLIO, 2001), vol. 1, p. 355.

technique to achieve; its 'complexity . . . dictated that young women depend on their stylists to sculpt their hair and keep it in place'.[51] There was both rigor and ritual in producing it, requirements that Imelda did not begrudge because she felt she owed it to the poor to labour adorning herself to look like a 'star'. Imelda's bouffant was distinctly exacting, seemingly monolithic and impermeable, with no hair out of place, as it were, at least when photographed or seen from afar. It appeared almost plastic and without porosity, largely concealing her natural long hair, and exuded power the way it did for a person like Margaret Thatcher, who also wore a bouffant. In Imelda's case, however, the formidability of her bouffant, which consists of both her own hair and a hairpiece, contrasted with the disarming softness of her femininity and the contours of her elegant dress. The bouffant likewise pulled all the hair away from her face to copiously reveal the neck, nape, and the jewellery. The bouffant likewise helped Imelda balance off her narrow forehead and accentuate her bone structure and porcelain skin. The dress and the bouffant co-produce the silhouette of Imelda, expressing the admixture of femininity and formidability. Place all these in the context of a tropical tableau at IRRI in Los Baños, and the image generates enchantment: How can a woman so wrought not wilt in this heat and humidity?

Second, Imelda as a figure eroticizes the visual space, and she does it with ambiguity. While she cuts a formal profile, a significant extent of her flesh is actually exposed, specifically the nape, neck, and collarbone, even amid the chill of either spring or autumn when she is in temperate countries. The said parts are presumed to be erotic zones. The foregrounding of Imelda as an erotic, tropical figure leads me to a relevant facet of her diplomatic image: coy but chameleon-like. When Imelda was in Washington, she was able to some-how convince Lyndon Johnson to carve out a portion of the war reparation fund for the Philippines for the construction of the Cultural Center of the Philippines. Imelda was a guest of Lady Bird Johnson at the opening of the Metropolitan Opera House at Lincoln Center in 1966, and she was impressed with the magnificent edifice. This got her to fantasize about a similar structure for Manila. And with swiftness, three years later, it opened in 1969, standing on land reclaimed from Manila Bay, with California Governor Ronald Reagan and Nancy Reagan sent by President Richard Nixon as guests to grace the gala. This alteration of nature into culture through the massive engineering of reclamation loops the discussion back into the site of the paradigmatic diplo-matic image in which Imelda politicizes nature and the Philippine pastoral. Such an exotic and erotic promise might not have been lost on Imelda.

[51] Ibid.

The appropriation of femininity in Imelda's practice as an emissary could be further seen in how she tried to seduce an official on her visit to the Nixon White House. This account is telling:

> the night before Imelda was to see Nixon, she revealed a larger aim to Richard Usher, the Philippine officer at the State Department. Attired in 'tight black slacks' and a 'low-cut leopard-skin top', Imelda greeted Usher in her hotel suite, motioned him to sit beside her, and remarked, 'Dick, you're not taking care of your baby. The Philippines is your baby.' The first lady warned that 'undemocratic elements' – the Catholic Church, Liberal Party, Communists, and students – would win a majority of delegates to an upcoming constitutional convention and 'turn the Philippines into a Marxist country'. Without a major infusion of US economic assistance, leftists would gain popularity and the Philippines would be lost to the United States.[52]

Third and finally, the statuesque Imelda is imagined in this chapter as a sculpture: autonomous and formal, rigid and coiffed, on the one hand, and kitschy and queer, on the other. That said, she proves to be a figure who transcends the said dualisms and is prone to the appropriations of camp and drag as may be seen in the musical *Here Lies Love* (2013), which conditions its ambience through Imelda's fascination with disco; in fact, she had one installed at the palace.[53] This is a theoretical challenge in which I constellate art history, diplomatic history, and art theory. Here I converse with Rosalind Krauss' well-known essay 'Sculpture in an Expanded Field' in which she talks about the tendencies of postmodern sculpture in the 1960s. Krauss annotates the drift of the sculptural form from the singular and the monumental to a series of negations in relation to other elements in the ecology: 'it was what was on or in front of a building that was not the building, or what was in the landscape that was not the landscape'.[54] The discussion of Krauss is important in my attempt to isolate Imelda as a monument, only to be reinserted into the environment via negation, thus enabling me to discuss the relationship between the natural and the cultural, the political and the aesthetic, the authentic and the excessive. Imelda as sculpture, therefore, brings together her social biography that is cobbled together to become a persona, one that needed an iconography so that it could circulate prodigiously, disseminated like a religious image or that of a Hollywood star. Such dissemination, however, does not diminish the sculptural integrity. In fact, it is constantly supplemented because the sculpture is an ornament as well, which imbricates enchantment and technology. A key aspect in this photographic image is the

---

[52] Kotlowski, 'The Possibilities and Limitations of First-Lady Diplomacy', p. 347.
[53] See Patrick D. Flores, 'Beautiful, Brutalist: Parks, Pageants, Photographs, Palaces', lecture, Ilham Gallery, Kuala Lumpur, 22 July 2017.
[54] Rosalind Krauss, 'Sculpture in the Expanded Field', *October* 8 (1979), 36.

impromptu wooden plank that raises the guests above the rice paddy. It is a supplement that is in the landscape but is not the landscape, and yet it allows us to see metaconceptually what is being done to the landscape or how it is transformed into something else through developmental experiments, rice and Imelda included. Without this plank, the image would just be a typical landscape. For it is the plank that makes the presence of the guests possible and visually coordinates the politics of the diplomatic image in relation to the politics of rice research in the Cold War. Synchronizing these articulations of both image and politics is the supplement that is Imelda herself. The raised platform is coextensive with the artifice or the stage that Imelda fabricates as a First Lady and as a conjurer of enchantment in a tropical landscape, exemplifying the political and diplomatic dimensions of a performative image.

Within the framework of the diplomatic image, the social construction of the First Lady looms as potentially overdetermining. In Imelda's modality, the sociality of the construction was aesthetically produced simultaneously. The surface quality, therefore, sustains Imelda's desires as a world figure, but it conceals the limits of her interventions in foreign affairs, at the same time. In other words, the enchantment of the technology of beauty is at once the source of transcendence of merely being First Lady and partly of the restoration of the same status.

The image of Imelda in Los Baños at the IRRI registers the political impulses of a First Lady who sent mixed signs of the Philippine post-colony: the mythological and religious cipher of nature and woman and the modernity of the televisual and cinematic celebrity, pageantry, and the avant-garde. It is simultaneously erotic, exotic, spectacular, modern, native, cosmopolitan, homespun, worldly. On this map, the coordinates offered up by Eva Peron in Argentina and Jackie Kennedy in the United States might be productive. Peron was more than just a First Lady to Juan Peron; she was a persona of her own who was adored and reviled by Argentinians for her place in the political and cultural space. Kennedy for her part was an indispensable part of the myth of Camelot, with her husband John F. Kennedy a self-anointed prince of Pax Americana. Imelda riffs on important facets from the semiotic catalogue of Evita, as she was known, and Jackie: melodrama and glamour, Hispanic piety and American celebrity.[55] And it is but propitious that all this would play out in the age of the pervasive television in which contentious sympathies resided in the local articulation of an international modernist ideal, be it in the form of

---

[55] See Berkeley Kaite, 'The Pink Suit: Jacqueline Kennedy and Celebrity Defilement', *Celebrity Studies*, 5:1–2 (2012), 175–96; and Marta E. Savigliano, 'Evita: The Globalization of a National Myth', *Latin American Perspectives* 24:6 (1997), 156–72.

nation or democracy in the Cold War. As Imelda once asked in mock confusion, 'What's the difference between America and the Philippines?'[56]

Imelda and Jackie partook of this celebritification and mediatization of politics, and may buttress the validity of the image as the idiom of diplomacy. When Kennedy was assassinated in 1963, an international drama of grief and adulation unreeled, attesting to the Kennedy mystique: 'Kennedy's policies, as understood by the people of the developing world, made them receptive to his image. Without this perception, the murder in Dallas would have struck the average resident of Cairo or New Delhi as a distant tragedy, not a universal calamity.'[57] Jackie may well have been Imelda's template in terms of myth-making and appearing as an artifice. As the equally sculptural Jackie once said: 'One should always dress like a marble column.'[58] Underlying such daunting persona was lavishness in sartorial imperatives befitting not only the First Lady of the United States but the royalty of the 'mythomania' of Camelot in Washington.[59] Jackie, like Imelda, teased out aspects of lineage from nobility to somewhat force an aristocratic provenance.[60] In the manner of a salonniere, she invited artists to the White House for prestige. Behind the image, however, was not a birthright: 'It was polished at Miss Porter's and Vassar and in the society of East Hampton and Newport. It was given depth by her avid reading of history, and particularly the history, in French, of the ancien régime.'[61] But Imelda and Jackie optimized this pastiche to purvey a distinction; it was not blithely dismissed as the opposite of blue-stocking hauteur. This is acutely seen in how a fashion curator would describe Jackie's Hubert de Givenchy opera coat, a tribute of the designer to Cristóbal Balenciaga: 'a palimpsest of historical references, suggesting by turns a Venetian domino, a Kabuki robe, and, as General de Gaulle himself remarked ... a costume in a Watteau painting'.[62]

Imelda was the exemplary First Lady in an expanded field of the post-colony. The two documentaries[63] produced long after the Marcoses were overthrown in 1986 announce Imelda's ability to discipline the narrative in her favour. She grants interviews that may ultimately be unflattering, providing content that satiates the popular appetite for both delusion and derision. She may come out of it defiled, but she gets to speak, and state her case. She does not permit the medium of the documentary to set the agenda through realism or critique. At the end of these documentaries, she emerges, paradoxically and

---

[56] *Imelda*, directed by Ramona Diaz (New York: CineDiaz, 2003).

[57] Rakove, *Kennedy, Johnson, and the Non-Aligned World*, p. xviii.

[58] Judith Thurman, 'Costume of the Country', in *Cleopatra's Nose: 39 Varieties of Desire* (New York: Picador, 2007), p. 383.

[59] Ibid., p. 389.   [60] Ibid.   [61] Ibid.   [62] Ibid., p. 386.

[63] See Ramona Diaz's *Imelda* (2003) and Lauren Greenfield's *The Kingmaker* (2019).

calculatingly, as the star and slave, basking in the traditional rebuke of her excess and corruption.

Imelda once stated that whenever she went overseas to represent the Philippines, she always wore the Philippine formal dress in which she would inscribe within its local design a motif of the country she was visiting. To paraphrase her spiel: In India, it was the lotus. In Iran, it was the Persian rug, the message being: I may be different, but I am a friend.[64] This was Imelda's diplomatic image that amalgamated sentimentality and style: soft enough a power for world leaders, who were mostly men, to suffer, but an unyielding star for a global public enamoured of tragic, because prohibitively self-regulating, women and a nation in search of worldly recognition. Such a dynamic unfolded in an era in which mass media aestheticized power and tended to reduce the woman in politics largely as femme fatale in a melodrama or soap opera. It alternated between the stark, almost cruel realism of television and the news, on the one hand, and the fuzzy, beguiling otherworldliness of the medium's mythologies, on the other. As Imelda puts it most aptly: 'When a person touches somebody, or kisses somebody, or embraces somebody, why do they do it? They want to see if you're real.'[65] The surrogate finally surpasses herself through the supplement.

---

[64] Imelda Romualdez Marcos, conversation with author, 2009.
[65] Roy Rowan, 'Orchid or Iron Butterfly, Imelda Marcos Is a Prime Mover in Manila', *People Magazine*, 29 March 1976.

3 Meeting of the Kings
The Dream Factory and Cold War Diplomacy

Jirayudh Sinthuphan

Tomorrow I shall depart Bangkok. I will first make a visit to the United States of America before traveling to another fourteen European nations. This visit is a state visit. It is my duty as the head of the state. Such a duty to maintain a good relationship is usually a responsibility for every member of the family. For nations with millions of citizens, it is almost impossible for every citizen personally to visit one another. Therefore, this duty is given to heads of the state. During this visit, I shall bring the goodwill of Thai people to the citizen of these nations. I will try my very best to make them know Thailand and have goodwill towards Thai people. I shall be away from you for nearly six months. It is natural that I will have worries about our nation. I would like to ask you all to tend to your duties and to remain calm. It is for your own good and for our nation.

> An excerpt from King Bhumibol Adulyadej's Speech to the Thai Nation,
> broadcast by the Thai National Radio Agency on June 13, 1960
> (author's translation)

One of the most endearing images of Thai-American Cold War diplomacy features two kings – Bhumibol Adulyadej, the king of Thailand, and Elvis Presley, the 'king of rock and roll' on the set of the movie musical *G.I. Blues*. Elvis Presley in an American military uniform engages in a friendly handshake with King Bhumibol, to the delight of the attendant audience (Fig. 3.1). In the background between the two kings, Queen Sirikit is looking radiant in her tailored three-piece ensemble, which the press noted resembled the colors of the American flag. The meeting between the two kings took place when King Bhumibol and Queen Sirikit went on their state visit to the United States in 1960. It was their first 'state' visit to the western bloc, and Bhumibol's first long trip away from home since his official return to the country in 1951. Their stopover in California, a preamble to the official state visit in which only the king and queen took part, was described at the time as more like an extended family holiday that included a trip to Disneyland.[1] While the image of the two kings, taken inside the soundstage of Paramount Studios, was an apparent sideshow to the 'real' diplomatic encounter that began in Washington days

---

[1] Paul M. Handley, *The King Never Smiles* (New Haven, CT: Yale University Press, 2006), p. 146.

Figure 3.1 Elvis Presley shakes hands with Bhumibol Adulyadej, King of
Thailand, while Queen Sirikit looks on, 1960.
Credit: Nat Dallinger, 1960. Copyright, Academy of Motion Picture Arts and Sciences.

later. Yet, over time it would play a crucial role in asserting the idea of a
special relation between Thailand and the United States, as well as between
Thais and their monarchy. To the present day, the picture has remained one of
the most powerful in shaping the Thai public's image of the royals and of itself
as a nation, indicating the importance of what was in fact an ingenious
diplomatic spectacle of fairy-tale kings in Tinseltown.

There are, in fact, many versions of this event in circulation, but the
particular photograph that I have chosen was taken by Nat Dallinger
(1911–2006), one of the most important photojournalists of the time of
Hollywood's golden age. Despite the obvious formality of the meeting at

Paramount Studios, Dallinger's lens captured non-hierarchical, spontaneous, and playful interactions between Oriental and Hollywood royalties. The two kings and the queen appeared to be relaxed, quite intimate, and yet glamorous – like proper movie stars.

A review of contemporary newspapers reveals that this image was never published in the press at the time of the visit. Rather, it grew in stature and significance over time as countless reproductions were produced for mass consumption by the Thai media and private consumption as cultural memorabilia. Despite the cosmopolitan and familiar nature of the image, its importance has been secured mainly for a Thai audience, as opposed to an international one. This prompts me to reconsider the nature of the royal visit in 1960 and the intended audience of this act of diplomacy. Borrowing from Susan Sontag's analysis of photography and Jacques Lacan's psychoanalytic theory of the mirror stage, I take a journey into the image to explore its meaning, appeals, usages, and afterlives in a Thai context through an analysis of its visuality and narratives.

The Image of Diplomacy and Its Power

> To photograph is to appropriate the thing photographed. It means putting oneself into a certain relation to the world that feels like knowledge – and, therefore, like power.[2]

A photograph is not only a documentation of an event. It is also knowledge about the event, and like all knowledge in the world, it is also shaped by a particular agenda and ideology. Looking at the image of the two kings today, I am fascinated by its power and its sociopolitical implications: a subtle marriage between Hollywood's publicity machine and American Cold War diplomacy.[3] Contrary to Thai popular belief, the meeting between Elvis Presley and Bhumibol was far from unique. In fact, a visit to the set of *G.I. Blues* was a repeated feature of American diplomatic spectacle in 1960. Princess Margrethe of Denmark and King Mahendra of Nepal were among foreign dignitaries who also visited the film set that same year, such visits providing Hollywood with a channel to promote their films and their stars to international markets. At the same time, the images skilfully crafted by Hollywood's publicity machine also helped disseminate American ideology and foreign policy further afield.

G.I. Blues was initiated in 1958 to be Elvis Presley's comeback vehicle after a two-year hiatus from the movies while he served in the US Army. For the US

---

[2] S. Sontag, *On Photography* (New York: Rosetta Books, 2005), p. 2.
[3] T. Shaw, *Hollywood's Cold War* (Edinburgh: Edinburgh University Press, 2007).

Army, the film was viewed as a public relations opportunity. The army had appointed its public information officer, John J. Mawn, as a technical advisor for the film, and supplied tanks to be used in the filming. Some scenes were shot on location eight months before Elvis' official discharge. In March 1960, Presley returned to the United States and began to shoot the movie at Paramount Studios in Los Angeles. Nat Dallinger was then hired by Paramount to produce publicity shots for the film. From the early 1940s to the late 1960s, Dallinger's syndicated photo column 'Inside Hollywood' provided worldwide readership with a candid and intimate view of Hollywood at play. A 1949 memo from MGM's publicity department explained to studio employees that 'the most important single outlet for pictorial material in Hollywood is Nat Dallinger ... Give him every possible service, even to the sacrifice of other things.'[4] In Dallinger's image of the two kings, his subjects appear naturally glamorous and at ease. Nonetheless, one can also observe a high level of choreography. By blending Hollywood's aesthetics with the national diplomatic agenda, the images of the King of Thailand and the King of Hollywood shaking hands embodied the idea of a strong and theoretically equal partnership between Thailand and the United States.

With the rise of Maoist China and the Viet Minh in Vietnam in the late 1940s Southeast Asia had become increasingly important to US policy makers. Increasingly, the Americans saw Thailand as a defensive wall against the spread of communism in the Far East.[5] During the late 1950s and the early 1960s, Thailand observed an increasing US military and civilian presence in its territory. This coincided with the escalation of US direct military involvement in the war in Vietnam and Laos throughout the 1960s. The *US Psychological Strategy Based on Thailand* (*PSB D-23*) was first developed in the early 1950s by General William J. Donovan, the former head of the Office of Strategic Services (OSS) who later became the US Ambassador to Thailand from 1953 to 1954, and was a blueprint for America's foreign policy and psychological warfare in the region.[6] Its main idea was to consolidate Thailand as a secure base for American operations in Southeast Asia, through effective overt and covert information programs. Along with the projection of US military prowess, the policy also sought to mobilize Thai culture and religious practice,

[4] A. Lewis, *Hollywood's First Paparazzo: Unseen Photos of Marilyn Monroe, Elizabeth Taylor, Elvis Presley* (2014). Retrieved from www.hollywoodreporter.com/news/marilyn-monroe-elvis-presley-unseen-681101.

[5] Daniel Fineman, *A Special Relationship: The United States and Military Government in Thailand, 1947–1958* (Honolulu: University of Hawai'i Press, 1997).

[6] Jim Glassman, *Drums of War, Drums of Development: The Formation of a Pacific Ruling Class and Industrial Transformation in East and Southeast Asia, 1945–1980* (Leiden: Brill, 2018), pp. 413–416.

along with the monarchy itself, as a means to win Thai hearts and minds.[7] The image of the royal couple's visit to the set of *G.I. Blues* and their friendly meeting with the lovable all-American GI portrayed by Elvis Presley thus contributed to preparing the Thai nation for a future encounter with real GIs when the US government stepped up its military presence in Thailand. The first U.S. base was set up in 1961. By 1965, the number grew into seven bases; these later became vital in fighting the war in Vietnam.

Internally, Thai politics from the early 1930s to the late 1950s was defined by a power struggle between royalists and anti-monarchists. Following a revolution in 1932, the monarchy had been significantly diminished and was subjugated to a limited presence in Thai society. Besides, the early days of King Bhumibol's reign was overshadowed by the mysterious death of his older brother, King Ananda Mahidol, in 1946, and the negotiation of war reparations as payment to secure Thailand's reintegration into the international community. During this time, diplomatic missions were mainly carried out by the liberal statesman Pridi Banomyong and/or the military leader Plaek Phibunsongkhram. The former travelled to the United Kingdom in 1946 and succeeded in securing a deal whereby Thailand was forgiven its war reparations, possibly with some help from the US government. The latter was invited to Buckingham Palace and lunched with Queen Elizabeth in 1955.[8]

The images from King Bhumibol's official state visit to the territory of its allies clearly delivered a powerful message about his country's allegiance to the United States. It also asserted the young king's position as the primary representative of the kingdom on both national and international stages. Images of the king as a westernized and down-to-earth young man during his visit to the United States and Europe in 1960 not only carved out a new career for King Bhumibol as a forward-looking leader of an aspiring democratic country aligned with the Western bloc. It also projected an image of Thailand as a legitimate and equal member of the Free World. After the 1960 royal visit, King Bhumibol and the rest of the royal family resumed more active roles in the country's affairs. The monarchy, along with the Buddhist religion, has since been perceived as an indispensable pillar of democracy and the Thai nation. In retrospect, such meanings also provided legitimacy for the Thai Army, which has claimed to act 'in defense of the nation, the monarchy and the religion'.

Nevertheless, Dallinger's image of Elvis Presley and King Bhumibol also benefitted Hollywood producers and Elvis as it helped to transform the Thai

---

[7] Matthew Phillips, 'For a love of "the Thais": US Imperialism and the Tender Violence of Thai Studies', *South East Asia Research*, 27:1 (May 2019), 97–114.

[8] Nicholas Tarling, 'Atonement before Absolution: British Policy towards Thailand during World War II', *Journal of the Siam Society*, 66 (1978), 22–65.

attitude towards the American singer. Up until 1960, rock and roll music, including singers such as Elvis Presley, was considered a symbol of youth defiance and gang culture, and was banned from public radio stations by the Thai authorities. After the meeting with King Bhumibol, however, Elvis' public image became more socially acceptable and ultimately secured long-lasting popularity in Thai society. To this day, Elvis Presley symbolizes an age of optimism underpinned by Thai-American friendship.

Image of Diplomacy: The Mirror Stage of a Thai Identity

> Photographs are a way of imprisoning reality, understood as recalcitrant, inaccessible; of making it stand still. Or they enlarge a reality that is felt to be shrunk, hollowed out, perishable, remote.[9]

Revisiting the image of the two kings and the narrative behind it has been an emotional experience for me. It was as if I was looking at the process in which my 'self' was being formed. As a result, I began to see the image of diplomacy as the mirror stage of a nation, in which a national self is formed through an interaction with the reflected moments of diplomatic practice. The idea of the 'mirror stage' derives from Lacan's critical reinterpretation of the work of Freud. For Lacan, the ego is fundamentally dependent upon interaction with external objects and with an 'Other'. He proposes that human subjects pass through a stage in which an external image of the body reflected in a mirror or represented to the subject by others produces a psychic response that gives rise to the mental representation of an 'I' and a perception of selfhood.[10] In the case of the 'two kings' it is thus possible to explore how the image shaped a nascent knowledge about our perceived place in the world: an ideal impression that we as a nation could both identify with in the present and strive towards in the future.

The image of the two kings sits within a wider portfolio of representations that became crucial in helping form a Thai national consciousness. We still largely identify with this image, culturally and politically. It informs our modern Thai aesthetics and physical appearance. It dictates our trade and foreign policies. It provides us with an identifier of a national self whose composite of 'the nation, the monarchy and the religion' becomes a part of our habits, our traditions, and our common sense. The 1960s seem like a distant memory, as does the Cold War, and yet we keep reproducing and recirculating its image. Even as the image has lost its vividness, it continues to create an ideal 'I', to which we perpetually strive at the expense of everything else.

---

[9] Sontag, *On Photography*, p. 2.
[10] J. Lacan, *Ecrits: A Selection,* trans. Alan Sheridan (London: Routledge, 1989), pp. 1–8.

Negotiating the 1960 Royal Visit

In 1959, King Bhumibhol himself brought up the idea of an official visit to the United States with the US Ambassador. On 29 January 1959, a telegram was sent from the Embassy in Thailand to the Department of the State. The US Ambassador at that time, Ural Alexis Johnson, wrote: 'King still intensely interested in paying State visit to U.S. in Spring 1960. Foregoing conversation took place during USIS function opening Lincoln Sesquicentennial attended by King last night.'[11] The US government appeared to be disinterested, and there was no follow-up on the matter after January 1959. Rather, communication between the embassy in Bangkok and the Department of the State during this period was dominated by the health of Prime Minister, Field Marshal Sarit Thanarat, who was suffering from liver disease, and who had to deal with the growing tension between Thailand and South Vietnam over the refugee crisis and the ongoing negotiation over a US aid program for Thailand.[12] Six months after it was first discussed, the invitation for the royal couple's first state visit to the United States finally arrived on 18 August 1959:

Ambassador is authorized to extend invitation through RTG to King and Queen of Thailand for ten days visit to United States at invitation of President. Late June 1960 has been tentatively set as approximate time during which visit could take place if this meets Their Majesties' convenience. Visit should begin on a Tuesday or Wednesday with first three days spent in Washington and remainder of time elsewhere in United States, depending on Their Majesties' interests and desires. Should King and Queen wish to remain in United States for longer period than ten-day state visit, expenses beyond that period would be responsibility of RTG. Official party should not exceed ten persons. Further details concerning visit will be forwarded as soon as acceptance received. If Their Majesties accept, it is proposed make agreed simultaneous public announcements Bangkok and Washington but essential no prior publicity pending receipt royal acceptance.[13]

The Preparation

Throughout the latter half of 1959 and the first half of 1960, preparations for the Thai monarch's first state visits were carried out by the Ministry of Foreign Affairs and the Royal Office. Since the overthrow of Plaek

---

[11]   Document 511, Telegram from the Embassy in Thailand to the Department of State, January 29, 1959, *Foreign Relations of the United States, 1958–1960, South and Southeast Asia*, volume XV.

[12]   Document 512–527, *Foreign Relations of the United States, 1958–1960, South and Southeast Asia*, volume XV.

[13]   Document 528, Telegram from the Department of State to the Embassy in Thailand, August 18, 1959, *Foreign Relations of the United States, 1958–1960, South and Southeast Asia*, Volume XV.

Phibunsongkhram's regime by Sarit in 1957, senior members of the Chakri dynasty, conservative politicians, civil servants, military personnel, and their business associates began to form an informal alliance to work towards a reinstatement of the monarchy's influence, to support the Sarit's regime and the US information program in the war against communism.[14] Members of this alliance were instrumental in the preparation of the royal visit to the United States and Europe in 1960.

Public Rehearsals

Preparation began by increasing the number of royal engagements with the Thai public. First, they were put back on their regional royal tour, which had been halted by the government of Plaek Phibunsongkhram in 1955.[15] Next, royal ceremonies were revived and expanded to give the king more visibility.[16] National holidays, which had been separated from the monarchy since 1932, were moved to days that were important to the monarchy.[17]

Prior to the shift away from absolute monarchy, the Royal Household had been responsible for the preparation of royal visits; the last official royal tour had taken place in 1934. In preparation for the trip to America, a group of advisors were thus called in to prepare the couple in every detail of royal protocol and international diplomacy. Apart from former ambassadors, this group of advisors included Princess Vibhavadi Rangsit, who later became a lady-in-waiting for the queen and who accompanied the royal couple on every one of their royal visits.[18]

By the end of 1959, the royal couple were ready for their first international visit. In December, the Ministry of Foreign Affairs sent them on a three-day trip to South Vietnam. This was followed by a visit to Indonesia in February 1960 and a trip to Burma in March of the same year. During the tour to these countries, they were scheduled to attend functions with heads of state and visit important cultural sites while government officials held intergovernmental meetings. The three Southeast Asian countries were at that time critical to

---

[14] Handley, *The King Never Smiles*, pp. 114–138.

[15] King Bhumibol and Queen Sirikit embarked on a series of regional tours in 1955, four years after they came back to permanently reside in the country. The tour began with visiting towns and villages of the Central provinces in September and of the North-eastern provinces in November. All the royal couple did was just travel to remote places and talk to their subjects with compassion and friendliness. The tour was such a success that the tour to the Northern and to Southern provinces were subsequently cancelled.

[16] Phillips, 'For a Love of "the Thais"', p. 102.

[17] Handley, *The King Never Smiles*, pp. 114–138.

[18] Somdej Pranangchao Sirikit Pra Barom Rajini Nath, *Kwam Song Jam Nai Karn Tam Sadej Tang Pradesh Thang Rajakarn*, 2nd ed., published on the occasion of the Queen's sixth cycle birthday 12 August 2547 BE (Bangkok: Siam Inter Multimedia, 2547 BE), pp. 88–89.

US operations in the region. Rangoon, for example, was the platform for the Thai–South Vietnam refugee crisis talks. Indonesia was the leader of the Non-aligned Movement, and the Thai government and the Thai public were agitated by the United States' plan to sell Thai rice to Indonesia.[19]

The king's South Vietnam trip appeared to be of special interest to the United States, as there was fear of a cancellation. A telegram from the Department of State to its embassy in Bangkok describes this concern in relation to a worsening Thailand and South Vietnam relations. Quite explicitly, it also stresses the importance of this trip to the American anti-communist agenda and requests the embassy to remind the Thai government that it should maintain a public airing of friendship between two anti-communist nations.[20]

The result of the king's visit to South Vietnam, Indonesia, and Burma had been favourable. The South Vietnam visit created a sense of camaraderie between two US allies. The tour of Indonesia lessened public agitation towards the US plan to sell Thai rice to Indonesia. In Rangoon, the refugee crisis between Thailand and Vietnam was resolved. Nonetheless, watching the video clips of these visits, one can clearly see that they were rehearsals for their grand introduction in June. There were moments of awkwardness and points of imperfection that would no longer be evident in the later US and European visits.[21]

The Cost

As stated by Washington, the US government bore the cost of the ten-day official visit, while the Thai government was responsible for the extended royal tour. But there were also other costs that the royal couple took on themselves. This included the expense for Queen Sirikit's outfits.[22] As she herself wrote in her 1968 memoir of the visits,

As for Western clothing, the Government at that time showed great concern to help me by offering to procure the service of a couturier from Dior to design and cut my clothes. Dior was a large Paris boutique and famous for haute couture. The King thanked the Government for their concern but refused the offer, requesting them not to worry about such a minor matter and confirmed that we would manage it ourselves.[23]

---

[19] Document 525, Note from the Acting Secretary of State to the Thai Ambassador (Visutr Arthayukti), August 6, 1959, *Foreign Relations of the United States, 1958–1960, South and Southeast Asia*, volume XV.

[20] Document 538, Telegram from the Department of State to the Embassy in Thailand, November 30, 1959, *Foreign Relations of the United States, 1958–1960, South and Southeast Asia*, volume XV.

[21] Videoclips of these three Southeast Asian visits can be found at the Thai Film Archive and are available on YouTube.

[22] Queen Sirikit Textile Museum, *Fit for the Queen* (Bangkok: River Books, 2016), p. 13.

[23] Somdej Pranangchao Sirikit Pra Barom Rajini Nath, *Kwam Song Jam Nai Karn Tam Sadej Tang Pradesh Thang Rajakarn*, pp. 88–91 (my translation).

The overall cost of the tour, however, has never been disclosed. The funds that were used to cover this extra cost probably came from their private assets, which were managed by Mom Davivongs Thawalyasak (Mom Rajawongse Chalermlarp Davivongs), who also served as the president of the Crown Property Bureau, the Bureau of the Royal Household, and the privy purse from the late 1940s until the early 1970s.[24] Moreover, Sarit's government also decided to double the palace budget, which steadily increased year on year from 1958, giving the family a substantial financial base.[25]

Building a Public Image

Another important element in the preparation for the visit was the construction of a recognizable public image for the king and the queen. This public image was a re-imagination of Thai identity through an intercultural marriage between Thai post-war aspirations and Western aesthetics. It was equally conceived for a Western gaze, as much as for Thai citizens to visualize their post-war identity. The same image remains an ideal that most still identify with to this day.

As also discussed in Chapter 4 in this volume, the king's public image during the Rangoon visit was unmistakably built on a Hindu-Buddhist cosmo-logical mapping of the divine state and virtuous monarch of a Buddhist kingdom. Although his attire for this trip was mostly western in style, the king also changed into a traditional white raj pattern jacket and a red *chong kraben*, or a lower body wrap-around cloth, when the group visited the Shwedagon Pagoda in Rangoon. As red dyed clothes were traditionally reserved only for royals and spiritual mediums, the king's choice for the red *chong kraben* and the queen's deep pink attire clearly channelled the divine. Furthermore, an image of a Siamese king walking barefoot all the way to pay homage to the Buddha's relics inside the pagoda, which holds such a historical significance to Thai-Burma relations, reflected an image of a devout Buddhist monarch and a concluding reconciliation between the two countries. Now with a little touch of Western modernity, the virtuous monarchs from a Buddhist kingdom in the East were set to conquer the West.

According to Queen Sirikit's memoir, the government took great interest in procuring the service of Dior for the queen. This would have been an obvious choice, Dior being the premier fashion house at the time with designs that in many ways embodied post-war ideals.[26] As a representative of the govern-ment, the royal couple's public image had to project an appropriate political

[24] Handley, *The King Never Smiles*, pp. 119–121.   [25] Ibid.
[26] R. Martin, and K. Harold, *Christian Dior*, exhibition catalogue (New York: Metropolitan Museum of Art, 1996), pp. 10–12.

and cultural message, while allowing them to stand out in the crowds. The king opted for simple Western suits and military uniforms to present himself as a westernized modern monarch and presumably to show his support to the Sarit regime. Much of the effort had been put into the construction of Queen Sirikit's image as the embodiment of Thai-ness and international elegance.

During the earlier trips through South Vietnam, Indonesia, and Burma, Queen Sirikit voiced her concern about the lack of a distinguishable set of Thai national costumes. Traditionally, citizens of Siam/Thailand wore attire in accordance with their ethnicity and regional preferences. There was no standardized Thai or Siamese attire. However, a State Convention for Dress was issued by Plaek Pibunsongkram's government in 1941, urging Thais to adopt Western-style attire to become a more civilised nation. There was some initial resistance from the public, but by 1944 Western-style clothing had become the norm.[27] On visiting the Southeast Asian nations, the first ladies all wore some sort of distinguishable national costume. Queen Sirikit, on the other hand, mainly wore Western-style dresses. In order to construct a unique image of Thai-ness for subsequent royal tours, Queen Sirikit asked her ladies-in-waiting and her dressmakers to design a set of Thai national costumes based on traditional Siamese fashion, which later became known as *Chood Thai Pra Rajaniyom* (Royal Convention of Thai Dresses). Queen Sirikit herself candidly recollected in her memoir that the design, which is a blend of Western aesthetics and an eclectic mix of Siamese elements, has gradually been adopted by Thai women and become known throughout the world as an image of Thailand.[28]

The French couturier Pierre Balmain was brought in by Princess Vibhavadi to design Queen Sirikit's Western-style outfits for the trip. The rationale was that it was beyond the ability of Thai dressmakers to understand what would be appropriate for each formal function and to create a unique design.[29] The design concept formulated by Balmain for Queen Sirikit's image during this royal tour has had a long-lasting influence on Thai identity, especially in the area of arts and design. He incorporated Thai materials and a Thai colour palette to his streamlined designs. Shades of violet, pink, and gold that were chosen for Queen Sirikit's outfits, particularly for her three-piece suit in the Dallinger image, became key visual elements when people think of Thailand.[30] Traditional Thai decorative patterns were adapted into embroidery patterns by

---

[27] S. Barme, *Luang Wichit Wathakarn and the Creation of Thai Identity* (Singapore: Institute of Southeast Asian Studies, 1993), pp. 156–160.

[28] Somdej Pranangchao Sirikit Pra Barom Rajini Nath, *Kwam Song Jam Nai Karn Tam Sadej Tang Pradesh Thang Rajakarn*, pp. 88–89.

[29] Queen Sirikit Museum of Textiles, *Fit for the Queen*, p. 15.

[30] The design of a new logo used for Thai International Airways that was carried out in 1975 was also based on similar concept and colour palette.

Maison Lesage in Paris for the decoration of her evening gowns as well as the newly redesigned Thai national costumes. Later on, Balmain also helped to fine-tune the design of Thai national costumes and give them a modern silhouette.[31]

Capturing the 1960 Royal Visit

After much preparation, the royal delegation departed Bangkok for Honolulu on 14 June 1960. Apart from the royal couple and their four children, the group consisted of officers on official state duties, and a royal entourage who travelled on the royal couple's personal expense. Reading though the list of people on the trip, one can observe the full operation of the Chakri network and their eagerness to succeed. The royal couple surrounded themselves with experienced diplomatic officers, devoted staff from the Bureau of the Royal Household, and close family confidants. Other than this, they were accompanied by a cameraperson from Channel 4 television; Mom Rajawongse Kukrit Pramote, who represented his own newspaper, *Siam Rath*; and staff from His Majesty's Personal Film Production Department. These men had an important responsibility to capture every detail of this fairy-tale tour for the public back home.

Channel 4 television at Bang Khoonprom was the first television station in Thailand. It was established in 1955, allegedly with assistance from the United States Agency for International Development (USAID), the United States Information Service (USIS), and the Radio Corporation of America (RCA).[32] At the beginning, the channel relied heavily on imported American technology and broadcasting materials, before producing its own drama, variety shows, and news programmes, with anti-communist, pro-monarchy, and pro-American overtones. There is also clear evidence of USIS's active operations in Thailand throughout the 1950s, particularly in the development of its mass communications and public relations machines. During that period, almost all who were working in the Thai media industries, the Thai Public Relations Department, and the communications departments at Chulalongkorn University and Thammasart University had received some sort of training from USIS or had been educated in the United States.[33] It has been suggested that by the early 1960s, USIS had almost taken over the Thai Public Relations Department, and might have been instrumental in bringing reports of the royal tour back to people in Thailand.[34]

---

[31] Queen Sirikit Museum of Textiles, *Fit for the Queen*, p. 15.

[32] S. Phokaew et al., *Jodmhaihaet Hok Sip Pee Thorathas Thai* (Bangkok: Office of the National Broadcasting and Telecommunications Commission, 2558 BE).

[33] Ibid.   [34] Handley, *The King Never Smiles*, p. 149.

His Majesty's Personal Film Production Department was and remains a private operation within the royal household. The films were probably intended as personal documentation for private viewing. However, the documentation of the 1950 royal wedding began to reach a wider audience when it was screened with great success two weeks after filming at Chalerm Krung cinema, a royal variety hall owned by the Crown Property Bureau.[35] Subsequent screening of other royal film productions also drew large crowds and raised considerable money for royal charities. His Majesty's Personal Film Production Department thus played an important role in creating positive images and more visibility for the Thai monarchy, particularly at a time when the government sought to restrict public exposure to the royal family.[36]

During the 1960 tour, both His Majesty's Personal Film Production Department and USIS produced newsreels of the royal couple's activities abroad to be shown at movie theatres, especially those owned by the Crown Property Bureau.[37] A close relationship between these two organizations can clearly be observed in identical copies of newsreels found in their respective collections. In terms of photography, film rolls were sent by air to be developed and published in leading magazines such as *Sri Sabdah*, *Siam Nikorn*, *Sakul Thai*, *Daily Mails*, or *Maeban Karn Ruen*. Kukrit Pramote, a conservative politician who was also a journalist and member of the extended royal clan, closely reported the tour for *Siam Rath* readers, glorifying it as 'our virtuous king's conquest of the West'. Princess Vibhavadi, who was an accomplished novelist and resident columnist for *Satreesarn*, the most popular Thai woman's magazine of the time, also published a series of letters addressed to a friend. Her writings described intimate details of the royal tour that included the decorations of royal residences, the food that was served at state dinners, and amusing incidents that happened along the way. She drew her readers closer to the queen's gorgeous outfits and the king's witty interactions with the foreign public, making them feel as if they were a part of Princess Vibhavadi's entourage. Beyond that, Princess Vibhavadi closely monitored daily media reports and included them in these letters, to let the Thai people know how much their sovereigns were loved by the foreign public. Her style of writings set a standard for future reporting of subsequent royal tours, including the trips to Pakistan, Iran, and Malaya. Her account of the 1960 royal tour was so well received that it was compiled into a single volume within a year. From 1962 to 1994, it was also reprinted again and again to be distributed at the cremation ceremony of many upper-middle-class Thais, including the princess's own ceremony in 1977.

---

[35] S. Chaichavalit, *Krongkran Sueksa Pue Karnanurak Papayont Suan Pra Ong* (Bangkok: Thai Film Archive, 2556 BE).
[36] Ibid.   [37] Handley, *The King Never Smiles*, pp. 148–149.

These newsreels and writings gave the Thai people at home an impression that the world was at their king's feet and that the queen had captured the hearts of the people wherever she visited.[38] They were encouraged to feel proud of their nation and to see it as a close ally of the United States. Never before in Thai history had ordinary Thai people felt such closeness between themselves and their sovereigns.

The Royals in Tinseltown

After Hawaii, the royal envoy landed in Los Angeles. They stayed at the residence of Henry Kearns, a head of the US Export-Import Bank and a close associate of Richard Nixon. It was where they left their four children before heading eastwards. The group was scheduled to stay in Los Angeles for nine nights. It was designated as a private visit by both Thai and American media. However, Princess Vibhavadi was rather bemused at their rather packed itinerary, full of activities organized by the Americans, which can be detailed follows:[39]

18 June 1960 Arriving in Los Angeles
19 June 1960 Free day
20 June 1960 Visiting Mobil Oil Refinery Plant and Douglas Aircraft Company
21 June 1960 Visiting Paramount Studios
22 June 1960 Visiting Disney's Land
23 June 1960 Meeting with Thai communities in California
              Official dinner with the Thai Consul in Los Angeles
24 June 1960 Visiting Vandenberg Air Force Base
25 June 1960 Lunch with American war heroes
              Tea with Mr. & Mrs. Henry Kearns
26 June 1960 Free day
27 June 1960 Departing for Pittsburgh

Looking through this itinerary, the royal stopover in California was clearly not an extended family holiday. As the point of entry to the United States for flights from Bangkok, California hosted the largest Thai diaspora and was the first destination for Thai people to experience American technological advancement and the greatness of the US Armed Forces. Most importantly, Los Angeles was the world's leading dream factory. Through movies produced in Hollywood, ideas and ideals were manufactured and projected to the world.

---

[38] Examples of newsreel reports can be accessed on YouTube and the website of the US Embassy Bangkok (https://th.usembassy.gov/th/vdo-remembering-king-bhumibol-adulyadejs-state-visit-u-s-1960-th/).

[39] H.S.H. Vibhavadirangsit, *Sadej Pra Rajadamnern Saharat America, Pakistan and Saha Bhandharat Malaya* (Bangkok: A commemorative publication on the cremation of H.S.H. Vibhavadirangsit on 20 April 2520 BE), p. 28.

During the Cold War, they provided global populations with an indirect experience of America and the very idea it embodied via their portrayals of home-life stability and private desire. Implicitly, film studios and movie stars were reliable instruments of American public diplomacy.[40]

In this respect, the California stopover offered a more relaxing and dreamier space to kindle a genuine people-to-people diplomacy than the royals' formal engagements on the East Coast. Images from California provided the Thai public with a window to imagine their post-war society and their position in the world. Through the photo taken during the royal family's informal visit to Disneyland, for example, the public were presented with a young, friendly, monogamous, and loving royal family. Separately, the photo of King Bhumibol and the future King Vachiralongkorn during their day trip to Vandenberg Air Force Base presented the Thai nation through a security relationship that connected the monarchy, the military, and the United States. Through the image of the king and the queen meeting Elvis Presley at Paramount Studios, Thai people found an image of a glamorous, modern, and down-to-earth people's monarch.

The Meeting of the Kings

A meeting between King Bhumibol and Elvis Presley in 1960 seemed like an outrageous idea to most people, since rock and roll music was still banned in the kingdom. Nonetheless, the meeting was indirectly prescribed by a US psychological strategy think tank. In 1959, the Special Operations Research Office at the American University in Washington published a report titled *Project PROSYMS-Thailand*, which was intended for use in planning and conducting psychological operations in Thailand. Among other ideas, it had already elucidated the increasing appeal of King Bhumibol in the advocation of new ways, and that of Elvis Presley among younger Thai people.[41]

The visit to Paramount Studios started in the morning of 21 June 1960. It was designated as an official full day visit and included a tour of several sound stages, which was closely followed by a meeting with the Hollywood press. The day ended with a charity dinner organized by the City of Los Angeles and the Los Angeles World Affairs Council. Princess Vibhavadi was amused by the arrangement of the whole event, comparing it to a theatrical production.[42] An issue of *LIFE* magazine published on 20 June 1960 also

---

[40] S. Nilsen, *Projecting America, 1958: Film and Cultural Diplomacy at the Brussels World's Fair* (Jefferson, NC: MacFarland, 2011), pp. 1–8.

[41] Project PROSYMS-Thailand, *AD 316 089*, pp. 91, 195. https://apps.dtic.mil/dtic/tr/fulltext/u2/316089.pdf.

[42] Vibhavadirangsit, *Sadej Pra Rajadamnern Saharat America, Pakistan and Saha Bhandharat Malaya*, pp. 40–41.

devoted three pages of coverage to the king as a welcoming message to the foreign guest, but the entire issue was in fact about the City of Los Angeles.

At Paramount, the royal couple were given a tour of the whole studio before being escorted onto the sound stage where *G.I. Blues* was being filmed. They were greeted by the producer, Elvis 'the King' Presley, as well as the film crews. Princess Vibhavadi described the first encounter between the two kings in detail:

After the tour of the studio, we were escorted onto the sound stage where they were filming G.I. Blues by Hal Willis. Mr. Willis was not well on that day. Mr. Paul Nathan, his representative, was there to greet us. He presented its two leading stars, Mr. Elvis Presley and Ms. Juliet Prowse, to the King. I thought I heard Mr. Presley say 'Hello, Your Majesty, Sir' to the King while shaking hands with him. Mr. Presley was more well-mannered and shier than I thought. He was much more handsome than in the movies, with baby-blue eyes, a clean-shaven face, a perfect set of teeth and a great smile. He had just left his military service; therefore, his hair was cut short like a normal American boy, and not left ghastly long like in his other movies. He had a full makeup on. It was rather brown but left the eyebrows and lips natural. Juliet Prowse was just like we could see in the movie.... After the two of them were presented to the King, the King sat down. They arranged for Elvis Presley to sit next to the Queen, and Juliet Prowse to sit next to the King. That girl had no manners. She still sat with her legs crossed as normal. Photographers rushed in to take their photos together. After a while, Elvis Presley and Juliet Prowse took their leave to shoot the film.[43]

The Thai press often described the event as a unique opportunity for the King of Thailand to give an audience to Elvis Presley. In fact, it was more likely the other way around. Early on that same year, Presley had already given many members of the world's royalty the privilege of visiting his kingdom. Three Scandinavian princesses – Margrethe of Denmark, Astrid of Norway, and Margaretha of Sweden – also paid a visit to the film set on 11 June during the inauguration of a direct flight to Los Angeles of the Scandinavian Airlines System (SAS). Elvis also entertained the young King Mahendra of Nepal and Queen Lakshmi Devi on 11 May during the Nepalese royals' private tour of the United States, just a few months before a coup d'état that ended the Nepalese king's father's decade-long democratic experiment and India-leaning foreign policies.

Thai media widely reported the meeting between King Bhumibol and Elvis Presley, but no stories could be found in the US press. Princess Vibhavadi, who usually monitored the American reception of the royal tour, did not mention any media report of the event in her writing. Nevertheless, the event was not about the royal guests. It was all about Elvis Presley, his movie, the City of Los Angeles, and the United States. The main focus of the image was

---

[43] Ibid., p. 31 (my translation).

Elvis Presley and what America can offer – military support and genuine friendship.

The Image of Diplomacy and Its Legacy

There are many other photographs depicting the meeting between King Bhumibol and Elvis Presley, but none could match Nat Dallinger's capturing of the event. While other photographers had to keep a certain distance, Dallinger was granted a privilege by the film studio to be up-close and personal with his subjects.[44] Most importantly, he had a rare ability to capture a fleeting magical moment in time. According to Susan Sontag, a photograph suggests that time consists of interesting events, and that the event itself is worth remembering. It gives the event an immortality and importance that it would never have enjoyed. Even if the event has long ended, the photograph and its meanings will always remain.[45]

In this particular image, that fleeting moment worth remembering was the spontaneity and the informality of the encounter, as well as the joy and the friendliness of an equal partnership. The royal couple appeared in the image as modern, smart, and down-to-earth human beings. Queen Sirikit looked remarkably radiant and alluring in her Thai silk suit. They were proud representatives of Thailand, traditional and yet contemporary, a star couple in post-war diplomatic spectacle. It sealed their image as the people's monarchs and as international darlings. The image also boosted Thai citizens' faith in their monarchy and their nation, as much as it did the king's confidence in himself. Following this visit, the royal family began to have more presence in Thai society and assumed a more active role in the country's internal and foreign affairs. The image also cemented the idea that the monarchy is an inseparable part of the nation, which provides legitimacy for those who claim to act 'in defence of the nation, the monarchy and the religion'. After decades of uncertainty, the monarchy finally reclaimed its position in Thai politics.

Furthermore, the 1960 royal tour must have also provided a space of reconciliation for the extended Chakri clan whose power struggles, questions of succession, and political discords had contributed to a rift among its cadet branches for several decades. Sitting behind the royal couple with her proud smile in the Dallinger image was Princess Vibhavadi, whose cadet branch was affected by such familial dissonance to a great extent. To me, her presence exuded the united force of the Chakri network where a century-old family feud was put to rest for a greater mission.

---

[44] The same moment of the meeting was also captured by photographers in a long shot. In that photograph, one can clearly notice Nat Dallinger taking a closer shot with his camera.

[45] Sontag, *On Photography*, p. 8.

Undoubtedly, the Dallinger image significantly benefitted Elvis Presley and his film. *G.I. Blues* did remarkably well in Thailand and established him as a symbol of 1960s youth culture, of an American dream, and of American friendship. Thai men of that generation, like my father, still relish their fond memories of the film and the good old days of the Elvis era. It was widely reported by the Thai press that King Bhumibol personally made a remark that 'Elvis is a good boy'[46] – a remark that transformed Elvis' 'bad boy' image to a more socially acceptable and likable one, but that also put an end to the ban on rock and roll in Thailand. For the Americans, it helped to procure a place, culturally as well as politically, in Thai hearts for decades to come – neutralizing claims of American imperial domination with a soft embrace.[47]

The Cold War may have long ended. Both Elvis Presley and King Bhumibol have passed away. Queen Sirikit has retreated into obscurity. Still, the image of the two kings has a powerful legacy in the cultural memory of Thai citizens. Since the 1960s, the Dallinger image has continually been reproduced for public consumption in countless magazines and other forms of publication. It was included in commemorative volumes marking the royal's special occasions, such as in *The Eagle and the Elephant*, published by USIS in 1997 to mark King Bhumibol's Golden Jubilee and in *Mitraphap Youngyuen* (Eternal Friendship) published by the Council of Thai Teachers on the occasion of his majesty's sixth-cycle birthday. Turkmenistan also included the image in a set of its postage stamps to celebrate the king's sixth-cycle birthday in 1999.[48]

Reproductions of the image can still be found hanging in private houses, in nostalgia shops, and in cafes around Thailand, as well as in Thai restaurants abroad. It was popularized by Mr Lek 'the Poster King' Wongsawang, a broadcaster, columnist, and publisher of Western popular music in Thailand. His company has published the Dallinger photo as a full-sized poster since the 1960s. Mr Wongsawang was also the promoter of *Koh Lang Wang* (Youths behind the Palace), an annual event where the experience of 1960s Thailand, including the meeting of the two kings, is remembered and relived. The event would have occurred in 2020 were it not for the COVID-19 pandemic.

Just before the death of King Bhumibol in 2016, the image of the two kings was again reproduced and exhibited alongside Queen Sirikit's suit from the visit in an exhibition titled 'Fit for the Queen' at the Queen Sirikit Museum of Textiles inside the royal palace. While the living memory of the visit fades

---

[46] N. Kanjanawan, *Kalanukrom Elvis Presley Thi Prakot Nai Sangkhom Thai B.E. 2500–2516* (Bangkok: Thai Film Archive, 2555 BE).

[47] Phillips, 'For a Love of "the Thais"', pp. 101–105.

[48] N. Kanjanawan, 'Roy Yim Nai Alai Wan Hang Kham Piti Mue Krang Song Yuen Saharat Pobkap', *Matichon Weekly*, 4–10 November 2559 BE, www.matichonweekly.com/column/article_13914.

away, these material and photographic relics ensure the moment can still be experienced, or at least imagined.

After the king's passing on 13 October 2016, the image has constantly been used as the king's obituary and as an object of mourning for Thais. It appeared in countless printed and online publications, as well as on every television channel. The US Embassy in Bangkok quickly published the photo and a video clip of the event on its website. The US Ambassador to Thailand also gave an interview to BBC Thai about a copy of the image at his Bangkok residence, and how it symbolized the people-to-people connectivity between Thailand and his nation. On social media, bloggers posted photos of the image hanging in various places and mourned the nation's loss of a father figure.

The ideal of the 'people's monarchs' and of 'American friendship' embodied in Dallinger's image clearly outlasted the king's own life. It would always be the way in which Thai people want to remember their King Bhumibol Adulyadej, their Thai identity, and their position in the world.

4   Conquering the World

King Bhumibol's 1960 Visit to Burma on Film

Matthew Phillips

Beneath a red, gold-lined umbrella, Thailand's King Bhumibol and Queen Sirikit proceed gracefully between pristinely dressed officials. The king wears a glistening white suit, the queen, a long red dress. Sheltered from the morning sun, and framed by the modern white façade of Bangkok's Don Mueang airport, the couple board a plane. As the aircraft moves gently down the runway, a hand holding a flag emerges from the cockpit window. The flag is yellow and emblazoned with the red Garuda bird from Hindu-Buddhist mythology: the national emblem of Thailand. The hand plants the flag at the side of the aircraft. With two fighter jets in tow, the plane floats through a radiant blue morning sky, then reappears in a foreign land. As the king descends from the plane, the Garuda once again glares from a yellow background placed on the door behind. The queen appears from above in a modern-cut sky-blue outfit. The royal procession continues: the entourage traveling away from the airport, passing through the streets of Rangoon (present-day Yangon) lined with gleeful crowds. A woman in traditional Burmese attire throws flower petals at the king's car. These sparkling scenes narrate the opening salvo of a diplomatic encounter between two neighbouring countries. They double as the conquest of a Buddhist king over a historic rival.

The visit of Thailand's king and queen to Burma (modern-day Myanmar) took place over four days in March 1960. It was the last of three short diplomatic trips made to neighbouring countries in preparation for nearly a decade of international travel.[1] Situated within the region, the journey represented the early deployment of Thai royal diplomacy in a distinct post-imperial world. As such, it presented publicists with a raft of complex moments of contradiction. Burma was a post-colonial nation, a vanguard neutralist power in the Cold War, and a proponent of socialism domestically. Conversely, Thailand was aligned with the United States and committed to American-informed capitalist development, underpinned by a conservative royalist ideology. More importantly, Burma had historically been considered by the

---

[1] Paul M. Handley, *The King Never Smiles: A Biography of Thailand's Bhumibol Adulyadej* (New Haven, CT: Yale University Press, 2006), p. 147.

Figure 4.1 King Bhumibol and Queen Sirikit walk from Don Mueang Airport to the plane. Still from the film *Nai Luang Somdet Phraboromrachanee Phraphat Saphap Phama 2–5 Minakhom* [The King and Queen visit to the Union of Burma 2–5 March], 1960.

Thai elite to be a rival polity that shared a similar Buddhist worldview and, with it, the same symbolic language of leadership.

The scenes described above are taken from a film produced by His Majesty's Personal Film Production Department and distributed for Thai audiences (see Fig. 4.1).[2] This was a critical time for the throne, with state propagandists focused on building national pride and identity around the figure of the young monarch. As such, the film is loaded with unmistakeable visual cues in which moments of potential disharmony were subtly restructured, reconciled, or smoothed out to placate Thai sensibilities. Most clearly, they emphasise King Bhumibol as a charismatic leader in the guise of his regional contemporaries. Drawing from long-standing regional diplomatic practices that emphasised the relative superiority of one leader over another, this

---

[2] Half of the film is currently available through YouTube: www.youtube.com/watch?v= fKk10P9LZAE&t=73s (accessed 2 September 2022). The full film was previously available on YouTube, but has since been removed. I originally viewed the film on Thai television in the aftermath of the death of King Bhumibol as part of the rolling coverage celebrating his life.

required a concerted effort from those around him. The effect was a film that asserted the superiority of King Bhumibol over his Burmese counterparts while elevating Queen Sirikit as the primary supporting character.

Buddhist Diplomacy Enters the Post-colonial Era

In pre-colonial Buddhist Southeast Asia, relations among political centres were underpinned by the constant battle for personal supremacy between kings. While kingdoms rose and fell according to complex social, economic, and political phenomena, the relative strength of each centre was linked in discourse to the perceived virtue of each ruler. The kings of the great regional centres, such as the city of Ayutthaya in modern-day Thailand or Ava in Burma, attracted tribute from lesser lords.[3] Monarchs also competed for influence over the region, each claiming titles celebrating their supposed divine superiority, and taking offence when not properly acknowledged. This meant perennial tension between leaders, with sporadic episodes of war.[4] In the royal courts, it also involved routine assertions of the king's moral standing through ritual and ceremonial practice that located him at the apex of a celestial and social order. The goal for any king was to ensure that representatives of other centres recognised his power as supreme through acts of tribute. Foreign embassies, even from afar, were thus required to participate in a series of activities that acknowledged the loftiness of the king and the power of the throne so that, in theory at least, the local population could imagine distant polities under the same royal umbrella.[5] As Stanley Tambiah explains, 'the king was seen as the pivot of the polity and as the mediating link between upper regions of the cosmos, composed of the gods and their heavens, and the lower plane of humans and lesser beings'.[6]

---

[3] Sunait Chutintaranond, 'Cakravartin: Ideology, Reason and Manifestation of Siamese and Burmese Kings in Traditional Warfare (1538–1857)', *Crossroads: An interdisciplinary Journal of Southeast Asian Studies*, 4:1 (1988), 46–56.

[4] While Southeast Asia had many powerful empires, with frequent conflicts, there was never a single hegemonic power. This has been explained by the unique environment, in which seas, mountains, and forests made it hard for a single leader to hold large territories, a feature that helped reinforce a model of sovereignty in which all individuals interacted in a multi-dimensional network of overlapping and crosscutting spheres of influence based on personal ties in which the power of any given centre was 'fluid and ever-changing'. See Hendrik Spruyt, *The World Imagined: Collective Beliefs and Political Order in the Sinocentric, Islamic and Southeast Asian International Societies* (Cambridge: Cambridge University Press, 2020), pp. 300–301. Also Thongchai Winichakul, *Siam Mapped: The History of the Geo-Body of a Nation* (Honolulu: University of Hawai'i Press, 1994), p. 88.

[5] H. G. Quaritch Wales, *Siamese State Ceremonies: Their History and Function* (London: Bernard Quaritch, 1931), p. 186.

[6] Stanley J. Tambiah, 'The Galactic Polity in Southeast Asia', *HAU: Journal of Ethnographic Theory,* 3:3 (2013), 505–34.

The colonial era ended the battle for tribute between kingdoms, replacing multiple centres with bound territories underpinned by modern notions of sovereignty and their associated diplomatic practices.[7] Yet, as the region entered the post-colonial era, nationalist propaganda continued to elevate respective leaders as exemplary amongst regional peers.[8] For the publicists working on King Bhumibol's trip to Burma this was a difficult task. Previously, kings did not travel to foreign capitals on acts of diplomacy, or indeed send envoys without good reason. As Wales explains, 'it was a maxim of Siamese kings to receive many embassies, but to send as few as possible', the idea being 'that the one who sent the first embassy was offering homage'.[9] From the late 1950s, those seeking to present Bhumibol's royal tours to a Thai audience were therefore required to draw from accounts that *did* describe a king in motion – travelling out from the centre and into war. Over hundreds of years, palace chronicles framed royal victory over foreign kings and their subjects as the restoration of righteous order over the world and, ultimately, the universe. Drawing from revered texts such as the *Ramakian* (the Thai version of the *Ramayana*) and the *Traiphum*, a fourteenth-century Thai treatise of kingship, these narratives ultimately portrayed success in war as a moral conquest, or *dhammavijaya*: victory achieved through displays of Buddhist virtue by a triumphant king. It was this paradigm that royal publicists used to elevate King Bhumibol on his trip to Burma, a feat that relied heavily on the technology of film.

The early mastery of moving images by Thai propagandists began in 1950, when King Bhumibol's coronation and marriage were filmed and subsequently shown in cinemas.[10] Throughout the decade, King Bhumibol had a tense relationship with the government, which was still largely committed to the revolutionary ideals that had deposed absolutism in 1932. Lacking access to state propaganda channels, the royal household instead relied on a small network of sympathetic elites to capture and reproduce images that suitably elevated the king in public discourse.[11] In so doing, they received help from

---

[7] Thongchai Winichakul, *Siam Mapped.*

[8] Jean Lacoutre, *The Demigods: Charismatic Leadership in the Third World* (New York: Alfred A Knopf, 1970).

[9] Wales, *Siamese State Ceremonies*, p. 186. Anthony Reid makes a similar point, noting that the chronicles of Southeast Asian polities 'acknowledged that it was a measure of a ruler's greatness that the harbour was full of foreign vessels and the court of foreign envoys'. See Anthony Reid, *Southeast Asia in the Age of Commerce 1450–1680, vol. 2: Expansion and Crisis* (New Haven, CT: Yale University Press, 1993), p. 234.

[10] Rebecca Townsend, 'Cold Fire: Gender, Development, and the Film Industry in Cold War Thailand', unpublished PhD dissertation, Cornell University (2017), p. 56.

[11] Chanida Chitbundid, *Krongkan an neuang ma chak phraratchadamri kansathapana phraratcha-amnat nam nai Phrabat Somdet Phrachao Yu Hua* [The Royally Initiated Projects: The Making of King Bhumibol's Royal Hegemony] (Bangkok: Foundation for the Promotion of Social Sciences and Humanities Textbooks, 2007), p. 73.

the United States. Particularly from 1953, the US Embassy in Bangkok supported those seeking to depict the king as a unifying figure. This included a tour of northeast Thailand in 1955, made up of train journeys and motorcades through the country's rural hinterland. As crowds of villagers flocked to witness the progression of a Thai king, cameras were on hand to film key scenes. In 1956, when King Bhumibol was ordained as a Buddhist monk, the United States Information Service (USIS) captured the king on film, ensuring the events were a public relations triumph for the palace.[12] Such efforts were strengthened by television, which was first established in Thailand in 1955, and provided new opportunities to disseminate the king's image. By the early 1960s, when the king and queen began nearly a decade of international travel, this same technology once again narrated their journey to the four corners of the earth, including their 1960 trip to the United States.[13] As explored in Chapter 3 in this volume, over time, these images helped secure internal narratives that placed Bhumibol at the apex of national life. Films of the king being welcomed by elated crowds in distant lands contributed to a sense that the Thai national community (*chat*) was exalted in world politics, while bestowing divine qualities onto the king himself.

One power of diplomatic images is the ability to not merely report but actively shape narratives of relation between states and their leaders. Features such the height, demeanour, or dress of one actor in relation to another along with visible aspects such as place or props impose meanings onto the value, purpose, and impact of the encounter. These dynamics are further enhanced through film, which, as Delueze notes, 'moves and temporalizes the images', tracking such relations through time and drawing on tools of duration or rhythm to influence how a narrative unfolds.[14] In the case of King Bhumibol, the moving image, captured and repackaged after the visit itself, proved a critical tool in overcoming the central contradiction of the trip: the need to present Thailand as an enthusiastic friend of a newly independent Asian neighbour, while retaining the suggestion of Thai regional superiority to domestic audiences.

To manage the discrepancy, Thai publicists engaged in what Christine Gray describes as a Janus ritual: practices that could simultaneously be interpreted in two radically different ways to Thai and foreign audiences, and which became critical to Thai statecraft in the nineteenth century. Keen to protect the monarch from charges of despotism, Gray notes how King Rama IV (1851–68) broke

---

[12] Townsend, 'Cold Fire', p. 56.

[13] P. Michael Rattanasengchanh, 'US-Thai Public Diplomacy, the Beginnings of a Military-Monarchical-Anti-Communist State, 1957–1963', *Journal of American-East Asian Relations*, 23:1 (2016), 70.

[14] Gilles Deleuze and Melissa McMuhan, 'The Brain Is the Screen: Interview with Gilles Deleuze on "The Time Image"', *Discourse*, 20:3 (1988), 50.

with the tradition of seclusion in the palace and began to take trips into the public realm. To western eyes, these journeys were interpreted as a sign of the monarch's democratic tendencies. But for Thai audiences they carried distinct symbolic meanings encoded in Buddhist-Hindu cosmology: the descent of a Buddhist deity from the heavens. Gray elaborates:

> The magical quality of his [the king's] descent from the heavens derives from beliefs about the potency of the sight of pure persons (gods) and pure actions in the Buddhist tradition; the sight of the king exercises a powerful sensory (visual) effect on his hot-hearted subjects, inclining them toward the dhamma.[15]

By harnessing the power of the moving image, royal publicists in the 1960s returned to the same coded messages, underpinned by the concept of moral conquest (*dhammavijaya*), to include foreign lands. In the case of the trip to Burma, the simple act of keeping the king and queen at the centre of the shot, always the primary focus of the camera, elevated Bhumibol to central protagonist. Through further careful editing, the trip resonated with the journeys of the 'great' conquering kings of Thai history, in turn evoking the exploits of victorious deities depicted on temple murals and motifs across the kingdom. Ultimately, the film served to locate the king and his nation at the centre of a new moral order, energised by anti-communism and American-led development.[16]

Two Polities, One Cosmos

King Bhumibol and Queen Sirikit left for Burma from Bangkok on 2 March 1960. They arrived at Mingaladon Airport at 9 am, where they were met by President U Win Maung and his wife Madame Win Maung. Following a twenty-one-gun salute, the president and the king were taken to their respective places on a dais where they received the first general salute and observed the Royal Anthem of Thailand. After a second salute, they proceeded to the terminal lounge where the president delivered his welcome address.[17] The president thanked the king and queen for visiting, and made it clear that

---

[15] Christine Gray, 'The Soteriological State in the 1970s', unpublished PhD dissertation, University of Chicago (1986), pp. 261–62.

[16] Matthew Phillips, 'Re-ordering the Cold War Cosmos: King Bhumibol's 1960 U.S. Tour', *Diplomatic History*, 45:2 (2021), 253–67.

[17] Programme of the State Visit of His Majesty King Bhumibol Adulyadej and Her Majesty Queen Sirikit, March 2nd–5th 1960, taken from *Set yuen: Sathan rat Viatnam, sathan rat Indonisia, sahaphap Phama, sahaphan rat Malaya, sathan rat Filippins* [Visit to: the Republic of Vietnam, the Republic of Indonesia, the Union of Burma, the Federation of Malaya, the Republic of the Philippines], *Samnak-phrarachawang ruap ruam lae jat phim sanong phra maha karunathikhun Phraphat Somdet Phramin somaha Phumiphol Adulyadet Neung nai Mahamongkhon Samai Chalerm Phrachonmapaasa* 1967, p. 197.

the Burmese people had been looking forward to the event: 'The Union of Burma and the Kingdom of Thailand are close neighbours and our two peoples have not only common culture and religion, but also a similar way of life.'[18] King Bhumibol responded that the 'Queen and I are delighted to set our feet upon Burmese soil'; the Burmese and the Thai were bound together in friendship, shared the same Buddhist faith, as well as the same aspirations of peace and co-operation.[19] Speeches complete, the entourage departed for the city, King Bhumibol and the president in the front car, Queen Sirikit and Madame Win Maung in the one behind.

In terms of aesthetics, this opening scene had clear echoes of the last time a Thai, or rather a Siamese, monarch had visited in 1872. The political context, however, could not have been more different. In the nineteenth-century iteration of the exchange, the British had just annexed southern Burma into British India, meaning that the young Siamese king of the time, Chulalongkorn, was welcomed by representatives of Queen Victoria. Dressed in European style, King Chulalongkorn arrived in Rangoon on a steam yacht accompanied by several naval vessels. The British chief commissioner met him at Iron Wharf, which was decorated with flags and laid out with a red carpet. They mounted a dai and listened to 'God Save the Queen' before departing to a twenty-one-gun salute. British officials pointedly noted how the young Siamese king and his entourage shunned 'native court prejudices, or restrictive conservation as regards manners and customs prevalent amongst neighbouring Asiatic cognate races'.[20] The *Rangoon Times* observed that the king was, 'in our English sense of the term, very well behaved'.[21]

For the Siamese elite, this early visit was situated within complex power dynamics rooted in the past. As a principal competitor to the city of Ayutthaya for regional supremacy, Burmese kingdoms routinely came into conflict with the Thai, each clash retold in royal chronicles as episodes of moral conquest over a rival that had fallen out of cosmic alignment. As Burmese chroniclers reported, when the King of Ayutthaya refused to pay his taxes and submit to the power of the Burmese throne in 1568, it was interpreted as an unnatural act, akin to conspiring against the Buddha. After defeating his enemy, the Burmese king exclaimed that

---

[18] Address of Welcome by His Excellency President U Win Maung to Their Majesties the King and Queen of Thailand on Arrival at Mingaladon Airport, Rangoon, 2 March 1960, taken from *Set yuen*, p. 203.

[19] *Set yuen*, p. 204.

[20] Major E. B. Sladen to C. U. Attchison Esq., C.S.I., Secretary to the Government of India, Foreign Department, 'Visit of King of Siam to India', from Sachchidanand Sahai, *India in 1872: As Seen by the Siamese* (New Delhi: B. R. Publishing, 2002), p. 400.

[21] Reprinted from the *Rangoon Times* in the Siam Repository, April 1872, Article 25, p. 241; 'The King of Siam in Burmah', in Sahai, *India in 1872*, p. 271.

the King of Ayutthaya who had already sworn an oath of loyalty which was not to be cast aside from son to grandson, perished because he broke the oath. Now, he is dead. As he was ungrateful to me, he will be thrown into the four nether worlds in the cycle of rebirth and become a stump in hell.[22]

For the Thais, this conquest set up the emergence of one of the most important figures in Thai history, King Naresuan. Known primarily for prising Ayutthaya back from Burmese control in 1590, today he is worshipped at shrines across Thailand as a god.[23]

In 1767 Burmese armies defeated the city of Ayutthaya, plunging the Siamese into a period of protracted political, social, and cultural crisis. The last of thirty-three sovereigns to have ruled over the kingdom was killed, and his brother, who had ruled as king before him, was forcefully removed to Burma. To the Siamese, the conquest upended the existing moral order, their palaces and temples devastated once again. Thai chroniclers later framed the events as symptomatic of a descent into a Buddhist dark age (*kali yuga*).[24] After a new kingdom was established in Bangkok, in 1782, conflict with the Burmese remained commonplace, confirming to the Thai elite that their neighbours belonged to the lower rungs of the cosmological hierarchy, along with the devils and demons.[25] A century later, in 1885, the Burmese monarchy was toppled after three wars with the British (1824–26, 1852–53, and 1885), while Siamese elites strengthened their position by aligning with European power. State administration was adapted to conform with European models, and Siam was integrated into new European-dominated trading networks. As part of this transformation, Siam's kings incorporated elements from European monarchic culture to attest to their superior character, constructing a cult of personality around their respective images.[26] Siamese historians actively adopted the British trope that cast the Burmese kings as despotic, having it converge with their own retelling of 1767. The most significant contribution to this endeavour was the 1917 publication of Prince Damrong's *Thai Rop Phama* [Our wars with the Burmese]. By adopting a standard western style and form, the text explored the story of

---

[22] Soe Thuzar Myint, *Siam-Myanmar Relations through the Perspective of Ayedawbon Treaties* (Bangkok: Institute of Asian Studies, Chulalongkorn University, 2018), p. 188.

[23] Prince Damrong Rajanubhab, *A Biography of King Naresuan the Great* (Bangkok: Foundation for the Promotion of Social Science Textbooks Project, 2008), p. 61.

[24] As quoted in, Sunait Chutintaranond, 'The Image of the Burmese Enemy in Thai Perceptions and Historical Writings', *Journal of the Siam Society*, 80:1 (1992), 90.

[25] Ibid., p. 91. Also see Pavin Chachavalpongpun, *A Plastic Nation: The Curse of Thainess in Thai-Burmese Relations* (Lanham, MD: University Press of America, 2005), p. 41.

[26] Attachak Sattayanurak, 'The Intellectual Aspects of Strong Kingship in the Late Nineteenth Century', *Journal of the Siam Society*, 88:1–2 (2000), 88.

the Siamese nation through wars with its neighbour, enshrining Burma as an eternal foe.[27]

In 1932 a revolution toppled the absolute monarchy in Siam and a new regime was installed. Yet state propagandists remained fixed to a chauvinistic version of history that emphasised Thai superiority in the region – one reason for changing the name of the country to Thailand in 1939.[28] This view was temporarily reinforced in the early 1940s, first with a military victory against the French in Cambodia, then after Thailand's wartime alliance with Japan enabled further territorial gains. The expansion of national borders into what became the Great Thai Empire (*Maha-Anajak Thai*) was only halted at the end of the Second World War, when Thailand's fractured political leadership was forced to return the territory and accept defeat. Many newspapers in Bangkok framed the loss of territory as a humiliation, contributing to a sense of national decay and rising anxiety about the future.[29] Having pinned Thai nationhood to pride in surviving the colonial period with sovereignty intact, Thailand was now just one of several independent Southeast Asian nations. To make matters worse, neighbouring states were generally led by a unique crop of popular and charismatic leaders who excelled in defying the so-called Great Powers and proclaimed strong and defiant visions of the future.

For the Burmese, the British removal of the king in 1885 and subsequent occupation was associated with a Buddhist dark age and the prospect of independence linked to a potentially new and prosperous era. When independence came in 1948, Burma was led by U Nu, who projected himself at home and abroad as a uniquely charismatic figure. In 1952 he merged socialism with Buddhist principles in a political plan underpinned by social justice and virtuous living.[30] Between 1954 and 1956, he hosted a synod to mark the year 2500 (in Burma 1956), an important date in the Buddhist calendar, in a newly constructed Peace Pagoda (*Kaba Aye Paya*).[31] Through these efforts, U Nu situated his leadership firmly within a Theravada Buddhist worldview, in which society was organised around a natural hierarchy where persons are ranked by degrees of religious purity, and where leadership is legitimised through demonstrations of virtue.[32] U Nu's actions routinely doubled as dramatic displays of his bountiful stores of good karma linked to a

---

[27] Prince Damrong Rajanubhab, *Our Wars with the Burmese: Thai Burmese Conflict 1539–1767* (Bangkok: White Lotus, 2001).

[28] Shane Strate, *The Lost Territories: Thailand's History of National Humiliation* (Honolulu: University of Hawai'i Press, 2015), pp. 2–4.

[29] Matthew Phillips, *Thailand in the Cold War* (Abingdon: Routledge, 2016), pp. 82–83.

[30] Maung Maung, 'Pyidawtha Comes to Burma', *Far Eastern Survey* 22:9 (1953), 117–19.

[31] Richard Butwell, *U Nu of Burma*, (Stanford, CA: Stanford University Press, 1963), p. 65.

[32] E. Sarkisyanz, *Buddhist Backgrounds of the Burmese Revolution* (New York: Springer, 1965), pp. 206–29.

corresponding ability to attract the love and affection of his people.[33] According to Tilman Frasch, efforts to bring Buddhist relics to the country reinforced U Nu's efforts to demonstrate *dhammavijaya* – 'winning over the people by the display of Buddhist virtues rather than by force'.[34]

Thailand's political elite remained fractured through most of the 1950s. In 1949, Prime Minister Plaek Phibunsongkhram declared an alliance with the United States in the emerging Cold War. The public remained unconvinced, however, and he was unable to foster enthusiasm. Meanwhile, US officials stepped up efforts to court the monarchy. This drive culminated in a coup in 1958 when Field Marshal Sarit Thanarat placed Thailand on a more distinctly pro-US trajectory and championed the monarch at home and abroad. Thus, King Bhumibol joined the raft of Southeast Asian leaders who established popular legitimacy through demonstrations of charismatic power. At home, traditional royal ceremonies were reintroduced, and in late 1959 the king began close to a decade of international travel.

The prospect of a royal visit to Burma was first proposed in 1955 following an invitation from U Nu for the king to attend the 2500-year Buddhist calendar celebrations in Rangoon. At that time, however, Bhumibol was not on good terms with Prime Minister Phibunsongkhram and lacked the authority to dictate how the visit should be represented back in Thailand. Plaek Phibunsongkhram travelled alone. Later, U Nu returned the favour by travelling to Thailand, where he appeared to demonstrate support for Phibunsongkhram by donating a large sum of money to repair temples in Ayutthaya and planting a tree at Wat Phra Sri Mahathat. Once again, the king would not meet with the Burmese leader.[35] By the late 1950s, U Nu was struggling. In 1958, he disposed of all belongings and retreated from public life after handing over power, temporarily, to army leader General Ne Win. In elections in February 1960 U Nu was once again victorious, celebrated by the Burmese Buddhist community as a spiritually advanced figure. When King Bhumibol and Queen Sirikit visited, he had yet to take up his position as prime minister.

The Conquering Monarch

At the heart of the battle for charismatic leadership by figures such as U Nu was a struggle over image, a consequence of the unique role played by visual communication in Theravada Buddhism. Across the region, subtle signals,

[33] Ian Harris, 'Buddhism, Politics and Nationalism', in David L. McMahan (ed.), *Buddhism in the Modern World* (Abingdon: Routledge, 2012), p. 188.
[34] Tilman Frasch, 'The Relic and the Rule of Righteousness: Reflections on U Nu's Dhammavijaya', in John Whalen-Bridge and Pattana Kitiarsa (eds.), *Buddhism, Modernity, and the State in Asia: Forms of Engagement* (New York: Palgrave Macmillan, 2013), p. 115.
[35] Kobkua Suwannathat-Pian, *Thailand's Durable Premier: Phibun through Three Decades 1932–1957* (Oxford: Oxford University Press, 1995), pp. 142–43.

including the dress, relative physical height, and the way such individuals interact with their environment are vital in communicating specific messages about relative status. As a result, the ability to control, manipulate, or secure a specific visual impression weighs heavily on the minds of leaders and those invested in their power.[36] While the Thai coup of 1958 did not bestow significant political power on Bhumibol, it did present royal officials with the freedom to exploit royal symbolism. As a result, the trip to Burma was duly transformed from a simple diplomatic visit into a narrative of spiritual conquest, captured for posterity.

Itineraries, memoires, and articles of the trip tell a story of speeches, formal dinners, and acts of mutual respect. Overall, they convey Bhumibol's journey through a series of backdrops, each designed to emphasise Burmese sovereignty in a post-colonial era. On day one, the king was invited to lay a wreath at the Mausoleum of Martyrs and to pay his respect to Burma's nationalist heroes. Later, at a state banquet held at the presidential residence, President U Win Maung noted in a speech, given in English, that due to European colonialism the countries of Southeast Asia had 'lost effective contact with each other'.[37] Now that states had regained their sovereignty, they were 'beginning to realise more than ever before that the maintenance of good neighbourly relations and the promotion of friendly co-operation among them are essential for their individual and collective progress and prosperity'.[38] The following day, the entourage paid a visit to Shwedagon Pagoda, Burma's pre-eminent site of spiritual power and an iconic symbol of independence. After that, the king and queen were taken to the Peace Pagoda and the Maha Pasana Guha cave, both built by U Nu as part of the 2500-year celebrations. On the final full day, the couple visited the Burma Pharmaceutical Industry.

In his own speech at the banquet, also in English, King Bhumibol noted the 'magnificence' of the hospitality and the 'generous words you have used about our country and ourselves'. Eschewing talk of physical boundaries, he focused instead on the 'invisible force' that brings the two peoples together. A force, he explained, 'that springs from the knowledge that the two peoples share the same noble heritage of the Buddhist faith'. Finally, while the president was keen to draw a line between the contemporary meeting and the past, the king was less willing to drop references to a historic rivalry: 'The two countries have learnt to overlook the differences of the past, and to promote friendly sentiments in the present.'[39]

King Bhumibol's emphasis on a shared Buddhist world-view located the Burmese and the Thai on the same spiritual plane. In so doing he evoked a

---

[36] Christine E. Gray, 'Buddhism as a Language of Images, Transtextuality as a Language of Power', *Word & Image: A Journal of Verbal/Visual Enquiry*, 11:2 (1995), 227.

[37] *Set yuen*, p. 207.   [38] Ibid.   [39] Ibid., p. 208.

common cosmology, within which Buddhist populations are understood to live together on the same continent of Jambu, one of four continents in the mythical version of the cosmos.[40] In so doing, he opened the door to the potential appearance of a great Buddhist leader, a *cakkavatti* king who, according to the *Traiphum*, can only be born on Jambu and who then conquers the world due to his sheer charismatic force, outranking all others he meets. As the *Traiphum* describes, this king will travel out from the royal capital by air and, upon arrival, to each ruler and king on Jambu, comes 'to offer gifts, to pay his respects, to bow down, and to do obeisance before the great Cakkavatti king, and the great Cakkavatti king teaches concerning merit and Dhamma'.[41]

On film, the story begins in Bangkok, where after a formal departure ceremony, the couple board a royal air force plane, a converted US-built Douglas DC 54 Skymaster (Fig. 4.2). The flag, installed outside the cockpit, indicates that the king is on board, and the overall scene emphasises unity. After a decade of political instability and factionalism, the military government, along with their American backers, are now working together in the service of the monarch – investing their labour and prestige, including the aesthetic of modern air travel, in him. This alone elevates King Bhumibol to the apex of the nation.

The next scene depicts two military planes following behind, chaperoning the royal flight through the sky. Text-based sources confirm that Thai fighters were replaced by Burmese fighter jets halfway, and, once again, the scene alludes to hierarchy – now loaded with more obvious cosmological implications. Specifically, it evoked the royal barge procession wherein the boats are modelled on the heavenly creatures of Thai-Buddhist cosmology, and the king sits at the apex of the arrangement, on occasion travelling in the Garuda barge. At times of war, the procession would leave the capital amidst a racket of conch shells and drums at a time deemed astrologically auspicious, taking the king and accompanying nobles into battle, joined by further lords upstream. In both Burma and Thailand, the inclusion of these nobles and foreign lords demonstrated the attractive power of the monarch, attesting to his heavenly status.[42] While the film does not mention where the fighter planes have come from, their presence takes on a similar role to accompanying barges in historic

---

[40] For a description of Jambu in Burmese cosmology, see Michael Aung Thwin, 'Jambudipda: Classical Burma's Camelot', *Contributions to Asian Studies*, 16 (1981), 51.

[41] Frank E. Reynolds and Mani B. Reynolds, *Three Worlds According to King Ruang: A Thai Buddhist Cosmology*, Berkeley Buddhist Studies Series 4 (Berkeley: University of California Press, 1982), p. 156.

[42] Wales describes how King Naresuan and his entourage, 'having attired themselves for war set forth in their royal state barges, with the brilliant royal insignia, tiered parasol, golden fans, and victory standards, beautiful and splendid with the whole procession of nobles' barges arranged in order before and behind'. Horace Geoffrey Quartich Wales, *Ancient South-East Asian Warfare* (London: Bernard Quartich, 1952), p. 173.

Figure 4.2 The pilot places a yellow Garuda flag on the front of the plane. Still from the film *Nai Luang Somdet Phraboromrachanee Phraphat Saphap Phama 2–5 Minakhom* [The King and Queen visit to the Union of Burma 2–5 March], 1960.

examples. Hovering below the royal flight, they are subordinate to the king. This also makes the association between the plane and the Garuda more obvious, as in both Burmese and Thai chronicles the appearance of a Garuda just prior to a victorious battle was ubiquitous.[43] Streaking across the sky at 8,000 feet, the plane is transformed into a sacred vehicle, carrying the king into battle as the Garuda carries the god Vishnu, with whom Thai kings associate.[44] When they arrive in Rangoon, and the king disembarks, the bird appears on the inside of the door, reinforcing the association (Fig. 4.3).

---

[43] In one story, the Garuda appeared at the camp of Naresuan as he prepared for war. Wales, *Ancient Warfare*, p. 174. In the Ayedawbon Treaties, the Burmese king, in his march on the Siamese is described as follows: 'just as the King of Garuda had chased the dragon, [the *naga*] (the king) ordered the soldiers to approach the town en masse'. Soe Thuzar Myint, *Siam-Myanmar Relations through the perspective of Ayedawbon Treaties* (Bangkok: Institute of Asian Studies, Chulalongkorn University, 2018), p. 187.

[44] Bryan Angelo Lim, 'Vehicle of Kingship and Sovereignty: Exploring Representations of Garuda in Siam', unpublished MA dissertation, SOAS University of London, 2018.

Figure 4.3 The king and queen descend from the plane. The Garuda (on the open door) once again has been placed in a key location. Still from the film *Nai Luang Somdet Phraboromrachanee Phraphat Saphap Phama 2–5 Minakhom,* [The King and Queen visit to the Union of Burma 2–5 March], 1960.

More visual cues appear throughout the first day. Rather than focus on the sites attended or the diplomatic activities completed, the film concentrates on the entourage as they travel through the streets of Rangoon. The car proceeds slowly down the road, flanked by Burmese horses and motorbikes, and crowds line up to cheer his arrival. A woman in Burmese dress throws flower petals in his path, in a manner that the narrator explains is 'in line with Burmese tradition'. Both the Thai press and international coverage emphasised the centrality of the king to the exchange. According to the Associated Press, many Burmese papers 'devoted editorial columns of comment which stressed the "charm and graciousness" of the Royal couple' who 'won the hearts' of the Burmese people.[45] The visual effect, however, was to show that Burmese

---

[45] 'Burma Press Praise Royal Thai Visitors', *Bangkok Post*, 4 March 1960, p. 2.

crowds were drawn to the king,[46] a demonstration of his royal *barami*. Described by Patrick Jory as 'an idealised form of personal authority characterised by moral superiority, spiritual prowess, and supernatural ability', *barami* is also a quality that is understood to draw people toward the person who possess it.[47] Foreign crowds, flocking to greet Bhumibol, appeared to attest directly to his charismatic potency.

Austere King, Glamourous Queen

At 8:30 in the morning the following day, the entourage departed from the President's House for Shwedagon Pagoda. On film, as the king and queen arrive at the eastern slope entrance, they are first met by the abbot and the rest of the Shwedagon Pagoda Trust. The narrator explains that the king removes his shoes 'in line with Burmese tradition'.[48] This was the central event of the trip. In the pre-colonial period, Shwedagon was the primary location of royal prestige in Rangoon. During British rule, the site became the focus of cultural contestation between the British and the Burmese – principally over shoes. For the British, the Burmese demand to remove shoes inside the temple was seen as unreasonable and symptomatic of the Burmese commitment to 'backward' traditions. For the Burmese, this refusal was emblematic of British condescension and, as such, became a key issue in the formation of anti-colonial sentiment.[49] Somewhat awkwardly, the practice was viewed differently by the Thai and Burmese, a fact exploited by the British.[50] When King Chulalongkorn and his party visited Shwedagon in 1872, they entered the temple enclosure in boots, and according to the British made offerings with 'little special regard to the strict observances, which are a cherished portion of Buddhistic ritualism'.[51] When Prime Minister Phibunsongkhram proposed that King Bhumibol visit Burma in 1955, palace officials refused, claiming he could not accept the requirement to remove his shoes.[52]

---

[46] Christine Gray, 'Royal Words and Their Unroyal Consequences', *Cultural Anthropology*, 7:4 (1992), 448–463.

[47] Patrick Jory, *Thailand's Theory of Monarchy: The Vessantra Jataka and the Idea of the Perfect Man* (Albany: State University of New York Press, 2016), p. 18.

[48] Police Chief Chumpol Lohachala, *Kan Set Phrarachadhamnoen Yuean Sathanrat Viatnam Sathanrat Indonisia Lae Sahaphap Phama* (Bangkok: Amarin Printing and Publishing, 1997), p. 123.

[49] For a discussion of the 'shoe question' in Burma, see Alicia Turner, *Saving Buddhism: The Impermanence of Religion in Colonial Burma* (Honolulu: University of Hawai'i Press, 2014), pp. 110–35.

[50] Donald M. Seeking, *State and Society in Modern Rangoon* (Abingdon: Routledge, 2011), p. 48.

[51] Major E. B. Sladen to C. U. Attchison Esq., C.S.I., Seceratry to the Government of India, Foreign Department. 'Visit of King of Siam to India', quoted from Sahai, *India in 1872,* p. 400.

[52] Handley, *The King Never Smiles*, p. 130.

When the royal couple arrive at the temple, the viewer is conducted through a series of luminous religious sites where the royal couple solemnly perform their ritual duties. The effect, combined with the lack of shoes, appears to show Bhumibol renouncing the trappings of kingship, even evoking the aesthetics of his time spent as a monk in 1956. No royal umbrella protects him from the sun as would be normal back in Bangkok, and for hours he endures the blistering morning heat. At the same time the king retains key markers of distinction. He makes the rare move of replacing his preferred western suit trousers with a pair of striking red pants (*chong kraben*), evoking Siamese kings of old. The theme of renunciation, combined with these subtle markers of distinction, pointedly conjures key kingly virtues, in Thai: *Pariccaga* (selfless sacrifice), *Maddava* (open-mindedness), and *Khanti* (patience and perseverance). Perhaps most significant, in light of Burma's historic defeat of Ayutthaya, the king demonstrates *akkodha*, an ability to not dwell on the misdeeds of the past, to show compassion to those who have done one wrong.

Another striking feature of these scenes is the role played by Queen Sirikit. At Shwedagon, her modern pink silk suit ensures she stands out, drawing the eye of the viewer in all scenes in which she appears. Always behind the king, her presence infuses the aesthetic with a sense of the contemporary. The queen walks alongside Madame Win Maung, yet the president's wife is barely visible. Dressed in white and blue textiles, the Burmese first lady disappears into the crowd of plain-clothed men in off-white Burmese suits. Sirikit, in contrast, comes across as somewhat lonely, engaged in a performance of distinction through a display of solitary radiance, serenity, and bodily discipline. By Sirikit's account, the trips to Vietnam, Indonesia, and then Burma were preparation for the later trips to the United States and Europe, during which time she invested heavily in a new wardrobe for the purposes of international diplomacy.[53]

Throughout the trip, the figure of Queen Sirikit manages contradictions that would otherwise undermine the king's status. At Rangoon airport, for instance, as the king descends the steps, Queen Sirikit momentarily adopts a position higher than her husband. Considering the taboo that nobody can be physically above the king, this raises an apparent question regarding celestial order. The queen's attire plays a critical function in overcoming the awkwardness. Having entered the aircraft in a regal body-length maroon dress, she exits in a light blue outfit in the guise of a modern jet-set celebrity. In line with the international trends of the time, the short cut and pastel tones do more to evoke

[53] Her Majesty Queen Sirikit, *In Memory of the State Visits of His Majesty the King*, 2nd ed. (first edition 1968) (Bangkok, 2004), pp. 84–86. Also see Melissa Leventon and Dale Carolyn Gluckman, *In Royal Fashion: The Style of Her Majesty Queen Sirikit of Thailand* (Bangkok: Queen Sirikit, Museum of Textiles, 2013), p. 43.

contemporaries such as Jacqueline Kennedy than traditional Buddhist queens. Yet the cosmological references remain. Having been born on a Friday, light blue is her astrological colour. At the same time, the modern outfit stands in direct contrast to the king, who remains clothed in the European imperial-style dress to which his predecessors had become accustomed. Situated both behind and above the king, Sirikit updates the scene, placing the couple at the apex of modern trends. While she plainly receives her status from him, she also boosts his charismatic power through a mastery of colour, fashion, and style.

Gem Queen, Warrior King

Prior to the twentieth century, queens or consorts were central to Thai court politics, and the harem was an extension of regional diplomacy. Based on the premise that the king occupied the highest spiritual point of the kingdom, wives often doubled as tribute from high-status families and vassal rulers who sought the king's protection.[54] As such, they served as another measurement of his power of attraction, further evidence of his charismatic potency.[55] Moreover, they directly indexed the kings' virility, with the number of wives, as Craig Reynolds explains, contributing 'to the mythology of the monarch as a source of prosperity, abundance, and fecundity'.[56]

By the turn of the century, the harem was no longer tenable. The integration of tributary states into a single nation at least partially ended the political rationale for polygamy. More critically, it was out of line with new moral codes imported from the West and, as such, a lightning rod for those who sought to cast the monarchy as moribund.[57] While rising incomes in the 1920s saw an expansion of the practice of polygamy, monogamy was increasingly proclaimed as the norm. Following the 1932 revolution, the government sought to elevate specific women as iconic representatives of progress. This was most notable through the Miss Thailand competition that ran annually from the mid-1930s, linking a world of expanded political opportunity with access to new consumables. Yet modern aesthetics were only possible within a

---

[54] Tamara Loos, *Subject Siam: Family, Law, and Colonial Modernity* (Ithaca, NY: Cornell University Press, 2006), p. 111.

[55] Chris Baker and Pasuk Phongpaichit, *The Palace Law of Ayutthaya and the Thammasat: Law and Kingship in Siam* (Ithaca, NY: Southeast Asia Program Publications, 2016), p. 62.

[56] Craig Reynolds makes the point that in the cosmology, the god Indra, to whom the Thai kings associate themselves, was said to have twenty-four million wives. See his *Seditious Histories: Contesting Thai and Southeast Asian Pasts* (Seattle: University of Washington Press, 2006), p. 193.

[57] Tamara Loos, 'The Birth of Mistresses and Bastards: A History of Marriage in Siam (Thailand)', in Julia Moses (ed.), *Marriage, Law and Modernity: Global Histories* (London: Bloomsbury, 2018), p. 84. Also see Scot Barmé, *Woman, Man, Bangkok: Love, Sex and Popular Culture in Thailand* (Oxford: Rowman and Littlefield, 2002), pp. 157–79.

tight set of social parameters – particularly for women. At the personal level, correct female behaviour was largely framed through a woman's relationship to the patriarchal institution of the family. At the national level, women were required to conform to prescribed notions of service, loyalty, and beauty. Throughout the period, state-backed media encouraged women to engage in a process of self-improvement that included maintaining good health, nurturing good behaviour, and dressing appropriately, each becoming an individual's responsibility to the nation.[58]

During the 1950s, the political drive to democratise the aesthetics of modernity fell away as expanded access to imported products and services began to give shape to a more overtly capitalist model of social advancement. While the emphasis on individual self-improvement remained, it was now more associated with one's wealth and knowledge of a particularly American-orientated culture. It also remained tied to a clear patriarchy. Women who were liberated into a world of love marriages and education continued to be responsible for taking care of the household, childcare, and entertaining guests, mastering domestic duties to allow the men to make their respective conquests in a world of expanded opportunity and freedom.[59]

It was in this context that Queen Sirikit presented herself as the country's primary female body: the sole individual able to reconcile the aesthetic demands of American-era consumerism with the modern ideals of the 1930s and the role of a dutiful queen. For Sirikit, this work primarily involved creating an elaborate and priceless wardrobe, made up of modern Thai dresses with references to tradition. To do this, she depended heavily on Thai silk, which had emerged as a new national product in the decade prior to the tours. While this process would really get going three months later, when the queen accompanied the king on their visit to the United States, the trip to Burma signalled both the work done and the work yet to be undertaken in her advancement to Thailand's queen of the American era.

Just as the queens in the harem substantiated the power of the king, Queen Sirikit's effort, demonstrated through her beauty and bodily perfection, served to boost the charismatic standing of the young king. Throughout the film, her aesthetic superiority to the crowd interacted awkwardly with the demands made upon her. This is particularly true in the second half of the film when, following the trip to Shwedagon, the couple are invited onto a boat along the Rangoon waterfront. As they arrive at the jetty, it is clear that the king and

---

[58] Kanjana Hubik Thepboriruk, 'Dear Thai Sisters: Propaganda, Fashion, and the Corporeal Nation under Phibunsongkhram', *Southeast Asian Studies*, 8:2 (2019), 233–58.

[59] This was a common feature of life for women in the post-colonial world. See Lila Abu-Lughod, *Remaking Women: Feminism and Modernity in the Middle East* (Princeton, NJ: Princeton University Press, 1998).

queen have, once again, undergone another sartorial transformation. Having completed his work at the temple, the king is now wearing a 1950s-style khaki suit, while the queen has changed to a fashionable white dress. As the boat moves away, the film displays a largely male crowd in relaxed conversation. The camera zooms in on the king, who is smiling and chatting with the abbot of Shwedagon. By moving in on the scene from afar, the viewer feels as if they are allowed to catch a glimpse of the king in this new guise, behind the scenes, so to speak. The viewer is then shown scenes of the river, replete with fast-moving human-powered river taxis. When the camera returns to the boat, the focus has shifted to a conversation between the president's wife and Queen Sirikit. The camera now places Queen Sirikit in the foreground. The two are sitting next to each other on a sofa, and Madame Win Maung is making small talk. Sirikit responds with a smile, yet she is not entirely comfortable. She looks away, and the camera pauses on her face from a new angle as she stares into space for an uncomfortably long period of time. As with the change of clothes, the scene reinforces a sense of discontinuity. Previously, Queen Sirikit had appeared either in the background or in a scene that replicated the king's previous actions. Now she is central.

Day three starts with a trip to a pharmaceutical factory. The king is again wearing an informal non-descript suit, while the queen wears a striking yellow dress – astrologically the colour of the king. Madame Win Maung again appears beside her, looking even more diminished: notably shorter, her face puffy and outfits uninspiring. The queen, in contrast, appears to dazzle all who talk with her, and while she dutifully listens to the men who encircle her, she can also have a room descend into laughter at will. After a tour of the industrial site, the couple are taken to meet uniformed female workers. Here, the camera brings the viewer into dialogue with the modern women of Burma. Moving down the line, blank faces slowly realise they are being filmed and burst into shy acquiescent smiles. Again and again, the camera enters their inner world as they blissfully chat to one another, until they realise they are on camera. Unlike Sirikit, who never looks directly at the camera, the film emphasises distinction, between the image of the modern queen and the disorderly women of Burma.

As Penny Van Esterik has described, elite Thai women were traditionally trained through literature and drama to be as virtuous as Sita, the wife of Rama from the Siamese epic the *Ramakian*.[60] In this idealised version of the relationship between a king and queen, Sita must prove herself pure to her husband by walking through flames – enduring suffering to attain a heavenly status by his side.[61] At the same time, only her acceptance by Rama confirms to the

---

[60] Penny Van Esterik, *Materializing Thailand* (Oxford: Berg, 2000), pp. 45–46.
[61] The implications of the Ramakien story of Sita are further elaborated by Rachel Harrison in 'Facing Demons: Sida Marries Totsakan in Sidaoreuang's Modern Thai Reinventions of the

world that she is worthy of that status. Similarly, Van Esterik describes how, like the core qualities of kingly virtue, beauty in Thai Buddhism is considered the effect of merit collected from past lives. Historically, women at the palace cultivated beauty in parallel with power.[62] Now, in the mid-twentieth century, at a time when 'old' models of kingship were being resurrected to project King Bhumibol as a modern, monogamous king, Queen Sirikit's duty was to demonstrate such degrees of radiance and beauty as to single-handedly attest to the king's potency, evoking a unique figure from the cosmology. As the *Traiphum* explains, 'because of the power of the merit of the one who qualified to be a great Cakkavatti king there is a gem woman':

She comes by air, just like a female devata, and comes down to pay her respects and bow down to the great Cakkavatti king. This gem woman is neither too short nor too tall, but is beautifully and suitably proportioned. She pleases and gladdens the hearts of the people. Her complexion appears polished and smooth; it is clean, clear, and very beautiful, and even the specks of dust do not settle on it or make marks on it – it is like a lotus being touched by the water. The features of this gem woman's entire body from head to toe are perfect, are beautiful, and please everyone in the human world.[63]

Conquest Complete

In the final scenes of the film (and visit), the viewer is transported back to the President's House for an afternoon tea party. Prime Minister Ne Win and his wife have joined the party; President Win Maung and his wife are also there. The leaders sit at the centre in a square arrangement, surrounded by tables of the most important guests. Further back, at the periphery of the event, ordinary Burmese and ethnic minority groups enjoy the party. As the narrator explains, this includes the Thai Yai – a Thai term used to designate the Shan of northern Burma. At the centre, the queen sits separately from the king, who has changed into full military garb.

Once again, the implications are hard to ignore. In both Burma and Thailand, political leaders were anxious to ensure their kingdoms were, as far as possible, reflections of the Buddhist heavens, most clearly demonstrated in the concept of the mandala. In this model, the king presides at the centre of the polity, with various tributary states conceived as concentric circles beyond palace walls. Just as Mount Meru lies at the centre of the universe, straddling the world of humans and deities, so royal power radiates out from the centre,

---

Epic Ramayana (Ramakien)', in J. Labarth (ed.), *Formes modernes de la poésie épique. Nouvellese approaches* (Brussels: P.I.E., 2003), pp. 339–69.

[62] Ibid., pp. 154–59.
[63] Reynolds and Reynolds, *Three Worlds according to King Ruang*, p. 166.

diminishing as it nears the outer reach.[64] Similarly, the palace itself was organised as a mandala, another replica of the universe and kingdom in microcosm.[65] So too, it would seem, was the tea party. The king's choice of clothes, combined with the narrative arc already traced, made sure that for Thai audiences, the Burmese mandala was gravitating around the central figure of Bhumibol – placing him at the centre of the polity. Ne Win, meanwhile, a figure who had his own ambitions for charismatic leadership, hardly appeared in the film, and appeared off-centre during this critical final scene.

While no longer dictated by the fierce military rivalry of the late eighteenth century, Thai-Burma relations during the 1950s retained a competitive character, in which the charismatic potency of the country's leaders appeared to directly indicate the relative power of the two states. Early in the decade, U Nu presented himself as a virtuous individual with a clear political vision. While in Thailand there were plenty of candidates, before 1958 there was no one leader who was able to do what U Nu achieved.[66] At the time of the king and queen's visit, however, the dynamics had begun to shift. As Burma floundered, the Thai economy boomed, and with U Nu temporarily out of the way, the stage was set for a diplomatic exchange that suited Thai sensibilities. The film's plot focused tightly on the royal couple. By carefully locating the two royal bodies in space and time and by drawing out the correct relationship with those around them, the final product attested to Thailand's ascendency in the region under the stewardship of a charismatic king.

---

[64] H. G. Quaritch Wales, *The Universe around Them: Cosmology and Cosmic Renewal in Indianized South-East Asia* (London: Probsthain, 1977), p. 137.

[65] Stanley J. Tambiah, *World Conqueror and World Renouncer: A Study of Buddhism and Polity in Thailand against a Historical Background* (Cambridge: Cambridge University Press, 1976), pp. 111–13.

[66] Hugh Tinker in 1957 claimed U Nu had 'in large measure come to occupy the role fulfilled in former days by the kings of Burma'. See Hugh Tinker, 'Nu, the Serene Statesman', *Pacific Affairs,* 30:2 (1957), 132. Also Matthew Walton, *Buddhism, Politics and Political Thought in Myanmar* (Cambridge: Cambridge University Press, 2017), p. 93; Ingrid Jordt, *Burma's Mass Lay Meditation Movement: Buddhism and the Cultural Construction of Power* (Athens: Ohio University Press, 2007), p. 177.

5   Between Style and Substance

West German President Heinrich Lübke in Indonesia in 1963

Christian Goeschel

At the centre of this chapter is an official diplomatic photograph that was commissioned by the West German government's press office (Bundespresseamt).[1] The image (Fig. 5.1) forms part of a series of photographs documenting Federal President Heinrich Lübke's 1963 visit to Indonesia, two years after the building of the Berlin Wall and a year after the Cuban Missile Crisis. Lübke's journey to Indonesia was part of a month-long tour of several Asian states. It started with Lübke's departure from Bonn to Tehran on 23 October and finished with his return to Bonn on 24 November 1963. The president travelled on a Lufthansa jet, which allowed him and his delegation to crisscross the Asian continent in a matter of hours, rather than several days or weeks. Lübke (1894–1972) was a Christian Democratic career politician with a keen interest in the 'developing world' and known for embarrassing slips. Elected president in 1959, he would fill this post, despite his deteriorating health and attacks by the East German government on his role in the Third Reich, until 1969. His trip had been meticulously prepared by the Protocol Department of the West German Foreign Ministry in coordination with Lübke's Federal Presidential Office (Bundespräsidialamt) and the West German government. As part of his itinerary, official state visits to Iran, the Philippines, and Japan, embedded in Western security alliances, were relatively straightforward matters for the West German government and its diplomats in charge of preparing the itinerary.

Indonesia turned out to be a trickier destination, since it was a non-aligned country run by Sukarno, whose foreign policy was flitting between the US- and Soviet-dominated spheres. Sukarno's foreign policy and his idea of 'guided democracy' would, according to official Indonesian propaganda, overcome the legacies of colonialism and turn Indonesia into a developed nation at the vanguard of the developing world. A growing personality cult of Sukarno was accompanied by a revolutionary language that included the naming of

[1] I should like to thank the participants of the Diplomatic Images workshops held at Yale-NUS College in Singapore in 2017 and 2018, the seminar audience at the National Museum of Ethnology in Osaka, and the editors and external readers for valuable feedback on an earlier version of this chapter.

Figure 5.1 Federal President Heinrich Lübke at the Kalibata Heroes Cemetery in Indonesia, 1963.
Bundesregierung, B 145 Bild-0009 1929. Photo by Ludwig Wegmann.

years. For instance, 1963, the year of Lübke's visit, was officially called 'The Ringing Out of the Sound of Revolution'. Jakarta had been rebuilt as the national capital as the symbol of the new Indonesia, a country characterised by ethnic and regional diversity. As part of his revolutionary and anti-imperialist zeal, viewed with increasing suspicion by the United States and its European allies, Sukarno had, a year previously, begun a campaign for the takeover of Western New Guinea, which, at that time, was still held by the Netherlands, Indonesia's former colonial power. In May 1963, West Irian, as it came to be known then, was incorporated by the Republic of Indonesia. In 1962, this conflict had cast a shadow over Lübke's earlier tour of Southeast Asia. At the request of the Dutch government, Lübke had bypassed Indonesia, to the disappointment of the Indonesian government, and travelled instead to Thailand.[2]

In 1963, Lübke was still reluctant to visit Indonesia, but the centre-right West German government convinced him to include the archipelago in his itinerary. Altogether, the German delegation spent a week in Indonesia with a tightly packed programme that included visits to Jakarta, Bandung, and Bali. With the exception of brief, largely conventional accounts in the biography of Lübke by the conservative historian Rudolf Morsey and Till Florian Tömmel's recent study of West German–Indonesian diplomatic relations during the Cold War, little has been written on Lübke's tour to Indonesia. One reason for this lacuna is that the trip looks more or less irrelevant from the perspective of conventional diplomatic history.[3]

But a different story of Lübke's visit is possible, inspired by recent work on the cultural history of diplomacy and a close reading of the diplomatic image (Fig. 5.1) at the start of this chapter.[4] If studied through the lens of official government documents and conventional diplomatic history, Lübke's visit to the cemetery seems indeed insignificant. No major political decisions were taken. But if we put the photograph at the centre of the analysis, a more insightful interpretation becomes possible that allows us to rethink the nexus between representational and 'real' politics in Cold War diplomacy. This chapter relies largely on unpublished official West German sources, which reflect the assumptions and biases of West German government functionaries that West Germany was more 'developed' than Indonesia. The West German sources also mirror a power asymmetry, as West Germany seemed far more powerful and significant on the global stage than the post-colonial Indonesia. One of the aims of this chapter is to deconstruct the official West German

---

[2] For the tour, see the standard biography of Lübke by Rudolf Morsey, *Heinrich Lübke: Eine politische Biographie* (Paderborn: Schöningh, 1996), pp. 377–9; for the itinerary, see Bundesarchiv Koblenz (hereinafter BAK), NL 216/111, Bl. 5–23: 'Vorläufiges Programm', 7 October 1963; Till Florian Tömmel, *Bonn, Jakarta und der Kalte Krieg: Die Außenpolitik der Bundesrepublik Deutschland gegenüber Indonesien von 1952 bis 1973* (Munich: Oldenbourg, 2018), pp. 170–80; for Indonesia under Sukarno, see Adrian Vickers, *A History of Modern Indonesia*, 2nd ed. (Cambridge: Cambridge University Press, 2013), pp. 147–54; for the end of the Dutch Empire in Indonesia, see Bart Luttikhuis and A. Dirk Moses (eds.), *Colonial Counterinsurgency and Mass Violence: The Dutch Empire in Indonesia* (Abingdon: Routledge, 2014).
[3] Morsey, *Heinrich Lübke*, pp. 377–9; Tömmel, *Bonn, Jakarta und der Kalte Krieg*, pp. 170–80.
[4] For recent work on post-war Germany, see Simone Derix, *Bebilderte Politik: Staatsbesuche in der Bundesrepublik 1949–1990* (Göttingen: Vandenhoeck und Ruprecht, 2009); Johannes Paulmann (ed.), *Auswärtige Repräsentationen: Deutsche Kulturdiplomatie nach 1945* (Cologne: Böhlau, 2005); for West Germany's self-understanding on the international stage, see Friedrich Kießling, 'Einleitung: Von "guten Nachbarn" und "deutschen Wegen"', *Geschichte und Gesellschaft*, 45 (2019), 471–96.

perspective on this diplomatic event that took place in Indonesia, one of the leading countries of the non-aligned movement. I will examine this picture, the moment it captures, and the story behind it in order to shed light on a broader question: How do official images of diplomatic events allow us to tell an alternative history of diplomacy and unlock insights that cannot be gained from a diplomatic history focused overwhelmingly on high-level politics and written documents?

To start with, the colour photograph, set in 6 × 6 cm format, was shot by Ludwig Wegmann, a well-known German press photographer and member of the official German delegation of journalists. Unlike the other pictures shot by Wegmann during Lübke's state visit, this image shows what was a conventional subject for German media audiences. This image, rather than Wegmann's more 'exotic' shots of Lübke's visit to a Buddhist temple or of an Indonesian woman making a batik fabric, will facilitate an analysis of how a staple of diplomatic rituals was adapted at a moment when Lübke, a Western statesman, met his non-Western counterpart, Sukarno.[5]

Recently decolonised states such as Indonesia had to fit into the global system of diplomacy and international relations heavily dominated by Western countries. In this sense, the Indonesian government's use of a war cemetery as a diplomatic space fulfilled Western expectations of a state visit. Nevertheless, it remains to be explored in the following pages how the power dynamics between post-colonial Indonesia and West Germany underpinned the photograph of the white-skinned, frail Lübke, standing bare-headed out of respect for the war dead in the scorching Indonesian sun.

Let us zoom in on the photograph. The picture was shot at Kalibata Heroes Cemetery (Taman Makam Pahlawan Kalibata) on the outskirts of Jakarta. This cemetery commemorates the dead of the Indonesian National Revolution in 1945–9. Some Japanese soldiers who had stayed on after the end of the Japanese occupation of the Dutch East Indies during the Second World War are also buried there. It is unclear whether the West German delegation knew about this fact, which brought up memories of the tripartite pact, the war-time alliance of Imperial Japan, Nazi Germany, and Fascist Italy, signed in 1940. The photograph is shot from an angle that draws in the spectator. It depicts a static scene, and the perspective blurs the distinction between Lübke and the viewer. Crowds were standing in the vicinity of the memorial, yet they are absent from the picture. Managed crowds were a central aspect of the choreography of state visits that had emerged in Europe over the course of the long nineteenth century amid the rise of mass society and the mass media.

[5] For the images, see www.bild.bundesarchiv.de/dba/de/search/?yearfrom=&yearto=&query=lübke+indonesien&page=1 (accessed 17 February 2020).

In non-Western societies too, crowds were central participants of diplomatic pageantry.[6]

One of the central concerns of the Indonesian government was to give the visit a distinctly national character, as Lübke was the first head of a European liberal-democratic state to visit Indonesia.[7] This particular photograph represented Lübke's visit in a way that catered to German media audience's expectations of the pomp and circumstance of a state visit. In the official press digest of Lübke's visit that was duly archived by the Federal Presidential Office, the photograph is not included, probably because the image does not stand out from the others, as it was illustrative of a standard diplomatic ceremony. Instead, the press digest contains photographs such as one depicting Sukarno dancing in front of his German guests. Another photograph showed a 'beautiful Bali girl [who] danced in front of the Federal President', as the caption declared. For similar reasons, this ceremony was not shown on the most popular German newsreel of the visit.[8]

Lübke's dress is worth investigating in more detail. Like other Western statesmen at the time, he is wearing a dark suit despite the sweltering heat. He is carrying out what seems like a typical diplomatic ceremony. He is standing respectfully in front of a wreath of white and yellow carnations, adorned with a ribbon in the colours of the German flag. An Indonesian officer, flanked by a guard of honour, is standing to attention outside a tomb of unknown soldiers. A reporter is squatting on the ground, eager to record sound bites for the radio, which seems strange given the solemn and silent atmosphere. The image is static, with a wall dividing the image, and with trees in the background. The picture suggests a sombre, reflective, and commemorative atmosphere. Lübke's stance also emphasises the pensive mood, with his hands folded in front of his body.[9]

---

[6] For crowd management, see Johannes Paulmann, *Pomp und Politik: Monarchenbegegnungen in Europa zwischen Ancien Régime und Erstem Weltkrieg* (Paderborn: Schöningh, 2000), pp. 367–80; Naoko Shimazu, 'Diplomacy as Theatre: Staging the Bandung Conference of 1955', *Modern Asian Studies*, 48 (2014), 225–52; Christian Goeschel, 'Staging Friendship: Mussolini and Hitler in Germany in 1937', *Historical Journal*, 60 (2017), 149–72; for context on decolonisation, see Jan C. Jansen and Jürgen Osterhammel, *Decolonization: a Short History* (Princeton, NJ: Princeton University Press, 2017); for the tripartite pact, see Christian Goeschel, 'Performing the New Order: The Tripartite Pact, 1940–1945', *Contemporary European History*, 23 (2024), 411–27; see also Daniel Hedinger, *Die Achse Berlin-Rom-Tokio 1919–1946* (Munich: CH Beck, 2021).

[7] Tömmel, *Bonn, Jakarta und der Kalte Krieg*, pp. 169–70.

[8] For the press digest compiled by Lübke's office, see BAK, B 122/ANH. 149; for the images, see ibid., copy of *Fürther Nachrichten*, 1 November 1963; ibid., copy of *Neue Rhein Zeitung*, 31 October 1963; *Ufa Wochenschau* of 8 November 1963 with coverage of Lübke's visit, see www.filmothek.bundesarchiv.de/video/584570?q=&xf%5B0%5D=CustomPlace&xo%5B0% 5D=EQUALS&xv%5B0%5D=Indonesien, accessed 10 September 2019.

[9] For the significance of gestures, see Michael J. Braddick (ed.), 'The Politics of Gesture: Historical Perspectives', *Past & Present*, 203, supplement 4 (2009), 9–35.

At a time when most newspapers were printed in black and white, it is striking that the image – unlike some of Wegmann's other photographs taken during the visit, is in colour. This was a visual strategy to emphasise the special character of Lübke's visit. It is noteworthy that Lübke, the guest of honour, casts a small shadow in relation to the shadows of the two Indonesian soldiers in the image. While this visual effect was probably unintended, it could suggest that Indonesia, not Germany, was the leading country in this bilateral relationship. Furthermore, Wegmann's picture captures a moment of Lübke in an oppressive and painful position, given that he is directly exposed to the scorching sun.

Two questions emerge from the image if one tells the story of the photograph from a European perspective: First, how did the West German government organise the visit and how did its choreography relate to earlier practices of state visits? The Federal Republic was a relatively new state established in Germany's three Western zones of occupation in 1949 on the ashes of the Third Reich.[10] Second, how do the German archives reflect what the West German government saw as an asymmetry of power between West Germany and Indonesia, one of the leading non-aligned countries where the West German government and German industry had close interests?

For those advocating a conventional diplomatic history, it might be tempting to gloss over the details of Lübke's visit and instead locate it in the context of Cold War diplomacy and the 'German' question. As William Glenn Gray, author of a study of early West German foreign policy, has shown, West Germany pursued a global campaign to isolate East Germany. This battle was fought in the developing world with a zeal bordering on obsession. Undoubtedly, Lübke's visit was a way for the West German government to remind the Indonesian regime that West Germany was the only legitimate German state.[11]

Yet, if we use this picture as the pivot to making sense of Lübke's visit, a different interpretation becomes possible that takes us further than official written sources and existing work on how the Global South became a battleground for the 'German question'. A cultural-historical interpretation of Lübke's visit, especially of the images produced during the visit, offers a more

---

[10] For previous West German state visits, see Frieder Günther, 'Gespiegelte Selbstdarstellung: Der Staatsbesuch von Theodor Heuss in Großbritannien', in Paulmann (ed.), *Auswärtige Repräsentationen*, pp. 185–203.

[11] William Glenn Gray, *Germany's Cold War: The Global Campaign to Isolate East Germany 1949–1969* (Chapel Hill: University of North Carolina Press, 2003); for a detailed account by a former West German diplomat, see Werner Kilian, *Die Hallstein-Doktrin: Der diplomatische Krieg zwischen der BRD und der DDR 1955–1973. Aus den Akten der beiden deutschen Außenministerien* (Berlin: Duncker & Humblot, 2001).

nuanced interpretation. As will become clear, culture is not simply a colourful add-on to diplomatic history, but one of its constitutive elements.[12]

In order to develop this point further, I demonstrate that visual sources such as the image at the centre of the chapter take us down an unexpected path that does not fit neatly into recent work on West Germany and the Global South. A deconstruction and contextualisation of Fig. 5.1 reveals a number of deeper sets of political implications.[13] But this does not mean that the image can be understood on its own, which is why I place the image into a broader context. A close reading of the image and unpublished documents from the West German Foreign Ministry's Protocol Department and the Federal Presidential Office allows for an examination of how seemingly unimportant cultural aspects of diplomacy and politics shape political meaning.

Particularly instructive for unlocking the meaning behind the image and Lübke's visit to Indonesia, part of the broader story of the global Cold War, is recent work by Jeffrey C. Alexander and others on 'social performance'. Such work has shed new light on how performative acts such as Lübke's standing in front of a wreath are not simply by-products but constitutive elements of politics and diplomacy.[14] The image taken during Lübke's Indonesian journey allows us to think afresh about the role of the representative and the symbolic in diplomacy and how these categories relate to each other. Clearly, the West German government used representational elements of diplomacy to attempt to bind Sukarno's Indonesia into the Western alliance system and make Indonesia distance itself from the Soviet bloc. A memorandum by the West German Embassy in Jakarta, written after Lübke's departure from Indonesia, concluded that the visit had been a success, as it had attracted publicity in Indonesia. According to the ambassador, Gerhart Weiz, the meticulous preparations of the West German government to promote West Germany to the Indonesian media had paid off. A crucial emphasis of this media strategy was, according to Weiz,

---

[12] Cf. David Reynolds, *Summits: Six Meetings that Shaped the Twentieth Century* (London: Penguin, 2007); Akira Iriye, 'Culture and Power: International Relations as Intercultural Relations', *Diplomatic History*, 3 (1979), 115–28.

[13] BAK, NL 216/111, Bl. 12–16: Vorläufiges Programm, 7 October 1963; for general context, see Agnes Bresselau von Bressensdorf, Elke Seefried, and Christian. F. Ostermann (eds.), *West Germany, the Global South and the Cold War* (Berlin: De Gruyter, 2017); Quinn Slobodian, *Foreign Front: Third World Politics in Sixties West Germany* (Durham, NC: Duke University Press, 2012).

[14] Jeffrey C. Alexander, 'Cultural Pragmatics: Social Performance between Ritual and Strategy', in Jeffrey C. Alexander, Bernhard Giesen, and Jason L. Mast (eds.), *Social Performance: Symbolic Action, Cultural Pragmatics, and Ritual* (Cambridge: Cambridge University Press, 2006), pp. 29–90; for an application of this approach, see Christian Goeschel, *Mussolini and Hitler: The Forging of the Fascist Alliance* (New Haven, CT: Yale University Press, 2018), 293–5.

that 'despite its capitalist economic form', West Germany could not be associated with 'any colonialist or imperialist pursuits'.[15]

Returning to Lübke's laying down a wreath, this diplomatic ceremony was in line with a broader international memorial culture that had been formalised after 1918, with the establishment of tombs of the unknown warrior to commemorate the experience of mass death in the First World War. European and non-European audiences were familiar with this pageantry.[16] In the official West German programme and the Indonesian 'State Committee for the Reception of Heads of Foreign States' programme of the visit, a mere twenty minutes were scheduled for the ceremony. It was held in the morning of 29 October 1963. The jet-lagged delegation had only arrived on the previous day from Iran after a brief stopover in India. The female members of the West German and Indonesian delegations, including Lübke's wife Wilhelmine, were not present. Instead, they were taken to a children's hospital. Wegmann's picture thus portrayed this diplomatic space in which Lübke laid down the wreath as all male, reflecting the idea that it was men, not women, who had died on the battlefield.[17]

Yet the photograph does not show the crowds behind Lübke's back. According to an Associated Press report, telexed to Bonn, 3,000 schoolchildren were present. Lübke greeted them in his rudimentary English, and they wished him *selamat pagi* (good morning). The German Press Agency noted that Lübke had briefly spoken to the crowds. They were essential performers in this show yet absent from the picture. For a German agency journalist, relying on the Indonesian Antara news agency and using condescending language, this ceremony was the 'first direct contact of the Federal President with the indigenous population'.[18]

What is clear from the discussion so far is that the photograph unlocks a story that is different from previous accounts of Lübke's state visit. Key to interpreting this picture and Lübke's tour more generally is that the role of the West German Federal President is largely ceremonial and representational. These are essential categories of politics and diplomacy. This observation forces us to rethink the dichotomy between 'representational' and 'real' politics, a distinction that had only emerged in Europe over the course of the long

---

[15] PA AA, B 37/56, Botschaft Djakarta an das Auswärtige Amt, 9 December 1963.

[16] For a recent study, with focus on Italy, see Laura Wittman, *The Tomb of the Unknown Soldier: Modern Mourning, and the Reinvention of the Mystical Body* (Toronto: University of Toronto Press, 2011), pp. 3–16.

[17] BAK, NL 216/111, Bl. 12: Vorläufiges Programm, 7 October 1963; PA AA, AV Neues Amt 196, copy of 'Programme for the State Visit to the Republic of Indonesia of His Excellency Dr. Heinrich Lübke, President of the Federal Republic of Germany, and Madame Wilhelmine Lübke, October 28–November 3, 1963'.

[18] BAK, B 122/ANH. 149, dpa 73 al, undated; ap 61 ausland, undated.

nineteenth century, as Brian Vick has shown in his study of the Congress of Vienna. The political significance of the cultural and ceremonial is thus an integral aspect of diplomacy.[19]

Interpreted through this perspective, Wegmann's photograph of Lübke prompts further questions about the political significance of representational matters. A central concern of West German officials was the dress code. Before the departure from Bonn, they had issued Lübke and his delegation detailed advice on what to wear. In a briefing paper, preserved in the files of the Federal Presidential Office, members of the delegation, largely unfamiliar with Indonesia, were instructed that the country was 'tropically hot'. High levels of humidity required 'dresses from light fabrics, cotton underwear, cotton men's shirts, not nylon', and suits made from 'light fabrics', such as 'dark tropic suits', and 'light summer hats'.[20]

It is striking that the West German Foreign Ministry's Protocol Department filled almost a dozen thick folders with minutiae of the visit because the diplomats themselves believed that these representational and visual details were politically significant.[21] Superficially, the choreography of Lübke's visit followed the conventions of international diplomatic protocol that had been established over many centuries and that had been gradually transformed to expectations of mass audiences at the turn of the nineteenth to the twentieth century. These conventions included public ceremonies, including commemorating the dead of past wars and mingling with the crowds, as well as photo opportunities.[22]

How precisely the West German state, as a relative newcomer to diplomatic protocol, especially in Southeast Asia, organised Lübke's visit is worth investigating more closely. West German diplomats in charge of preparing the visit were nervous because state visits were still a relative novelty to the Federal Republic, as Simone Derix has demonstrated in her book on state visits to West Germany. The presumed asymmetricality of power reflected in the West German archives, with German officials adopting a perspective of superiority on Indonesia, was reversed when it came to the relative weakness, insecurity, and lack of confidence of West German diplomats in organising state visits. They remained unsure about questions of protocol, in particular, what kind of diplomatic protocol would be appropriate to the new Federal Republic, which

---

[19] A good summary of the visit is in the press coverage; see, e.g., BAK, B 122/ANH./149, *Trierische Landeszeitung*, 4 November 1963; Brian Vick, *The Congress of Vienna: Power and Politics after Napoleon* (Cambridge, MA: Harvard University Press, 2014).
[20] BAK, B 122/5448, Bl. 156–8: Merkblatt, 15 October 1963.   [21] PA AA, B 8/533–44.
[22] Paulmann, *Pomp und Politik*; for older literature, see Garrett Mattingly, *Renaissance Diplomacy* (Boston: Houghton and Mifflin, 1955); more recent work is Markus Mösslang and Torsten Riotte (eds.), *The Diplomats' World: A Cultural History of Diplomacy, 1815–1914* (Oxford: Oxford University Press, 2007), and Shimazu, 'Diplomacy as Theatre'.

was anxious to distance itself from the Third Reich and its bombastic-militaristic diplomatic style that had reflected its belligerency. But matters were complex. Most West German diplomats in positions of authority had served under the Third Reich and wanted to demonstrate West Germany's alleged clean break from the Nazi past. There was a strong sense of uncertainty as to how West Germany should represent itself on the international stage, especially during state visits. Some diplomats in charge of protocol issues even did internships with their French, British, and Italian colleagues, as they believed that these countries had a longer, more continuous tradition of diplomatic protocol than West Germany. Thus, in December 1963, after Lübke's return to Bonn, a West German diplomat wrote a lengthy memorandum about the protocol arrangements during Lübke's visit and made some suggestions as to how these could be improved for future official visits. Particularly significant for the author of the memorandum were the display of flags on the roads linking the airport to the centre of the capital city visited by Lübke and the size of the official programmes distributed to delegation members. The general concern was to appear not as triumphant German bullies, even though Asia had not suffered from Nazi occupation, but instead as considerate and friendly representatives of the 'free' world.[23]

Turning to the detailed preparations of West German officials, it is instructive to ask what they knew about Indonesia. A working bibliography for the West German delegation illustrated the lack of general knowledge about Indonesia within the West German government. The reading list contained a mere three titles, including a 1960 guide published by the obscure Safari Publishing House (Safari-Verlag), a Nazi-era publication by Anton Schwägerl about German expatriates in the Dutch colony (*Das Auslandsdeutschtum im Niederländischen Kolonialbereich*), and a guide titled 'Indonesia Today'.[24] Indonesia, according to a briefing by the West German Embassy in Jakarta, was a dangerous country, where many diplomats had been attacked on the street and had their property stolen. The embassy in Jakarta

---

[23] PA AA, B 8/544, 'Aufzeichnung', 30 December 1963; for context, see Derix, *Bebilderte Politik*, pp. 30, 42, 49; for Nazi legacies in the Foreign Ministry, see Eckart Conze, Norbert Frei, Peter Hayes, and Moshe Zimmermann (eds.), *Das Amt und die Vergangenheit: Deutsche Diplomaten im Dritten Reich und in der Bundesrepublik* (Munich: Blessing, 2010); for a critique, see Richard J. Evans, 'The German Foreign Office and the Nazi Past', *Neue Politische Literatur*, 56 (2011), 165–83; see also Thomas W. Maulucci, Jr., *Adenauer's Foreign Office: West German Diplomacy in the Shadow of the Third Reich* (DeKalb: Northern Illinois University Press, 2012), pp. 64–91; for West Germany's self-understanding, see Friedrich Kießling, *Die undeutschen Deutschen. Eine ideengeschichtliche Archäologie der alten Bundesrepublik, 1945–1972* (Paderborn: Schöningh, 2012); for nation branding, see Carolin Viktorin, Jessica C. E. Gienow-Hecht, Annika Estner, and Marcel K. Will (eds.), *Nation Branding in Modern History* (New York: Berghahn, 2018).

[24] BAK, B 122/5446, Bl. 384–6: undated note by VLR I Bassler.

even forwarded detailed lists of items such as watches that had been stolen or robbed from diplomats and their families.[25]

In the mindset of the West German government, Lübke's visit, with all its representational aspects, was part of a broader strategy to establish West Germany as the only legitimate German state around the globe. Communist East Germany, almost completely isolated on the global diplomatic stage, had been trying to increase its influence in the Global South. East Berlin saw the Global South as an arena where East Germany (the German Democratic Republic, GDR) could exercise influence and obtain the much-coveted diplomatic recognition from non-aligned countries such as Egypt or Indonesia.[26]

Through the so-called Hallstein doctrine, a policy named after the former Under Secretary of State in the West German Foreign Ministry Walter Hallstein, any state, except for the Soviet Union, that recognised the GDR diplomatically would have its ties severed with West Germany. (In reality, the Hallstein doctrine had been formulated by a leading German diplomat, not Hallstein, in 1955 when West Germany had regained its sovereignty from the Western allies.) West Germany only applied the doctrine twice: first in 1957, when the non-aligned, Socialist-run Yugoslavia recognised the GDR; and second in 1963, when Cuba began official diplomatic relations with East Berlin. Until the détente of the early 1970s, there were no official relations between the two German states, and the West German government insisted on the *Alleinvertretungsanspruch*, in other words on being the only legitimate German state. Recently decolonised countries such as India, Egypt, and Indonesia were particularly contested ground, as the GDR's government, lacking any realistic chance to be recognised by Western states in the early Cold War, appealed to Socialist notions of anti-imperialism and decolonisation from the Western capitalist colonial powers. This rhetoric, the East German rulers expected, would be received favourably in the developing world. Yet, if any state or its officials made gestures that the GDR existed, such as allowing East German flags to be hoisted at trade fairs, furious West German diplomatic interventions were not slow in coming. These included threats to stop development aid payments.[27]

Indonesia is a good case study for exploring the West German government's policies towards the developing world. Sukarno, one of the leaders of the

---

[25] BAK, B 122/5446, Bl. 623–5: 'Spiegeldoppel', 29 July 1963.

[26] See, for instance, Katherine Pence, 'Showcasing Cold War Germany in Cairo: 1954 and 1957 Industrial Exhibitions and the Competition for Arab Partners', *Journal of Contemporary History*, 47 (2011), 69–95.

[27] For context, see Bastian Hein, *Die Westdeutschen und die Dritte Welt: Entwicklungspolitik und Entwicklungsdienste zwischen Reform und Revolte 1959–1974* (Munich: Oldenbourg, 2006), pp. 20–1; see also Amit Das Gupta, *Handel, Hilfe, Hallstein-Doktrin: Die bundesdeutsche Südasienpolitik unter Adenauer und Erhard 1949 bis 1966* (Husum: Matthiesen, 2004).

non-aligned movement, oscillated in his policy towards the two Germanies. On the one hand, Sukarno's Indonesia maintained official diplomatic relations with West Germany. Sukarno had travelled to West Germany in 1956. For the West German government, Sukarno's visit had been helpful in terms of legitimising the Federal Republic in global politics. Sukarno's state visit had even included a trip to West Berlin, the Western enclave in East Germany under joint French, British, and American sovereignty that was a thorn in the side of the East German government and the Soviet Union.[28]

At the same time, Sukarno maintained semi-official relations with Soviet-bloc states. Like Egypt's leader Gamal Abdel Nasser, he allowed East Germany to open a consulate. This policy was meant to reinforce the independence of Indonesia vis-à-vis the Western bloc and display Indonesia's commitment to create an anti-imperialist world order. In September 1961, at the Belgrade Conference, when the non-aligned movement was formally launched, matters escalated when Sukarno and other leaders of non-aligned countries declared that there must be a de facto recognition of the two German states. The West German government was furious and put diplomatic pressure on Sukarno to refrain from any further statements or gestures that implied the GDR even existed.[29]

Tensions continued between West Germany and Indonesia. In 1962, when the Indonesian foreign minister had received the exequatur of the new East German consul in Jakarta, the West German government protested. In early 1963, the West German government even recalled its ambassador for consultations, after the Indonesian government had issued a joint communiqué with Communist Czechoslovakia that included a reference to the two German states. The ambassador's recall made the Indonesian government, reliant on West German developing aid and trade, relent and issue an apology to West Germany. In a briefing paper for Lübke's visit, the West German Foreign Ministry hoped that West German–Indonesian relations would improve as a result of Lübke's visit, which is why so much effort was put into the representational aspects of the event. After all, West German officials deliberated, Sukarno wanted West German aid for his prestige project, the Lamping steelworks, a project that was related to his quest to create a strong Indonesian national economy.[30] Sukarno's government was thus playing the

[28] For Sukarno's visit to West Germany, see Tömmel, *Bonn, Jakarta und der Kalte Krieg*, pp. 101–3; Derix, *Bebilderte Politik*, p. 90.

[29] Gray, *Germany's Cold War*, pp. 127–9; for the non-aligned movement, see Lorenz Lüthi, 'The Non-aligned Movement and the Cold War, 1961–1973', *Journal of Cold War Studies*, 18 (2016), 98–147.

[30] BAK, B 122/5446, Bl. 525–33: Die politischen Beziehungen zwischen der Bundesrepublik und Indonesien, undated.

diplomatic register between West and East Germany, not least in order to extract more development aid from West Germany.[31]

For the East German regime, Lübke's visit was irritating. East Berlin feared that Lübke's state visit anticipated a change to Sukarno's ambiguous position towards the two German states. Just before Lübke's journey to Indonesia, the East German Ministry of Foreign Affairs provided the GDR's Consulate General in Jakarta, led by Gustav Hertzfeld, with discrediting material on the West German ambassador Weiz, who had been involved in the Nazi movement. This information was to be released to the Indonesian press. Other material circulated by the East German regime claimed that the West German government had sided with the Netherlands in the dispute over Western New Guinea. East Berlin also spread rumours about an alleged slander campaign against Sukarno in the West German press.[32] Yet such attempts had a limited impact, and Lübke's visit went ahead as scheduled.

That representational and 'real' politics are not mutually exclusive categories and stand in a reciprocal relationship with each other applies to Lübke's tour to Indonesia more generally. Lübke's arrival address to Sukarno at Jakarta airport had gone through various drafts in the Federal Presidential Office and the Foreign Ministry. The speech included the usual diplomatic niceties, such as thanks for the invitation and polite platitudes such as a reference to the 'intellectual and commercial links between Indonesia and Germany' that had allegedly been existing for centuries. Lübke's remarks about the 'revolutionary development of your country, talent and industriousness of your people, wealth and tropical diversity of its islands' were couched in the simple language typical of the president. Yet platitudes and polite remarks aside, he reinforced the message that the Hallstein doctrine was the official policy of the West German government.[33]

Behind the scenes of the diplomatic play of West German–Indonesian friendship, West German diplomats worked hard to maintain the Hallstein doctrine. Lübke's arrival in Jakarta almost turned into a diplomatic accident. For the Indonesian government had invited the East German Consul General to the airport. He duly appeared, as this opportunity to officially represent the GDR was too good be missed. Just before Lübke's plane landed, a West German diplomat persuaded the Indonesian government to ask the East

---

[31] Gray, *Germany's Cold War*, pp. 136–7.

[32] Politisches Archiv des Auswärtiges Amts (hereafter PA AA), MfAA, M1/A 16129, Gehler to General Consulate Jakarta, 9 September 1963; ibid., Berichterstattung über den Lübke-Besuch in Indonesien in der BRD-Presse, 28 October 1963.

[33] BAK, NL 216/111, Bl. 145–6: Ansprache des Herrn Bundespräsidenten bei der Ankunft auf dem Flughafen Djakarta, undated.

German official to leave the scene because his presence would have undermined official West German policy.[34]

Concern to represent West Germany in the best way possible made West German diplomats focus on the details of the Federal Republic's official reception in Jakarta. Because the West German Embassy did not have a sufficiently large room to host the party, it was held at the Hotel Indonesia (a modernist flagship hotel opened in 1962). Official documents show how ignorance about Indonesian culture was coupled with a strong sense of condescension bordering on arrogance. For instance, before Lübke's arrival, the West German ambassador sent a telegram to the Foreign Ministry in Bonn, insisting that a chef be sent from Germany to Indonesia. Otherwise, the ambassador warned, the cook of the Hotel Indonesia would provide 'overcooked food, lukewarm buried in sauce, in incorrect bowls'. The ambassador also recommended that food and drink, including Nescafé, seen as a symbol of modern consumer culture, must be sent in advance from West Germany to the coffee-growing nation.[35]

Another job for West German diplomats was the selection of gifts for Sukarno and other Indonesians in positions of authority. This task took up a considerable amount of diplomatic correspondence. Gifts play a significant role in diplomacy, as they delineate rank and demonstrate appreciation and respect, both on an individual level but also on an official level. Gift-giving creates a reciprocal relationship of receiving and giving between the guest and the host. But gift-giving also reflected the assumptions of West German diplomatic officials, influenced by national and racial stereotypes. They thought that in the case of 'developing countries' such as Indonesia, heads of state had to be given particularly abundant presents in order to make sure that they would support West Germany and not East Germany.[36]

A list of suggested gifts for members of Indonesia's military and political elites has been preserved in the files of the West German Foreign Ministry, together with the cost of each item. The higher the rank of a gift recipient, the more costly was the present. For instance, the suggested presents for Foreign Minister Subandrio included a hunting rifle, worth 1,500 DM, and a signed and framed photograph of Lübke, while Subandrio's wife was to receive an assortment of music records worth 300 DM.[37]

---

[34] Tömmel, *Bonn, Jakarta und der Kalte Krieg*, p. 174.
[35] PA AA, B8/538, Telegramm, 26 July 1963; ibid., undated note by Holleben.
[36] Simone Derix, 'Assembling Things Right: The Material Dimensions of West German Diplomacy (1950s to 1970s)', *European History Yearbook*, 17 (2016), 128–48; more generally, see Zoltán Biedermann, Anne Gerritsen, and Giorgio Riello (eds.), *Global Gifts: The Material Culture of Diplomacy in Early Modern Eurasia* (Cambridge: Cambridge University Press, 2018).
[37] PA AA, B 8/533, Geschenkvorschläge für den Staatsbesuch in Djakarta (Indonesien), undated.

For Sukarno, the German ambassador had suggested a mobile water purification unit because Indonesia was prone to earthquakes, and water purification
units were needed in the eventuality. The ambassador recommended other
gifts, including a Mercedes. Conveniently, this particular car model had not
been released yet, which gave the cost-conscious officials in Bonn the excuse
to shelve the idea. Eventually, Sukarno, a known womaniser, was given a bust
of Eve, worth 15,000 DM that had been bought from a prestigious art dealer in
Cologne. The bust was sizeable, as the West German ambassador had warned
that a small sculpture might offend Sukarno, who had, on a previous occasion,
ridiculed the Czechoslovak ambassador for giving him a small bust.[38]

Even the smallest details of Lübke's visit received the abundant attention of
German diplomats. For instance, the West German Embassy in Jakarta wrote
an alarming letter to Bonn, cautioning that the delegation should only expect
Western-style lavatories in Sukarno's palace and the Hotel Indonesia, but not
elsewhere. 'Very sensitive' delegation members were even encouraged to
bring along their own plastic lavatory seats. This important information
prompted the chief of the West German foreign ministry's protocol department
to request an urgent telegram from the Jakarta embassy giving details of the
size of Indonesian lavatory bowls. Eventually, the West German Foreign
Ministry sent three plastic lavatory seats by air freight to Jakarta. Thus, the
matter was brought to a satisfactory conclusion.

More letters were exchanged between Bonn and the Embassy in Jakarta,
suggesting menus for the dinner officially hosted by Lübke. Meals are an
integral aspect of diplomatic ceremonial, and allow the host government to
present its own national traditions. The meal at the West German dinner
included expensive items such as clear turtle soup and more mundane food
such as potatoes in order to remind the guests of the unpretentious, down-to-
earth diplomatic style of the Federal Republic, which stood in contradistinction
to the pomp and circumstance of the Third Reich, even though the Indonesian
hosts were probably oblivious to such concerns. The anxieties of West German
officials to represent the newly created West Germany on the global stage thus
overshadowed Lübke's visit.[39]

While programmes of state visits tend to be negotiated between the host and
the visitor nation, the West German government displayed a bossy attitude that

---

[38] PA AA, B 8/533, Weiz to Foreign Ministry, 16 August 1963; ibid., Weiz to Foreign Ministry,
13 August 1963; ibid., note by Holleben, 28 August 1963; ibid., telegram, 16 September 1963;
PA AA, B 8/541, Rechnung, 17 October 1963.

[39] For the lavatories, see PA AA, B 8/541, Büronotiz, 1 October 1963; ibid., telegram Holleben to
German Embassy, 5 October 1963; PA AA, B 8/542, note by Neumann-Dr Schulte, 15 October
1963; ibid., Merkblatt, 17 October 1963; for the menu, see PA AA, B8/534; for diplomatic
meals, see Iver Neumann, *Diplomatic Sites: A Critical Inquiry* (London: Hurst, 2013),
pp. 45–72.

revealed a German sense of superiority. The West German Foreign Ministry effectively told the Indonesian hosts that there must not be too many dance performances on the programme in order to avoid boring the German delegation. The politics of gesture also concerned the West German protocol department. Since Lübke was increasingly frail, his staff had proposed the idea that the president should use his left rather than right hand to greet Sukarno and other members of the Indonesian government. The chief of the West German foreign ministry's protocol department was aghast and insisted that the president would have to use his right hand or, instead, put his right arm into a sling in order to avoid offending his hosts by using his left hand, deemed unclean in many parts of Southeast Asia.[40]

During the visit, gaffes and misunderstandings on both sides led to some embarrassment. Sukarno, who spoke some German, enjoyed showing off his linguistic skills to Lübke. In a particularly noteworthy incident, Sukarno allegedly began to sing German songs. Suddenly, to the consternation of the West German delegation, Sukarno was singing the 'Horst-Wessel-Lied', the Nazi party's official anthem.[41]

For the West German government, the result of the state visit was mixed. The West German press reported that the visit had been harmonious and published images of Sukarno dancing with young women and 'pretty Bali girls danc[ing] in front of the Federal President'. Sukarno continued his ambivalent policy towards the two Germanies. On the one hand, Indonesia accepted West German development aid and continued to refrain from recognising the GDR. On the other hand, the Indonesian government allowed East Germany to keep running its consulate in Jakarta. Regional German newspapers, duly archived by Lübke's staff, boasted that the visit had been a great success in this regard. One such paper, the *Nord West Zeitung*, firmly emphasised that 'Indonesia is not a tropical copy of an Eastern people's democracy.'[42]

Behind the scenes, the West German government faced some direct criticism from the British government, whose focus in Southeast Asia during this era of decolonisation was to establish an independent Malaysia. A Frankfurt tabloid newspaper even titled one article 'London Is Angry with Federal President Lübke', based on his friendly attitude towards Sukarno. Sukarno

---

[40] BAK, B 122/5448, Bl. 174: Telegramm, 18 October 1963; BAK, B 122/5446, Bl. 225–7: Der Chef des Protokolls, 23 September 1963; ibid., Bl. 363: Der Chef des Protokolls, 14 October 1963; for the menu, see also PA AA, B 8/538, Weiz to Foreign Ministry, 5 August 1963; ibid., Weiz telegram, 26 July 1963; for the politics of gesture, see Braddick, 'The Politics of Gesture'.
[41] Horst H. Geerken, *Der Ruf des Geckos: 18 erlebnisreiche Jahre in Indonesien* (Books on Demand, 2015), pp. 77–8.
[42] BAK, B 122/ANH./149, *Neue Rheinzeitung*, 31 October 1963; ibid., *Nord West Zeitung*, 12 November 1963.

opposed the creation of the Federation of Malaysia in 1963, and started a guerrilla campaign against the forces of the British Commonwealth in Borneo and peninsular Malaya. In this context, in September 1963, crowds had attacked the British Embassy in Jakarta when the Federation of Malaysia was established. The British government had high hopes that Lübke's visit would help maintain at least some links between the Western alliance and Sukarno, lest Indonesia would drift off into the Soviet sphere. On the advice of the West German government, Lübke did not visit Malaysia, a concession to Sukarno's anti-British position. The West German Foreign Ministry offered a lame excuse and insisted that the runway at Kuala Lumpur airport was too short for the presidential plane.[43] The British Foreign Secretary Rab Butler subsequently told Lübke that Britain did not trust Sukarno, who was, after all, an iconic leader of the struggle for decolonisation. Lübke, reflecting West Germany's subservient status to Britain, reinforced the point that the principal reason for his visit to Indonesia was to ensure that Sukarno would not recognise East Germany.[44]

Through ceremonies and gestures, which this chapter has deconstructed, Lübke performed a show of respect towards Sukarno and Indonesia. The result of the performance, staged largely by the West German Foreign Ministry, was a success for West Germany, namely, that Indonesia refrained from recognising the GDR, at least for the time being.[45] Given the broader geopolitical changes in Southeast Asia at the time, with the escalation of the conflict in Vietnam and the independence of Malaysia, the West German government's obsession with the German question was out of touch with reality.[46] Within two years, Sukarno's fall from power would begin, although he remained formally in office as president of Indonesia until 1967. In the wake of the 30 September 1965 military coup, Suharto and the army pursued a violent anti-Communist genocidal campaign that cost the lives of at least 500,000 people.[47]

In the global Cold War, less established powers such as the two Germanies pursued their own interests that were broadly aligned with those of the global super powers, the United States and the USSR, respectively, both of which

---

[43] BAK, B 122/ANH./149, *Abendpost*, 13 November 1963; Tömmel, *Bonn, Jakarta und der Kalte Krieg*, pp. 172–3.

[44] BAK, B 122/5526, Bl. 520–4: Aufzeichnung, 19 December 1963; for the anti-British campaign, see Vickers, *A History of Modern Indonesia*, p. 154.

[45] Cf. Morsey, *Heinrich Lübke*, p. 383.   [46] Gray, *Germany's Cold War*.

[47] Robert Cribb, 'Political Genocides in Postcolonial Asia', in Donald Bloxham and A. Dirk Moses (eds.), *The Oxford Handbook of Genocide Studies* (Oxford: Oxford University Press, 2010), pp. 445–65; Jess Melvin, *The Army and the Indonesian Genocide: Mechanics of Mass Murder* (London: Routledge, 2018); Geoffrey B. Robinson, *The Killing Season: A History of the Indonesian Massacres, 1965–66* (Princeton, NJ: Princeton University Press, 2018); see also the essays in Katharine McGregor, Jess Melvin, and Annie Pohlman (eds.), *The Indonesian Genocide of 1965: Causes, Dynamics and Legacies* (Basingstoke: Palgrave Macmillan, 2018).

tried to increase their diplomatic, economic, and ideological superiority over one another. What many recent histories of the Cold War, however sophisticated, tend to overlook in their reliance of written documents is that gestures and performances mattered as much as political substance in this global conflict. This conclusion has been facilitated by a close reading of a 'diplomatic image'.[48]

The style and substance of diplomatic encounters mutually condition each other. This observation takes us back to the image of Lübke's visit to the war cemetery. Seemingly unimportant, at least for conventional historians of high politics and diplomacy, this image has facilitated a deconstruction of Lübke's state visit that has led to unexpected conclusions. While the West German archives adopt a perspective of superiority over Indonesia, the West German itineraries and plans demonstrate a great deal of insecurity and anxiety of officials on how the newly established West German state should represent itself on the global stage.[49]

Sharp distinctions between representational and 'real' politics, between 'important' and 'unimportant' aspects of diplomacy, and between style and substance are hard to sustain. Instead, using images as a starting point for writing diplomatic histories takes us on unexpected paths that make us question such simplistic assumptions and remind us of the reciprocity between politics and culture.[50]

---

[48] For the global Cold War, see Odd Arne Westad, *The Global Cold War: Third World Interventions and the Making of Our Times* (Cambridge: Cambridge University Press, 2007).
[49] Derix, *Bebilderte Politik.*   [50] Goeschel, *Mussolini and Hitler*, pp. 291–6.

6 A Photograph with Two Stories
Lisa Larsen and the Bandung Conference of 1955

Naoko Shimazu

A black and white photograph shows a street scene of spectators excitedly looking and some even pointing at something (Fig. 6.1). Noticeably, there are a number of women in the photograph, with the front row taken up by three women in Chinese dress. One of two older women, possibly twins, has a look of rapturous delight in spotting someone or something afar. The younger woman, with a parasol on the right, also wears a huge smile, her hand jutting forward, almost into the camera and out of the picture, pointing at something. Yet it is the slightly befuddled look of the other woman who complicates and enriches the image because she makes us aware of the temporal tension in the photograph. It must be only a matter of seconds before she is likely to break into a wide grin, and partake in the collective delight of recognizing what the other two have already seen.[1]

***

The power of the photograph lies in its ability to evoke emotions. We feel connected with these women, as if we were sharing this moment with them. Indeed, they were roadside spectators to the Asian-African Conference (popularly known as the Bandung Conference) taking place in Bandung, a mountain city in West Java. Most likely, they were standing on Asia Africa Road (Jalan Asia Afrika), the conference's main thoroughfare, where famous leaders from newly post-colonial Asia and Africa walked towards the Freedom Building (Gedung Merdeka) to attend the opening ceremony on 18 April 1955. The conference was attended by twenty-nine Asian and African nations, and represents a decisive moment in the global history of the twentieth century.[2]

---

[1] I would like to thank Claartje van Dijk at the International Center of Photography (ICP) at Mana and the New-York Historical Society for assistance on materials on Lisa Larsen.
[2] From 18 to 24 April 1955, the Colombo Powers (Ceylon, India, Burma, Pakistan, and Indonesia) hosted the Asian-African Conference (popularly known as the Bandung Conference) attended by twenty-five Asian and African states, in Bandung, Indonesia. For a cultural history of the conference, see my 'Diplomacy as Theatre: The Bandung Conference of 1955', *Modern Asian Studies*, 48:1 (January 2014), 225–252.

Figure 6.1 Lisa Larsen, 'Crowd of People Waiting', 1955.
Subseries 1.7.1 (Bandung Conference, Indonesia), Series 1. Prints, Lisa Larsen
Collection, International Center of Photography, New York. Shutterstock.

This photograph is special and distinct from many other photographs of diplomacy. It is almost counter-intuitive that global diplomacy can evoke such strong positive emotions in the everyday. The powerful allure emanates from its apparent authenticity of the conflicting emotions we see on the faces and bodily gestures of the three Chinese women. It also conveys authenticity of the situation and the moment because of the seeming obliviousness of the women to the photographer. They are no longer anonymous spectators who blend into the backdrop of street scenes. Instead, they are singled out and illuminated, as individuals with emotions in the theatre of diplomacy unfolding in front of their eyes and, simultaneously as if by magic, enfolding them into it. To capture their emotions so expressively, the photographer is clearly in sympathy with these women.[3]

Lisa Larsen, the American photographer, captured the fabulous explosion of emotions in the three Chinese women. Her photograph helps to de-centre the traditional way of thinking about diplomatic images, which are often determined by journalistic conceptions of what these images ought to contain – as photojournalist Tom White's insightful chapter in this volume (Chapter 10) points out. Instead of important men in suits, Larsen's focus on women illuminates gender and the crowd in the retelling of global diplomacy.

In 'reading' the photograph as a diplomatic image – that is, seeing and interpreting diplomacy from the image – we are led to a variety of stories. Out of many one could tell from this particular photograph, I decided on two: one a story of China and the Chinese in Indonesia through the visual signals we glean from the photograph, and ultimately what ethnic politics meant for China's diplomacy at Bandung. The other story of the United States and its perspective on the Bandung Conference through engaging with the provenance of the photograph, which was featured in *LIFE* magazine and was taken by a celebrated woman photographer. Connecting these two stories is the role of women in diplomacy – yet a relatively under-developed field in our understanding of global diplomacy.[4]

A Story of China and the Chinese in Indonesia

Who or what is the object of enthrallment of these local women? For the Chinese population of Bandung, the only leader who could possibly have elicited this level of excitement was Zhou Enlai, the premier of the People's

---

[3] Wilson Hicks, *Words and Pictures: An Introduction to Photojournalism* (New York: Harper and Brothers, 1952), p. 16.

[4] In the past few years, we have seen notable works emerging, e.g., Glenda Sluga and Carolyn James (eds.), *Women, Diplomacy and International Politics since 1500* (London: Routledge, 2015), and Ann Towns and Karin Aggestam (eds.), *Gendering Diplomacy and International Relations* (Basingstoke: Palgrave, 2018).

Republic of China. Zhou was the most talked about leader to attend the conference – which was a pageantry of 'who's who' in the newly post-colonial world of Asia and Africa, boasting an illustrious line-up of Jawaharlal Nehru (India), Gamal Abdel Nasser (Egypt), U Nu (Burma), Prince Sihanouk (Cambodia), Prince Feisal (Saudi Arabia), Sir John Kotelawala (Ceylon), and Mohammed Ali Bogra (Pakistan), to name but a few, and presided over by the indomitable Sukarno. Zhou Enlai's presence in Bandung caused quite a stir[5] – everything about him was fair game for the media, as inches and inches of column space were dedicated to obsessing about the Chinese leader in many different languages – his dark eyebrows, his elegant hands, his beautiful grey suit now renamed the Zhou suit, his lavish dinner parties, his calm dignity in the face of calamity, and so on. Zhou was a new diplomatic celebrity – as were many other leaders at Bandung.

The photographer's decision to focus on the Chinese women opens up a further layer to the story of Asian-African diplomacy at Bandung. We are made to confront the Chinese-ness of their identity, which speaks to us primarily through their dress. What the delightful expressions of the local women veiled was the complex political situation of the 'ethnic Chinese' population in Indonesia, or what became known as the 'Chinese problem' in Sukarno's Indonesia.[6]

Historically, the ethnic Chinese were 'foreign Orientals', a distinct category that came in between the Dutch and the 'Inlanders' (Indonesians) under the Dutch colonial administration. In addition, they had been restricted in their habitation and mobility through the combination of *wijkenstelsel* (ethnic Chinese had to live in designated quarters in cities) and *passenstelsel* (they needed a pass to move from one residential jurisdiction to another).[7] Bandung, which is located in the mountainous regions of Priangan about 100 kilometres inland in the southeast of Jakarta, did not have a Chinese population to speak of until fairly late. Chinese communities developed predominantly along the coastal port cities in Java and Sumatra. It was the construction of a trans-Javanese trunk road called the Grote Postweg (Great Post Road) in 1812, followed by the railways in 1885, that made Bandung gradually attractive for ethnic Chinese. The Chinese quarter in Bandung was situated on the present-

---

[5] For a media analysis of Zhou at Bandung as well as how such media images might have had historical roots, see Sally Percival Wood, '"Chou Gags Critics in Bandoeng" or How the Media Framed Premier Zhou Enlai at the Bandung Conference, 1955', *Modern Asian Studies*, 44:5 (September 2010), 1001–1027.

[6] Mary Somers Heidhues, 'Studying the Chinese in Indonesia: A Long Half-Century', *Sojourn: Journal of Social Issues in Southeast Asia* 32:3 (November 2017), 604.

[7] Charles A. Coppel and Leo Suryadinata, 'The Use of the Terms "Tjina" and "Tionghua" in Indonesia: An Historical Survey', in Charles A. Coppel (ed.), *Studying Ethnic Chinese in Indonesia* (Singapore: Singapore Society of Asian Studies, 2002), p. 371.

day Jalan Otto Iskandar Dinata road, formerly known as Pasarbaroeweg.[8] With the abolition of the pass system and the quarter system (in which the city was divided into sections) in 1910 and 1914, respectively, the Chinese population in Bandung increased quite rapidly in the twentieth century.[9] Bandung was known as a sleepy mountain village (*bergedessa*), but the Dutch plantation owners from the surrounding areas of Priangan started coming into the city. By the end of the nineteenth century, there was a Western enclave with some 600 Europeans.[10]

What made the 'Chinese problem' in Indonesia complex was the changing political fortunes of mainland China in the first half of the twentieth century, which influenced intra-communal politics among the ethnic Chinese, especially after the birth of the People's Republic of China in 1949. Around the time of the Bandung Conference, approximately 2.5 million ethnic Chinese lived in Indonesia, largely divided into two categories: the *totoks* (40%) looked towards China as their home, either physical, ancestral, or spiritual; while the *peranakans* (60%) grew roots in Indonesian society, often with familial ties through inter-marriages with local women.[11] Indonesia had been a significant destination of overseas Chinese for years, particularly for those of Hokkien, Cantonese, and Hakka origins, compared with other Southeast Asian countries.

To complicate further, the *totoks* were split between the pro-Beijing and pro-Taipei groups, representing the ideologically distinct two Chinas of the mid-twentieth century. Both groups possessed powerful networks of media, schools, and civic associations, which were buttressed by Beijing and Taipei. Interestingly, quite a few ethnic Chinese capitalists sided with the pro-Beijing camp, mainly because they were primarily interested in 'a strong Chinese government' – whether Nationalist or Communist – which could protect and promote their interests. Tellingly, one of them said that the overseas Chinese were like shareholders in 'the Chinese government'. This meant that the contest between the 'Reds' (pro-Beijing) and the 'Blues' (pro-Taipei) became one of legitimacy to governing 'China'. By 1957, the pro-Beijing camp might have had a slightly higher upper hand than the pro-Taipei camp in winning allegiance of the *totoks*.[12]

---

[8] Devisanthi Tunas, 'The Chinese Settlement of Bandung at the Turn of the 20th Century', unpublished MA thesis, National University of Singapore (2007), p. 50, note 127.

[9] The Siau Giap, 'Socio-economic Role of the Chinese in Indonesia 1820–1940', in Angus Maddison and Ge Prince (eds.), *Economic Growth in Indonesia 1820–1940* (Dordrecht: Foris Publications, 1989), p. 172.

[10] Haryoto Kunto, *Wajah Bandoeng Tempo Doeloe* (Bandung: P. T. Granesia, 1984), p. 68.

[11] Leo Suryadinata, *Pribumi Indonesian, the Chinese Minority, and China* (Singapore: Heinemann Asia, 1992), p. 95.

[12] Taomo Zhou, *Migration in the Time of Revolution: China, Indonesia, and the Cold War* (Ithaca, NY: Cornell University Press, 2019), p. 90, and chapter 4 generally. This is a superb study that disentangles the very complex intra-communal identity politics of the ethnic Chinese population in Indonesia.

Regardless of the infighting among the *totoks*, the Indonesians (*pribumi*) and their government tended to see ethnic Chinese as one and the same, as evidenced in their conceptualization of the so-called Chinese problem. For them, ethnic Chinese continued to be a source of disloyalty (because of their identity politics, which had more to do with Beijing and Taipei than Jakarta) and were perceived to create unfair economic competition and consequently to gain unfair advantages. Hence, the general attitude was that they needed to be managed and contained. The rivalry among the *totoks* might have needlessly complicated Jakarta's relationship with Beijing. Nonetheless, Beijing preferred not to interfere too much in the domestic politics of ethnic Chinese in Indonesia. After all, Indonesia was one of the first states to recognize the PRC and was considered an important part of Mao's conception of the 'intermediate zone' in China's foreign policy (which regards the superpower rivalry from a China-centric position).[13]

The photograph of the ethnic Chinese women, hence, is more complicated than first meets the eye. With the benefit of having now a cursory understanding of the complexity of the 'Chinese problem' in Indonesia, how are we to interpret their rapturous delight? Assuming that Zhou was their object of delight, then should we see them as part of the pro-Beijing *totoks* in Bandung? Or are we complicating the issue too much and should instead simply see them as ethnic Chinese women delighted to catch the sight of the famous Chinese leader, cast as a global celebrity? To be fair, it was not only these women who had been enamoured with Zhou at Bandung; contemporary media coverage reveals that nearly everyone fell for Zhou, even if reluctantly, and often in spite of themselves. Hence, it is not an exaggeration to say that Zhou's attendance at Bandung, not to mention his exemplary 'performance', came at a critical juncture in many respects, possibly affecting the rivalry among the *totoks* and boosting the confidence of ethnic Chinese in Indonesia generally.

What the photograph does not reveal is the larger complication caused by the Beijing-Taipei standoff, which affected Asian-African diplomacy at the Bandung Conference, particularly interfering with Zhou's attendance. A few days before the conference, a Lockheed Constellation aircraft chartered from Air India, the 'Kashmir Princess', crashed into the sea off the northern coast of Borneo on its way from Hong Kong to Jakarta, killing eleven passengers, with three crew rescued. Earlier intelligence interception that a bomb would be planted by a 'Chinese Nationalist agent' during a stopover in Hong Kong had saved Zhou's life. Nevertheless, the flight went on as scheduled as a 'decoy', killing those on board, including some members of the Chinese delegation and

---

[13] Chen Jian, 'Bridging Revolution and Decolonization: The "Bandung Discourse" in China's Early Cold War Experience', *The Chinese Historical Review*, 15:2 (2008), 212.

some Chinese journalists.[14] Zhou had asked the Indonesian authorities for an additional security arrangement to protect him and the Chinese delegation from a possible terrorist attack from the Blood and Iron Group, a Chinese Nationalist terrorist group reported to have infiltrated Indonesia just before the conference. In this way, Liang Yingming, the twenty-four-year-old, second-generation, pro-Beijing *totok* who was a high school history teacher from Surakarta in Central Java, became involved in the conference. He became Zhou's bodyguard, following a call made by the Chinese Embassy asking the pro-Beijing *totoks* to help reinforce the security of the Chinese delegation. By early June of that year, Liang boarded a ship bound for the PRC in search of a new and better life.[15]

A long-standing problem facing the ethnic Chinese population concerned dual nationality. On the one hand, ethnic Chinese would automatically obtain Chinese citizenship based on the 'right of blood' principle, while on the other, all Indonesian-born ethnic Chinese obtained Indonesian citizenship. On 22 April 1955, Zhou signed the Sino-Indonesian Dual Nationality Treaty in Bandung, giving choice to ethnic Chinese to obtain citizenship of either the People's Republic of China or Indonesia. Although the new treaty had put an end to the dual nationality problem, not all ethnic Chinese were happy, as it created a new problem of ethnic Chinese who could be denied Indonesian citizenship for discriminatory reasons. Nevertheless, Zhou was portrayed as a man of action, which helped to project a positive image of the PRC in Indonesia.

After the conference, Zhou's Indonesian visit metamorphosed into an official state visit. Arriving in Jakarta, Zhou was given a grand welcome, including an open car parade with Sukarno, throbbing with crowds cheering the two leaders. A welcome reception was arranged by the representatives of ethnic Chinese in Indonesia, when 600 selected guests from all over Indonesia came to greet Zhou. Notably, female representatives (including a medical doctor hailing from a fifth-generation ethnic Chinese family in Indonesia) were presented in the front row to shake hands with Zhou. Many such photographs were featured in the special issue of the association's conference book, *Buku Peringatan Konperensi Asia-Afrika*, an invaluable visual source for casting light on Zhou's activities with ethnic Chinese communities in Bandung and Jakarta.[16] Earlier in Bandung, the Bandung Chinese Association feted Zhou,

---

[14] The most comprehensive research on the Kashmir Princess crash so far is by Steve Tsang, 'Target Zhou Enlai: The "Kashmir Princess" Incident of 1955', *The China Quarterly*, 139 (September 1994), 766–782.

[15] Zhou, *Migration in the Time of Revolution*, pp. 1–2, 65.

[16] *Yafei huiyi shilu: Buku Peringatan Konperensi Asia-Afrika* (Jakarta: Inhua N.V. Penerbit Madjalah Ekonomi, 1955), pp. 22–24, 96; 'Chou Addresses Bandung's Chinese', *Indonesian Observer*, 26 April 1955.

inviting 300 local ethnic Chinese. In this way, Zhou was used as a catalyst for improving ethnic Chinese relations with the local *pribumi*, as the mayor of Bandung, the governor of West Java, and the deputy chief of the West Javanese police attended the reception. Attired in his grey Western-style suit, Zhou thanked numerous people, including the Chinese of Bandung, for their 'very warm welcome'.[17]

In all, the fundamental significance of Zhou's presence for ethnic Chinese communities in Indonesia was not lost on others, as reported in the *Times of India*:

> Chinese communities in Jakarta, Bandung and adjoining towns put up thousands of Chinese Communist flags – the largest number ever seen anywhere outside the Chinese mainland – to greet the visiting Premier.... the Chinese Embassy tipped off local Chinese communities, who managed to turn out in thousands to welcome him. Doll-like Chinese children, beaming with joy, rushing forward with bouquets of flowers as the smiling Premier stepped down from the plane. Despite elaborate security precautions, today was a gala day for the local Chinese since Mr Chou En-Lai's visit was a symbol of the growing power and prestige of the New China. Here, in Bandung, foreign visitors were surprised to see that Chinese Communist flags were almost as numerous as Indonesian and other Asian-African flags combined. Not many of these local Chinese are by any means Communists or Communist sympathizers. They are essentially Chinese with a strong sense of loyalty to China no matter which Government is in power.[18]

Zhou did play his China card very well, especially in basing his appeal on his Chinese identity. Such an approach enabled him to overcome the intra-communal *totok* politics, as well as playing up his Asian identity, in tune with the conference's mantra of Asian-African solidarity. No doubt, the orchestration of a pro-Zhou propaganda campaign behind the scenes by Ambassador Huang Zhen played not a small part in the remarkable success of Zhou's Bandung diplomacy.

An American Story of Bandung

By focusing on the photographer, we are led to another story – this time 'an American story' of the Bandung Conference. Born Lisa Rothschild in Germany in 1925, Larsen fled Germany to the United States with her parents before the Second World War. When she covered the Bandung Conference, she was thirty-two years of age, having already won the Woman Photographer of the Year award from the National Press Photographers' Association–Encyclopaedia Britannica (NPPA-EB) in 1958, as well as the prestigious

---

[17] Hong Liu, 'Constructing a China Metaphor: Sukarno's Perception of the PRC and Indonesia's Political Transformation', *Journal of Southeast Asian Studies*, 28:1 (May 1997), 28.

[18] 'Chou Accorded a Big Welcome in Jakarta', *Times of India* (Bombay), 17 April 1955.

Mathew Brady Award in 1953.[19] In her early days, she worked freelance for a wide range of media outlets, including *Vogue*, the *New York Times*, *Parade*, *Glamour*, *Charm*, *Holiday*, and *LIFE*. For eleven years from 1948, she worked at *LIFE* as a contract photographer. Apart from Indonesia, she undertook many other foreign assignments in her career, including in the Middle East (Turkey, Iran), Latin America (Guatemala, Mexico), East Asia (Hong Kong, Tokyo, Vietnam, Cambodia, Laos, Thailand, and China) and, in her final three years, Eastern Europe (Russia, Poland, Hungary) for which she became very well known. Her familiarity with the United Nations 'circuit' meant that she had already come across some of the leaders she photographed in Bandung, including Carlos Romulo, the head of the Philippines delegation, who served as the president of the UN General Assembly from 1949 to 1950. Her photographs of the 1955 conference constituted part of her portfolio, leading her to win the Mathew Brady Award again in 1956, and the third prize for the NPPA-EB award in the same year.[20] Tragically, she died prematurely in 1959 from cancer, only four years after the Bandung Conference.

As a contract photographer for *LIFE* magazine, Larsen and her fellow photographer Howard Sochurek (flown in from *LIFE*'s Singapore bureau) first arrived in Jakarta and moved on to Bandung to cover the conference.[21] It was a 'full-time task', as she recalled, starting early in the morning and continuing late into the night. They covered not only the official proceedings held in the Freedom Building and the Dwi-Warna Building (the secondary conference venue), but also the 'blanket' social events including numerous nightly dinners and parties, some secret, some public, while they were 'always on the run'.[22] Together they took some of the most iconic photographs of the conference, leaving their visual legacy in memorable ways.

Of the hundreds of rolls of film they took, the *LIFE* editorial chose forty-six photographs, which were featured in a nine-page lead photo-essay of the issue, entitled 'For Nehru and Zhou, a Rude Awakening at Bandung: Friends of the

---

[19] 'Lisa Larsen Awards', from George Karas to Ray Mackland, 11 March 1959, Lisa Larsen. Time Inc. Bio Files (MS 3009-RG 2), The New-York Historical Society.

[20] 'Lisa Larsen', in 'Encyclopedia of Photographers', Time Inc. Bio Files (MS 3009-RG 2), New-York Historical Society. There is useful biographical information on Larsen by Mary O'Donnell Hulme in the webpage of the International Center of Photography, www.icp.org/browse/archive/constituents/lisa-larsen?all/all/all/all/0, accessed 26 November 2019.

[21] Donald Wilson, a *LIFE* journalist who worked with Sochurek in Vietnam, recalled him as 'talented but humorless'. In 1954, they covered Dien Bien Phu, and Sochurek temporarily changed places with Robert Capa, who famously died within a few weeks in Vietnam. Sochurek returned to Vietnam after Capa's death. Donald M. Wilson, *The First 78 Years* (Xlibris US, 2006), pp. 102–104.

[22] Series 4, Subseries 4.1 Papers, Bandung Conference (April 1955), Lisa Larsen Collection, International Center of Photography, New York.

West Speak Up', published on 2 May 1955.[23] In *LIFE*'s lingo, the 'frontis-piece' for this story is a photograph of Zhou smiling and facing Nehru (only the latter's head can be seen), intended to set the tone for the entire story.[24] In this photo-essay, Larsen's photograph of the three Chinese women was the only one selected that did not feature a conference participant or a famous face such as Nehru's or Zhou's. What is more, it is the only image depicting a street scene in Bandung and portraying local women. As such, it is the only visual clue that relayed any indication of the popular excitement felt by the public in Bandung. Indeed, it is entitled 'Waiting for Chou'. Getty Images, which now owns the copyright, has given it a different title: 'Crowd of People in Bandung'.

Wilson Hicks, the executive editor, recalled, 'It is not an unusual spectacle in the managing editor's office for 15 people to stand staring at a single photograph.'[25] Any picture story in *LIFE* would have gone through a compli-cated process involving people of many different roles – managing editor, chief writer, writer, reporter, assignment editor, photographer, and graphic designer, among others. For a major diplomatic event such as the Bandung Conference, the chief writer of the Foreign News department would have suggested a story to the managing editor (if the latter did not do so him- or herself), and a hypothetical script for that story would have been prepared by the writer and reporter (researcher), suggesting picture points for the photog-rapher to aim for. This is communicated by the assignment editor, who picks a photographer whose sympathies and sensibilities are likely to result in the meeting of minds with the word team (editor, writer, and reporter). Then, the selected photographer and the assignment editor come up with a storyline based on the pictures. Hence, both words (writer and editor) and pictures (assignment editor and photographer) together form the story. Once the photo-graphs are available, the managing editor together with his team would start the layout of the story by selecting the photographs first. In this process, even if the photographer had been there in the room, they would not have had a voice.[26]

At *LIFE*, the managing editor held a tremendous control over the story:

Having determined the story he wishes to tell, the editor selects those pictures which relate themselves most readily and effectively to other pictures in developing the story's theme or advancing the question.... In addition to answering the question, "*Does the*

[23] 'For Nehru and Zhou, a Rude Awakening at Bandung: Friends of the West Speak Up', *LIFE*, 2 May 1955, 29–37; Wilson Hicks, *Words and Pictures: An Introduction to Photojournalism* (New York: Harper and Brothers, 1952), pp. 62, 69.
[24] 'For Nehru and Zhou, a Rude Awakening', 29; Hicks, *Words and Pictures*, p. 72.
[25] Hicks, *Words and Pictures*, p. 77.   [26] Hicks, *Words and Pictures*, pp. 47–78.

picture say what it is intended to say?" the editor asks and answers another question, *"Does it say what I want it to say?"*[27]

Once the frontispiece and the ender – that is, the first photo and the last photo in the sequence in the story – are decided, the rest of the selection tends to fall into line more quickly. Importantly, the frontispiece signals the main content of the story. Then, the managing editor instructs the writer to write the story to fit the storyline layout based on the tightly selected sequence of photographs. In this way, we can see the powerful agency of photographs in *LIFE*'s photo-essays. Don Wilson who worked as a *LIFE* correspondent lamented that 'Pictures were always the main focus, and the print copy supported them.'[28] Even though a story would usually be initiated by the 'word team', at the point of layout, pictures take precedence, and the word team come up with the text to complement them, in order to complete the 'picture story'. The logic is based on reductive process – how best to encapsulate the story by distilling it through the most persuasive sequence of photographs, achievable only after repeated culling.[29] Usually, the editorial team goes through about 7,000 photographs from which they pick 200 for an issue. In total, the office goes through 350,000 photographs per year, out of which about 10,000 are used. The degree of control held over the selection of photographs and the story being told by the managing editor meant that not all *LIFE* photographers were happy. In 1947, the famous agency Magnum Photos was formed by a group of disgruntled former *LIFE* photographers such as Henri Cartier-Bresson, Robert Capa, George Rodger, and W. Eugene Smith, seeking greater freedom and agency for photographers.[30]

Likewise, we can safely assume that *LIFE*'s story on the Bandung Conference would have been produced with a similar process and equally tight editorial control. We know from Larsen's travel diary that there was a crew of *Time-LIFE* correspondents who covered Bandung, in addition to Larsen and Sochurek as contract photographers. From the Singapore bureau came Dwight Martin, who once covered the Korean War, and Don Wilson, who had been covering the war in Indo-China. These foreign news correspondents would have supplied information back to the head office in New York.[31]

What is fascinating about this particular story is the apparent disconnect that can be detected between words and images. Intriguingly, the photographs on

---

[27] 'Wilson Hicks, the Former Editor of *LIFE* Magazine, Dies at 73', *New York Times*, 7 July 1970. Emphasis in original.

[28] Wilson, *The First 78 Years*, p. 86.   [29] Hicks, *Words and Pictures*, pp. 47, 49–62, 72, 84.

[30] Erika Doss, 'Looking at *LIFE*: Rethinking America's Favorite Magazine, 1936–1972', in Erika Doss (ed.), *Looking at LIFE Magazine* (Washington, DC: Smithsonian Institution Press, 2001), p. 17.

[31] Series 4, Subseries 4.1 Papers, Bandung Conference (April 1955), Lisa Larsen Collection, International Center of Photography, New York.

their own tell a story of confident, post-colonial international statesmen, who were 'conferencing the international', while the words betray a narrative that emphasises the fractious.[32] Perceptively, Jeff Guy calls this disjoint a 'paralysis of perspective' where 'an intrinsic ambiguity in the photograph which has created a conflict between text and image … [leads] to a "paralysis of perspective" among the observers'.[33] We may experience a degree of cognitive dissonance because of the apparent discrepancy in the meanings conveyed through the text as opposed to those conveyed through the images. Our customary expectation that images and text complement each other in a story becomes destabilised. Granted, some of the images in the photo-essay show Nehru looking disgruntled as noted in the text. Still, there is enough of a disjoint there that the tenor of the text is not always in tune with the tenor of the visual. Why did the editorial team decide to leave this tension in the photo-essay?

LIFE's word team might have wanted to tell a story about how neutralist Nehru and communist Zhou were in cahoots with each other, manoeuvring to make friends at the conference. To their 'chagrin', their collusion came to nothing because they were ultimately outmanoeuvred by friends of the West, spearheaded by Ceylon's Sir John Kotelawala and his 'fiery anti-communist speech'. What the photo-essay's 'words' attempt to do is to undermine Asian-African unity by emphasizing how deep the distrust was between the pro-Western and neutralist-communist camps, and, moreover, how disparate and diverse the Bandung nations were. The tone is decidedly anti-Nehru, focusing on Nehru's anger and disappointment, as well as his deputy, Krishna Menon, who 'glares about assembly in unconcealed fury' – accompanied by a photograph to prove the point.[34]

Let us suppose that the tension between the text and the photos was a carefully contrived 'dialogue' to produce that fractious, and dissonant, effect in the reader. The way *LIFE* was conceived, the reader would usually view the pictures first, then go to the text, and revert back to the pictures. Because of the use of high-quality photographs (in this story, forty-six photographs), the text (usually not more than 400 words in total) would have to compete by having headlines and captions 'screaming out' of the pages in pithy, eye-catching words. It may even be the case that the reader might simply look at the photographs and the headlines or captions, and not bother with the words. In any case, *LIFE* expects the reader to do some imaginative legwork so that

---

[32] 'Conferencing the International: A Cultural and Historical Geography of the Origins of Internationalism (1919–1939)', School of Geography, University of Nottingham, https://gtr .ukri.org/project/5B92827E-11D6–45D2-A805–06682ED17018, accessed 7 February 2020.

[33] Jeff Guy, '"A Paralysis of Perspective": Image and Text in the Creation of an African Chief', *South African Historical Journal*, 47:1 (2002), 51.

[34] 'For Nehru and Zhou, a Rude Awakening ', 29–37.

the cumulative effect of pictures plus words becomes 'greater than the sum of [their] parts'.[35]

In fact, the portrayals of the Bandung leaders featured in the photo-essay reflected the US State Department's attitudes towards the various Asian leaders present at Bandung. As mentioned previously, photographs of Nehru that are unflattering, with sub-heads or captions such as 'a frowning Nehru', 'a study in anger', 'temper tantrum', and 'a chagrined Nehru', feature rather prominently.[36] What the *LIFE* reader may not have known was that such an attitude towards the Indian premier reflected the general official attitude held by the US State Department towards Nehru:

The personal failure of Nehru was one important outcome of the conference.... It is probable that Nehru in the near future cannot again speak with the same weight he claimed in the past, in spite of his aspirations to be 'the voice of Asia' and 'the conscience of the world'. This loss of prestige on the part of Nehru was probably partly responsible for failure of the neutralists to win more ground.[37]

By coincidence or by design, it is striking that the most popular American graphic magazine with a circulation figure of 5,655,000 in 1955 happened to articulate through its lead photo-essay on the Bandung Conference the State Department's attitude towards Nehru.[38]

It was not only the story about Nehru that was 'coincidental'; Sir John Kotelawala – a known friend of the Free World (together with Carlos Romulo of the Philippines and Prince Wan Waithayakorn of Thailand), who stood up against communism in his divisive speech – is given the place of honour as the ender, that is, the final picture, featuring a charismatic portrait of him taken by Larsen. Zhou, who was supposedly the real enemy of the United States, fared better than Nehru. Images of Zhou are in the charismatic and dignified mode. *LIFE*'s visually favourable portraiture of Zhou was mirrored in the analysis of the Bandung Conference submitted to the State Department by Ambassador Hugh S. Cumming of the US Embassy in Jakarta:

While it is true that the West enjoyed a very considerable success substantively, it is equally clear that Chou En-lai enjoyed a tremendous triumph. In his public appearances, Chou possessed great stage presence. He was dignified, calm, affable, and subtly conveyed the feeling that he ought to be the main figure of the conference.... He made a tremendous impression on all the press, the delegates and other observers.[39]

[35] Hicks, *Words and Pictures*, pp. 6–7.   [36] 'For Nehru and Chou, a Rude Awakening', 34–35.
[37] 'Evaluation of the Bandung Conference', in Elmer B. Staats, 'Secret: Memorandum for the Operations Coordinating Board: Bandung Conference of April 1955', 12 May 1955, US Department of State, RG59 Subject and Special Files, 1953–1961, Box 35, A1 1586C, NARA, College Park, Maryland.
[38] Theodore Peterson, *Magazines in the Twentieth Century* (Urbana: University of Illinois Press, 1956), p. 56.
[39] 'Evaluation of the Bandung Conference'.

What is arresting is that the general tone of the photo-essay mirrored very closely the tone of Ambassador Cumming's confidential, 'secret' report.

As Larsen's travel diary of her visit to Bandung reveals, the relationship between some American journalists and American diplomats were cosy, to say the least: 'Off to Jerry Donahue's house [in Jakarta], central Time Life hang out, drinks, cocktails, dinner, etc., reception at the embassy. Cumming [US Ambassador to Indonesia] surrounded by newsmen giving them top secret information, so it looked.'[40] Most of the American correspondents from major newspapers were hanging out at the US Embassy and at Bill Palmer's, who was the director of the Association of American Film Importers.[41] Then, the *LIFE* story might have been one of the remarkable 'American stories' to have developed on the ground at the Bandung Conference, probably in close interaction with the US Embassy, whose ambassador had been more favourably disposed to Zhou than his boss, Secretary of State John Foster Dulles. Only those who experienced the conference at first-hand would have been able to appreciate fully the psychological enormity of Zhou's diplomatic success. This is what Ambassador Cumming's report stated, and what the photographs of Zhou in *LIFE* hinted at.

The Photographed Photographer

Larsen's sympathetic and humane gaze made all subjects come alive, whether they were the big men of politics and diplomacy or women of the everyday. She was a photographer who brought out emotions in her subjects: 'One of the best women news photographers, Lisa Larsen gets great emotional intensity into her work.'[42] Ray Mackland,[43] who was the *LIFE* picture editor, wrote movingly on her death:

Lisa Larsen was a photographer with a blithe spirit. Gay, charming, fun-loving, she nevertheless had an absorbing interest in the world's peoples and their plight, and it was these qualities, which so captivated them, that enabled her to show them with such realism and such sympathy.[44]

---

[40] Series 4, Subseries 4.1 Papers, Bandung Conference (April 1955), Lisa Larsen Collection, International Center of Photography, New York.

[41] Palmer was accused of being a CIA agent in Indonesia at the time by the Indonesian Communists. See Beb Vuyk's 'A Weekend with Richard Wright (1960)', in Brian Russell Roberts and Keith Foulcher (eds.), *Indonesian Notebook: A Source Book on Richard Wright and the Bandung Conference* (Durham, NC: Duke University Press, 2016), p. 205, note 29.

[42] 'Lisa Larsen: A Bio', Time Inc. Bio Files (MS 3009-RG 2), New-York Historical Society.

[43] Charles Ray Mackland (1910–1989), known as Ray Macland, joined *LIFE* in 1942, and was the picture editor from 1950 to 1961 when he joined the United States Information Agency as its director of the photographic division until his retirement in 1978. See his obituary in the *New York Times*, 6 September 1989.

[44] 'Lisa Larsen: An Appreciation', 13 March 1959, Time Inc. Bio Files (MS 3009-RG 2), New-York Historical Society.

Was Larsen's gender relevant in the choice of her subject matter – the three unknown local Chinese women? Larsen did take many shots of women in Bandung, but also on her other assignments for *LIFE*.[45] In 1955, for instance, the front cover of the German magazine *Camera* featured a photograph of Turkish women taken by Larsen. Her contact sheets of trips to Hong Kong in 1955 also contain many shots of women, at various types of work. Patryk Babiracki's essay on Larsen's 1956 trip to the Soviet Union sensitively examines her work in capturing women in their multiple roles and complexities.[46] In going through her archives, we can see clearly that women mattered greatly as subjects for Larsen. In the case of Bandung, Larsen gives these local women a presence in the diplomatic context – and opens up the possibility of retelling a diplomatic narrative inclusive of local women.

None of this would have happened without the intervention of the *LIFE* editorial, as Larsen's powerful photograph would not have reached its zenith as *the* image that represented 'the people'. It succeeds in capturing the 'most meaningful moment' in which the image presents 'a climax of … action or emotion or both together'.[47] The three Chinese women became an integral part of *LIFE*'s retelling of the conference, by underlining popular participation as a necessary ingredient to making a good story on global diplomacy. It may also have helped to underscore Zhou's diplomatic success, to visualize the extent of the overseas Chinese networks, and to realign China's position as an influential alternative 'pole' within the East in the Cold War frame. The photograph is compelling because of the emotional intensity it embodies. Larsen's photograph stands out in the genre of 'the crowd' because she gives powerful agency to the anonymous crowd. Larsen was not the only one to have felt popular energy in Bandung, as the local people featured rather prominently in the visual evidence of the conference – a reminder that the people contributed to making the Bandung experience special.

Emotional intensity – the hallmark of Larsen's photography – is evident also in her other notable work on Bandung. During the conference, she embarked on a personal project of taking portraits of some of the key leaders:

In addition to the regular coverage, this correspondent embarked hopefully on a special project – a series of calm, undisturbed interviews and portrait sittings of the leading African and American statesmen. This required luck and organization. Handwritten notes asking permission, time and place for the interviews were channeled through

---

[45] See Series 4, Subseries 4.1 Papers and 4.8 Papers, Bandung Conference (April 1955), Lisa Larsen Collection, International Center of Photography, New York.

[46] Patryk Babiracki, 'Searching for the Soviet Woman: Photojournalist Lisa Larsen in the Soviet Union, Spring–Fall 1956', *Apparatus: Film, Media and Digital Culture in Central and Eastern Europe*, 15 (2022). DOI: https://dx.doi.org/10.17892/app.2022.00015.325. I thank the author for bringing this to my attention.

[47] Hicks, *Words and Pictures*, p. 122.

fourteen Aide-de-camps. The appointments requested, were for the early morning hours from 6 to 8 a.m., or lunchtime from 1 to 2.20 p.m. The resulting interviews are not interviews in the ordinary sense. They do not necessarily deal with the news of the moment. They attempt rather to give a glimpse of the personalities behind the news. A small portable tape-recorder and two Leica cameras, one for color and one for black and white were the total equipment used. Conversation during the actual portrait sitting was recorded.

A man who sits in front of a camera is less likely to be interview conscious. His words appear less carefully chosen for the printed page and his concern focuses primarily on 'how he looks'. This casual approach can reveal much of a man's personality.[48]

'Working with a Leica in color and black-and-white, Larsen produced warm, realistic and sympathetic portraits.'[49] Her innovative approach helped her gain access to the inner sanctum of some of the Bandung leaders, as Larsen 'ambushed' them during breakfast or lunch in order to take unguarded photographs of them. Some sitters were less forthcoming than others – such as Nasser and Prince Wan Waithayakorn, who seemed uncomfortable about this unorthodox intrusion in the early morning. 'You [Larsen] have taken enough pictures of me,' declined Zhou. 'I am too busy, I have no time,' protested Prince Sihanouk, although U Nu, Mohammed Ali, Sir John Kotelawala, and Carlos Romulo seemed to have enjoyed her outlandish mode of portrait-taking. This special project resulted in some of the most charismatic portraits taken of the key Bandung leaders. Nehru relaxed with the help of his daughter, Indira Gandhi: 'Nehru's face is intriguing. He has a wonderful bone structure and a rapid change and variety of fleeting expressions. Never once did Panditji show a sign of impatience.'[50] Even with Nasser, who claimed, 'If you photographed me in Cairo in my uniform, I would never smile,' Larsen managed to extract a matinee idol image.[51] She was an accomplished diplomat herself.[52]

Larsen's gender and her physical attractiveness – the 'glamour girl of press photography' – had turned her into a sexualized photographer. She presents an ambiguous role as a photographer – as both an image-maker and an object of the image being created by the media. Her beauty, coupled with her dogged determination to get her job done, had turned her into a minor celebrity during the conference. In particular, the Indonesian media were fascinated by the blond female American photographer, and took photographs of her taking photographs – the photographer at work.

---

[48] Series 4, Subseries 4.1 Papers, Bandung Conference (April 1955), Lisa Larsen Collection, International Center of Photography, New York.

[49] 'Lisa Larsen', in 'Encyclopedia of Photographers'.

[50] Series 4, Subseries 4.1 Papers, Bandung Conference (April 1955), Lisa Larsen Collection, International Center of Photography, New York. She took portraits of fourteen leaders.

[51] Ibid.   [52] Hicks, *Words and Pictures*, p. 108.

In October 2022, Lisa Larsen's stand-up, poster-sized photograph in the Asian-African Conference Museum in Bandung acts an important reminder of the globality of the 1955 moment.[53] It seems not uncommon for photographers and photojournalists to feature in diplomatic images, as per Tom White's personal experience in his essay in this volume (Chapter 10) has also shown. White remarks on the irony of himself being photographed as one of the 'journalists from around the world' at the time of the Trump-Kim Summit in Singapore in 2018, even though he had been a resident in Singapore for some time by then. In both cases of Larsen and White, it is the 'whiteness' of their presence that stands out in the largely 'Asian' crowd, supposedly contributing to the global nature of the events.

On arrival at the airport in Bandung, a Boy Scout waiting for the dignitaries asked for her autograph.[54] *BERITA*, an Indonesian magazine, referred to her as 'The Stubborn Female Journalist':

Among the foreign journalists who had a lot of attention in restaurants is a female journalist called Lisa Larson [*sic*] from LIFE, and her female American colleague from the NY Times. Though prohibited many times by the state apparatus, they keep approaching Nehru, U Nu and Nasser to take their pictures, and sometimes they climbed the chair or the fence which is rather high to perform their duty. The assistant police inspector often pulled their legs and call them '*wanita, wanita bandel* [lady, stubborn lady]'.[55]

Such antics in balletic poses did bemuse the bystanders, though Larsen herself would have been totally focused on taking *that* picture. In another Indonesian press reference, such public demonstrations of Larsen's professionalism were posed as a challenge: 'Can our women follow her?'[56] After the conference, the *Indonesian Observer* reported that Larsen's next assignment was to photograph the famous Komodo dragons in the zoo of the East Javanese city of Surabaya.[57]

Bob Rouveroy, a photographer in Bandung, reminisced about her:[58]

A few years ago I met Lisa Larsen when we were both covering the Asian-African Conference in Bandung, Indonesia.... I had ample time and opportunity to study her all-consuming drive to get that picture, the one that stands out. Nearly all delegates were Moslems and so frown on forwardness of women in general. But after awhile, they and

---

[53] The author thanks Kathleen Ditzig for bringing this to attention.
[54] Series 4, Subseries 4.1 Papers, Bandung Conference (April 1955), Lisa Larsen Collection, International Center of Photography, New York.
[55] 'Pusparagam Konferensi (Conference Miscellanies)', *BERITA* 3 (April 1955).
[56] 'The AA Conference Situation in Bandung" (Suasana A.A. meliputi Bandung), *Star Weekly*, 486 (23 April 1955).
[57] 'A-A Roundup', *Indonesian Observer*, 27 April 1955.
[58] Robert Rouveroy (1927–2009) was born in Bandung as Emile Leonardus van Rouveroy van Nieuwaal.

I all fell in love with her because of her humanity and friendliness, and her honest reporting. It was impossible not to like her, even if she crowded one out of a good camera position.[59]

Alas, he was only one of many admirers, as revealed in her obituary, 'Lisa Larsen: An Appreciation':

Few photographers were as well-known, and as well-remembered, as Lisa. Alben Barkley whom she accompanied on a barnstorming trip, called her Mona Lisa.... In Russia, Khrushchev singled her out for attention – and comment. Ho Chi Minh said, 'If I were a young man, I'd be in love with you.'[60]

She died from cancer in 1959, only four years after the Bandung Conference.

***

What is powerful about the photograph shown in Fig. 6.1 is its everyday-ness – in having these local Chinese women with wondrous expressions in engagement with one of the defining diplomatic moments in twentieth-century history. As such, it represents an unlikely 'diplomatic' image, and enables us to think more expansively about what a diplomatic image could be. For that, we needed Lisa Larsen, who through her sympathetic eye and humanity gave agency to these local women as rightful players in the role of audience in the theatre of global diplomacy taking place in their backyard. It is a striking photograph, 'a great photograph', evidently acknowledged even with the most careful scrutiny of the editor at *LIFE*.

Let us pause a little to consider what it means to bring diplomacy into the wider context of everyday society. Is it about recasting our understanding of diplomacy within our practical experience of 'everyday familiarity with objects and events'?[61] Is it about reframing the understanding of diplomacy within the repertoire of objects, events, and meanings of everyday familiarity, so that we – the general public – can appropriate diplomacy as objects and events with which we can identify in the everyday? To that extent, is it any different from any other spectacle that is presented to the audience in the context of the everyday? Evidently, our journey of understanding diplomacy in the everyday has only just begun.

What Larsen had managed to do in the photograph of the local Chinese women was to seamlessly interweave the everyday with the extraordinary in

---

[59] 'Photographer's Legacy: Friends', 13 April 1959, Lisa Larsen, Time Inc. Bio Files (MS 3009-RG 2), New-York Historical Society.

[60] 'Lisa Larsen: An Appreciation', 13 March 1959, Time Inc. Bio Files (MS 3009-RG 2), New-York Historical Society.

[61] Erwin Panofsky, *Studies in Iconology: Humanistic Themes in the Art of the Renaissance* (New York: Harper & Row, 1967), p. 4.

global diplomacy. Hosting a diplomatic event in any local milieu has the extraordinary effect of transplanting the global to the local, by the physical presence of a temporally bound cosmopolitan community of international statesmen, the foreign press corps, and various foreign hangers-on. At the same time, the local landscape including the local people as mise-en-scene becomes inadvertently globalized by their integration into a larger diplomatic narrative. If we are to push this line of thinking further, the audience elsewhere observing the conference through newspapers, newsreels, and magazines might have imagined sharing the experience of being the audience vicariously through the local people of Bandung. Certainly, the memorable photograph of the local Chinese women of Bandung provides us with an alternative 'window' through which to understand the layered meanings of what global diplomacy might have meant for the Indonesian public, but which also has global resonance.

Lisa Larsen's status as a rare female photographer at the time demonstrated the ambiguity of her dual positionality – one as a photographer, and another as an object of photography. Whatever we can say about the photographer, the photograph itself speaks volumes about the meanings it contained. The two stories told in this chapter are not by any means the only stories that can be told from the photograph. Far from it – and this brings us back to the nature of photographs as sources – their ambiguity as well as their exciting potential for unravelling many untold stories about diplomacy.

7 Waxwork Wars

Exhibiting the Japanese Surrender over Half a Century in Singapore

Paul Rae

When General Seishiro Itagaki, Commander of the Japanese 7th Area Army, applied the seal of the Japanese Army to the instruments of surrender at the City Hall Chambers in Singapore on 12 August 1945, what was he putting his stamp on? Most immediately, it was the surrender of the Japanese Army in Southeast Asia, and an end to Japan's imperial project of creating the 'Greater East Asia Co-prosperity Sphere'. More broadly, Itagaki was submitting to Emperor Hirohito's acceptance of the terms of the Potsdam Declaration, and the order that Japanese military personnel surrender. The first and most significant such surrender ceremony had taken place on board the USS *Missouri* in Tokyo Bay on 2 September 1945, followed by similar events throughout Southeast Asia. Each reiterated the complex negotiations in the transfer of power that surrender entails. Hirohito had requested a conditional surrender and been rebuffed. Prior to accepting the surrender in Singapore, Admiral Lord Louis Mountbatten, Supreme Allied Commander South East Asia Command, announced that the event was 'no negotiated surrender. The Japanese are submitting to superior force, now massed here.'[1] Yet surrender marks the transition from war to peace, and from a military to a civilian state (even if under a transitional military administration). The terms of surrender dictate to a significant degree the basis on which participating states and others will relate in future. And the semiotics, aesthetics, and performance of the surrender all bear on its legitimacy in the eyes of those on whose behalf the agreement is made. As such, the Japanese surrender can be said, like other surrenders, to inhabit a liminal realm, bearing upon post-war relations in the region precisely by dint of its ambivalent relation to that domain.

Such ambiguities at the heart of a momentous occasion ramify across a wide spectrum of human activities. Here, I narrow the question of the complexities of Japan's surrender to what may seem an insignificantly literal answer to my opening question: Itagaki was putting his stamp on 'vermillion-coloured wax'.[2] Insignificant, but not irrelevant. As Robin Wagner-Pacifici writes, in

---

[1] 'Japanese in Malaysia Surrender at Singapore', *Straits Times*, 13 September 1945, p. 1.
[2] Ibid., p. 4.

surrender contexts, '[g]iven the enormous weight of the signature (part demonstrative, part performative, part representational), we should not be surprised to find a fetishistic attachment to the actual instruments of signing'.[3] She notes that the presence of the imperial seal in the Tokyo Bay ceremony, and the authorisation of Foreign Minister Mamoru Shigemitsu to sign the documents, provided the 'fragile thread'[4] by which the emperor sustained his authority – itself a condition somewhat at odds with the Allied insistence on unconditional surrender. But there is an even more basic way of thinking about wax, whose cultivation and fabrication is an ancient human technology, whose practical uses are highly varied, and whose phenomenological appeal remains mysterious, almost otherworldly. The capacity of wax to hold an imprint is both useful and puzzling, testifying as it does to the presence of an absence. Its ability to be moulded, combined with the fact it maintains visual and tactile similarities with human flesh, means it has played an instrumental role in the history of three-dimensional representations of the human body. When Itagaki put the Japanese Army's seal and subsequently his personal seal to the surrender instruments in Singapore in 1945, little did he know that one such three-dimensional representation of the human body – his own – awaited in the future. For the obverse of Itagaki's imprint would be his own likeness in wax, reproduced alongside those of his six fellow officers, and twenty representatives of the Allied forces (Fig. 7.1). In March 1974, a waxwork display of the surrender opened in Singapore's City Hall Chambers where the ceremony had taken place almost three decades earlier. Relocated to the resort island of Sentosa later that year, the exhibit remains on display today. Half a century old, the waxworks are past their heyday, and relatively little-visited. Indeed, their endurance is itself anomalous in Singapore's novelty-hungry, footfall-driven tourist environment. With so little left to chance in land-scarce, resource-intensive Singapore, and even less to obsolescence, this in turn raises an interesting question: While today there is little love lost for this unlovely and timeworn exhibit, what *would* be lost that makes it worth holding onto?

The short answer is that the waxworks have more than one story to tell, and task to perform. Here, I consider what this seemingly minor imprint of the Japanese surrender can tell us about post-war Japan-Singapore relations, and what work – historical or otherwise – it continues to do by dint of its low-key but persistent durability. My enquiry focuses on three salient periods in the life of the exhibit: when it was created, what it represents, and the experience it offers today. In concluding, I reflect further on the ambivalent relation to diplomacy that the waxworks, as a representation of surrender, retain, and to the ambivalent qualities

---

[3] Robin Wagner-Pacifici, *The Art of Surrender: Decomposing Sovereignty at Conflict's End* (Chicago: University of Chicago Press, 2005), p. 50.
[4] Ibid., p. 52.

Figure 7.1 The waxwork figure of General Seishiro Itagaki (centre) signing the Instrument of Surrender in the tableau depicting the formal Japanese surrender to the British in 1945, Surrender Chamber at Sentosa, Singapore. Photo: Paul Rae.

of diplomacy that, in their fundamental oddness as an exercise in Singaporean nation-building, they exemplify. Both of these qualities, I suggest, are grounded in the specific form the exhibit takes: a static, figurative tableau made of an unstable, uncanny material. We begin with the story of the waxworks' creation a quarter of a century after the event it would come to depict.

The 1970s: What the Waxworks Were For

In December 1970, the Singapore Tourist Promotion Board (STPB) convened a Special Committee for Selective Historic Sites into Tourist Attractions to improve the attractions available to arriving visitors. Having identified a site by the Singapore River where Sir Stamford Raffles was thought to have landed in 1819 to 'found' modern Singapore, a white polymarble reproduction of Thomas Woolner's 1887 bronze statue of Raffles was subsequently erected in 1972. Later that year, an 8.6-metre fountain depicting the STPB's hybrid fish-lion mascot, the Merlion, was sited at the mouth of the Singapore River. And by March 1974, the waxwork reconstruction of the formal Japanese surrender was complete. These initiatives spoke to the complexity of Singapore's self-imagining, in terms of the stories it told about itself and the appeal it held for visitors. Tellingly, Singaporeans were not represented in any of the attractions. Yet more intriguingly, of the three – an imperialist, a cartoon, and a historical tableau – the latter would prove most contentious.

How so? In 1967, two years after independence, Singapore had been dealt a blow to its economy and security when Britain announced a pull-out of its military, which had vouchsafed Singapore's defence, employed 25,000 local workers, and contributed 20 per cent of gross national product.[5] Tourism was identified as an important alternative source of foreign currency and local employment. The STPB's annual report for 1970–71 highlighted that, with visitor arrivals passing the half-million mark for the first time, the industry was now earning $300 million annually, or 5 per cent of GDP.[6] The long aftermath of World War II, which had seen protracted efforts at decolonisation and independence, was now coming to an end, and new regional alignments were forming. That same report announced a study into the Japanese tourist market, which aimed to build on the introduction of Japanese-language tour guide training in 1969, and the opening of a tourist office in Tokyo (along with Sydney and San Francisco) in 1970.[7] Successive annual reports trace the development of this initiative. Japanese tour operators were hosted in Singapore in 1971, leading to a 54.4 per cent increase in arrivals from Japan in 1972[8] and contributing substantially to the materially and symbolically significant milestone of one million annual visitors in December 1973.[9]

This development said as much about Japan as Singapore. As Shinji Yamashita reports, '[a]fter Japan's defeat in the Pacific War in 1945, overseas tourism was restricted for most Japanese, but in 1964, the year of the Tokyo

---

[5] Malcolm H. Murfett, John N. Miksic, Brian P. Farrell, and Chiang Min Shun, *Between Two Oceans: A Military History of Singapore from 1275 to 1971*, 2nd ed. (Singapore: Marshall Cavendish, 2011), pp. 327, 329.

[6] Singapore Tourist Promotion Board [hereafter STPB], *Annual Report April 1970–March 1971* (Singapore: Singapore Tourist Promotion Board, 1971), p. 4.

[7] STPB, *Annual Report April 1970–March 1971*, p. 7.

[8] STPB, *Annual Report April 1972–3* (Singapore: Singapore Tourist Promotion Board, 1973), p. 1.

[9] STPB, *Annual Report 1973–4* (Singapore: Singapore Tourist Promotion Board, 1974), n.p.

Olympics, the restrictions were removed. In that year, 128,000 Japanese went abroad'.[10] This new-found freedom coincided with a diplomatic and commercial effort by Japan to engage with Southeast Asia and to overcome lingering regional animosity. These complex issues crystallised over war reparations. Singapore had demanded reparations in 1959, but Japan refused because Singapore was a colony of the United Kingdom, which it had already paid in accordance with the 1951 Treaty of San Francisco. The March 1962 discovery in Singapore of forty-nine mass graves holding the remains of Chinese massacred by the Japanese during the war reignited demands for payment of a 'blood debt'. Upon Singaporean independence in 1965, negotiations were reopened, with diplomatic relations formally established between the two countries in 1966. In 1967, Japan agreed to pay 2,940 million yen to the Singapore government and to offer as much again in low-cost loans,[11] and in the 1970s Japan would become Singapore's largest foreign investor and trading partner.[12] In December 1971, the yen, which had been undervalued after being tied to the dollar from 1949, was revalued under the Smithsonian Agreement, another motivating factor in the STPB's targeting of Japanese tourists at that time.

These developments left a complicated legacy. Although reparations were paid before the Surrender waxworks were mooted, the story of how the exhibit was proposed to Singaporeans highlights how fraught the situation remained. In January 1971, the *Singapore Herald* reported that the STPB was planning 'a Madam Tussauds of sorts', which would represent the British surrender to Japanese General Tomoyuki Yamashita (the so-called Tiger of Malaya) on 15 February 1942. To be located on the British surrender site at the Ford Factory in Bukit Timah, the goal was 'to lure more Japanese tourists here'.[13] This caused a furore. The Appeal Committee for Singapore Chinese Massacred by Japanese, dormant since suing for the blood debt in the mid-1960s, described the plan as 'disgraceful',[14] and MP Low Yong Nguan castigated it in Parliament as 'an insult to the dignity of our people'.[15] The STPB countered that the waxworks were part of a larger initiative that would

---

[10] Shinji Yamashita, 'Southeast Asian Tourism from a Japanese Perspective', in M. Hitchcock et al. (eds.), *Tourism in Southeast Asia: Challenges and New Directions* (Copenhagen: NIAS Press, 2008), pp. 189–205 (p. 190).

[11] Hiroshi Shimizu, *Japanese Firms in Contemporary Singapore* (Singapore: NUS Press, 2008), p. 40.

[12] Narushige Michishita, 'Japan, Singapore, and 70 Years of Post-war Ties', *Straits Times*, 11 February 2015. Available at www.straitstimes.com/opinion/japan-singapore-and-70-years-of-post-war-ties (accessed 20 May 2020).

[13] 'Singapore Plans for a Mini Madam Tussauds', *Singapore Herald*, 27 January 1971, p. 20.

[14] 'That "Tiger" in Wax Idea Is Disgraceful', *Singapore Herald*, 3 February 1971, p. 5.

[15] In Parliament of Singapore, 'Debate on Annual Budget Statement', *Hansard*, 17 March 1971, column 678.

also include the Japanese surrender, and that the plan was not simply to please tourists 'to earn a few more yens [*sic*]'.[16] However, in response to the outcry from representatives of the Chinese community who had been violently impacted by the Japanese occupation, several voices were raised *in support* of the Japanese. In a letter to the press arguing that Yamashita helped 'Asia to regain her self-respect and identity', one D. E. S. Chelliah outlined the rationale:

As a Singaporean and an Asian, I am of the opinion that not only would it be proper for Singapore but also for every other Asian country which has been liberated from the shackles of the colonial powers a[s] a result of the last World War, to erect a statue in memory of Tomoyuki Yamashita.[17]

Further letters echoed the sentiment:

I am of the view that the three Wise Men of Singapore as discoverers of modern Singapore are Stamford Raffles, Tomoyuki Yamashita and Lee Kuan Yew ... As a Singapore citizen of Eurasian descent ... I think it is high time that a proper statue was erected in memory of Tomoyuki Yamashita.[18]

I for one am satisfied that but for the Japanese victory we would have had to live with the concept that it is the White man's divine right to rule and the Asian's divine right to serve the White for many a day to come.[19]

The British surrender waxworks plan was suspended, while research proceeded on details of the Japanese surrender, in preparation for *its* re-creation. This created its own frictions, however, this time in Singapore-Japan relations. One journalist suggested that 'Tokyo leaked out the [Tourist] Board's intentions after they have [*sic*] been approached for the return of records taken away during the Occupation.'[20] A note in an STPB research document on the surrender indicated that the chairman of the board had twice raised the project with the Japanese Ambassador, 'and on each occasion the Japanese Government had expressed a firm refusal to cooperate'.[21]

The Japanese surrender waxworks opened in the City Hall Chamber in March 1974 at a cost that dwarfed other tourist initiatives: Merlion Park had cost $135,935; the ornamental Siong Lim Garden $22,349; the waxworks,

---

[16] 'Not Merely to Earn Yen Says Tourist Board', *Straits Times*, 4 February 1971, p. 5.
[17] D. E. S. Chelliah, 'Why It Is Proper to Erect Statue of Yamashita', *Singapore Herald*, 8 March 1971, p. 5.
[18] C. I. Danker, 'One for Lee Kuan Yew, One for Yamashita', *Singapore Herald*, 12 March 1971, p. 2.
[19] 'Yamashita Did the Asians a Great Service', *Singapore Herald*, 13 March 1971, p. 8.
[20] J. Sam, 'Memorials Are Anything but Reminders of a Shameful Past', *New Nation*, 21 October 1971, p. 10.
[21] STPB, *Historical Research on the Surrender Ceremony at City Hall on 12th September 1945* (Singapore: Singapore Tourist Promotion Board, 1975), p. 35.

$430,338.[22] In September, at a further cost of $179,183,[23] the exhibit was relocated to Sentosa, where it has remained on almost continuous display. In November 2017 it was re-launched, accompanied by an automated audio-visual framing.

In 1980, it was reported the Japanese surrender scene would be joined by that of the British. Whereas the Japanese surrender had been made in Britain, the British surrender was manufactured in Japan (for $130,000) and opened on 1 August 1981.[24] The Japan scholar and former military intelligence officer Louis Allen suggests the British surrender scene was created at the instigation of a journalist from the *Nihon Keizai Shimbun* newspaper, who had expressed dissatisfaction at its absence, and had been told the reason was lack of funds: 'Nothing loth, Mr Saito promptly obtained the required waxworks from a Japanese company, and had them transported on a Japanese vessel, free of charge, from Japan.'[25] Publicly available accounts tell a slightly different story. The initial March 1980 *Straits Times* article announcing the new display specified it was the Sentosa Development Corporation (SDC) that had 'embarked on a project'[26] to re-enact the British surrender; a year later, it was reported that the SDC had 'received proposals from British and Japanese firms for commissioning of the wax figures'. An SDC team was researching the surrender, explained the report, although, echoing the Japanese government's earlier unwillingness to assist with the creation of the Japanese surrender, the British High Commission expressed itself 'unable to help' with details of the British surrender.[27]

Clearly, in the decade since such a display had been controversially mooted, a shift in attitudes had taken place. To be sure, sensitivities remained. The *Straits Times* reported rumours that the SDC had initiated the new project because 'the influx of Japanese tourists caused some embarrassment ... over the incomplete picture given in the Surrender Chamber'. An SDC representative insisted the rumours were 'unfounded,' but went on to say that while the

---

[22] STPB, 'Singapore Tourist Promotion Board Income and Expenditure Account for the Year Ended 31 March 1974', *Annual Report 1973–4*, n.p.

[23] STPB, 'Finance', in *Annual Report 1974/5* (Singapore: Singapore Tourist Promotion Board, 1975), n.p.

[24] 'Second Waxworks Museum Opens today', *Straits Times*, 1 August 1981, p. 13.

[25] Louis Allen, 'Japan as Occupying Power: The Revision of History', in Adriana Boscaro, Franco Gatti, and Massimo Raveri (eds.), *Rethinking Japan*, 2 vols. (Folkestone: Japan Library, 1991), vol. 2, p. 68.

[26] 'Sentosa Adds New Scene to Its Surrender Chamber', *Straits Times*, 23 March 1980, p. 6.

[27] 'Waxworks of British Surrender', *Straits Times*, 10 March 1981, p. 7. Allen's account of the genesis of the British surrender waxworks might give one to believe that the Japanese bankrolled the $130,000 attraction. However, the SDC's accounts for FY1981/2 include a cost entry for the Surrender Chambers of $128,588, which suggest otherwise. See 'Notes on the Accounts, 4a) Fixed Assets', in Sentosa Development Corporation, *Sentosa Development Corporation Annual Report 81/2* (Singapore: Sentosa Development Corporation, 1982), n.p.

original waxworks were drawing big crowds, including Japanese tourists, 'the new wax works may interest them more'.[28] Nevertheless, this was a far cry from the accusations that had greeted the first such announcement in 1971. Numerous reasons can be adduced. No doubt some memories of the war had faded, and those with lived experience of the Japanese Occupation were passing away. Japanese trade and investment in Singapore grew significantly in the 1970s, over-reaching that of Britain[29] and providing opportunities for strengthened ties. In 1980, for instance, the mayor of the Japanese city of Urawa, leading a twenty-three-strong delegation, presented to the SDC a replica plaque of Hirohito's formal surrender message, for display alongside the Japanese surrender waxworks.[30] Moreover, as the Singaporean writer Janadas Devan argued in the 1990s with reference to Singapore-Japan relations, the ruptures and discontinuities of Singapore's past, combined with the economic and social exigencies of its present and future, mean that 'Singapore occurred, and continues to sustain itself, as a result of recurrent acts of forgettings.'[31]

Taken together, these factors testify to a broader transformation in how Singapore was beginning to see itself, both reconceiving its relations with pre-independence occupying powers and working out what its own identity as a nation-state would be. It was now acceptable, indeed desirable, for the general manager of the SDC to justify the opening of the new waxworks by saying: 'We got the tail end but no beginning ... We want Singaporeans to know the whys of the Second World War in relation to Singapore.'[32] The seven years during which hundreds of thousands of visitors annually had gazed exclusively upon the capitulation of the Japanese will also have played a role in rendering the British surrender scene more palatable to Singaporeans.[33] And that will

---

[28] 'Sentosa Adds New Scene to Its Surrender Chamber'.

[29] According to Shimizu, direct investment in Singapore manufacturing by Japan and Britain were, respectively, $68 million and $199 million in 1970, and $801 million and $791 million by 1978. Shimizu, *Japanese Firms in Contemporary Singapore*, p. 40.

[30] 'Chamber Gets the Message', *New Nation*, 26 November 1980, p. 2.

[31] Janadas Devan, 'My Country and My People: Forgetting to Remember', in Kwok Kian-Woon, Kwa Chong Guan, Lily Kong, and Brenda Yeoh (eds.), *Our Place in Time: Exploring Heritage and Memory in Singapore* (Singapore: Singapore Heritage Society), p. 22.

[32] 'Second Waxworks Museum Opens Today'.

[33] SDC took over the management of the waxworks from STPB in February 1976, with successive annual reports from 1976 to 1982 (the first full year of the British Surrender display's operation) giving visitor numbers to the Surrender Chambers as follows: 1976 (252,000, out of a total of 695,081 visitors to Sentosa); 1977 (238,000/632,000); 1978 (263,000/657,000); 1979 (323,000/872,100); 1980 (number not given); 1981 (512,000/1,245,549); 1982 (625,199/1,900,685). During the years when figures were available, Japan was consistently among the top two countries of origin for international tourists to visit Sentosa, and by some margin. For example, 67,312 Japanese tourists visited Sentosa in 1980. By 1982, that number had gone down to 56,789. But with the exception of Malaysia (89,816), no other country's citizens numbered above 20,000 visitors. Sentosa Development Corporation, *Annual Reports*, 1976/7 to 1982/3.

have played its own part in shaping perceptions of the war, especially among the rapidly increasing number of Singaporeans born after 1945.[34] But how accurate would those perceptions have been? What *was* the relationship between the scene depicted and what took place?

1945: What the Waxworks Show

What do the waxworks show? Two rows of men – Japanese officers on one side, Allied representatives on the other – sit at long tables facing each other, flanked by standing Allied personnel. This aesthetic austerity contributes to a seemingly straightforward answer: the waxworks show the formal surrender of all Japanese forces in Southeast Asia to the Allied nations of South East Asia Command (SEAC). Yet the composition actually points to a basic paradox of surrender, namely, that representatives of the losing side must retain sufficient legitimacy to admit defeat, so they and those they represent may thereby be divested *of* that power. The relative symmetry of the waxwork display suggests parity between the two sides; only Mountbatten's raised writing desk and a microphone signal otherwise. This contrasts with the waxworks of the 1942 British surrender to the Japanese that today's Surrender Chamber visitor encounters first. There, Yamashita, backed by the standing figures of his retinue, glares fiercely at Lieutenant-General Arthur Percival and his seated fellow officers, demanding immediate and unconditional surrender (Fig. 7.2). And yet, as already noted, Mountbatten made clear in opening remarks delivered into that now-unattended microphone that the Japanese surrender, too, was unconditional. It is in the relationship between aesthetic parity and power asymmetry that the significatory interest of the Japanese surrender waxworks resides.

The ceremony could take such a simple form because it drew on a vast citational hinterland. Broadly speaking, it referenced established conventions of military surrender. More specifically, it alluded to the multiple surrender ceremonies that preceded it across Southeast Asia and the Pacific.[35] As is always the case where citationality is at issue, an animating tension therefore

---

[34] By 1980, 70 per cent of Singapore's resident population of almost 2.3 million was under thirty-five, and therefore born after the war. Calculated from data available at data.gov.sg, 'Singapore Residents by Age Group, Ethnic Group and Gender, End June, Annual', available at https://data.gov.sg/dataset/resident-population-by-ethnicity-gender-and-age-group (accessed 27 May 2020).

[35] The *Reports of General McArthur* lists Japanese surrenders in thirty-one Asia-Pacific states or territories in the run-up to the surrender in Singapore on 12 September 1945, beginning in Morotai and Halmahera, on Indonesia's Maluku Islands, on 27 August 1945. The actual number is higher, since in some areas, there were multiple ceremonies (e.g., surrender ceremonies on Borneo took place both in Balikpapan in the west and on Labuan island, to the north). See Supreme Commander for the Allied Powers, *Reports of General MacArthur*, 2 vols. (Washington, DC: Centre for Military History, US Army, 1994 [1966]), vol. 1, pp. 458–66.

Figure 7.2 Wax figures of General Tomoyuki Yamashita (second seated
figure from left) and officers in a tableau of the 1942 British surrender
of Singapore.
Photo: Paul Rae.

prevailed between the informing conditions of the ceremony, which resided
elsewhere, and the requirement that the event carry performative force in its own
right. In the case of the Singapore surrender, both features were heightened.

First, the ceremony was subject to a notable logic of displacement that
speaks in part to the unstable nature of citationality, but also to the disorderly
realities of war's end and the transition to civilian rule. Itagaki himself was
standing in for Field Marshal Hisaichi Terauchi, commander of the Southern
Expeditionary Army, who had suffered a stroke in Saigon and was unable to
travel. Terauchi would surrender to Lord Mountbatten in person in
November 1945, before dying the following year of a second stroke.
Although it was reported on the day before the ceremony that the Japanese
officers would surrender their swords at the ceremony,[36] they did not. Itagaki,
his chief of staff, and fourteen other generals would go on to participate in a
further ceremony for this purpose on 22 February 1946 in Kuala Lumpur.

Still more notable in this logic of displacement and surrogacy was the fact
that, in addition to standing in for Terauchi at the 12 September ceremony,

---

[36] "'Victory Day' in Singapore', *Straits Times*, 11 September 1945, p. 1.

Itagaki was, in a sense, standing in for himself. This is because he and his delegation had *already* effectively surrendered to the Allies aboard the HMS *Sussex*, off Singapore, on 4 September, leading to the withdrawal of 35,000 Japanese troops to the peninsula over the ensuing twenty-four hours.[37] This, in turn, placed all the more emphasis on the theatrical and symbolic aspects of the 12 September event. Indeed, in historian Romen Bose's view, the formal ceremony 'was significant purely as a tool to restore British pride and status among the local population'.[38] This was itself part of a broader pattern of performative projections of power by SEAC. The initial planned Allied invasions of Malaya – Operation Zipper, which involved landings on the west coast, to be followed by the massive southwards sweep of Operation Mailfist – were rapidly reworked after it became apparent that Japanese surrender was imminent. A scaled-down version of Zipper went ahead on 2 September, as Air Chief Marshall Sir Keith Park, SEAC's Air Commander-in-Chief, would put it, 'having quickly transferred a proportion of its original strength to Operation "Tiderace" and leaving itself more in the nature of a display of show the flag'.[39] Tiderace was a non-combative replacement for Mailfist, in which a flotilla of ships landed 100,000 Allied personnel in Malaya and Singapore, although, as Bose puts it, 'the fact that they were not fully assault-loaded meant that there would have been significant Allied losses and civilian casualties if the Japanese had resisted'.[40] The reduction in firepower and the changed circumstances of the operations led contemporary and subsequent observers to emphasise their performative dimensions. Describing the flotilla anchored off Morib Beach in Selangor, Park wrote: 'The scene, with every vessel twinkling lights, resembled more a Cowes regatta than one of the largest amphibious operations of the campaign.'[41] Historians Christopher Bayly and Tim Harper write that '[t]he whole series of events was carefully choreographed to impress on the peoples of Asia that Japan had been defeated by force of arms, and to erase the memory of the earlier Allied capitulations'.[42] And Murfett et al. describe Tiderace as 'a three-day propaganda spectacle offering photographic opportunities galore for the British media'.[43] Following the 12 September surrender ceremony itself, Allied representative Admiral Arthur Power lodged a complaint about the number and behaviour of the press in the chamber,

---

[37] Romen Bose, *The End of the War: Singapore's Liberation and the Aftermath of the Second World War* (Singapore: Marshall Cavendish, 2006), p. 157.

[38] Ibid., p. 127.

[39] Air Chief Marshall Sir Keith Park, 'Air Operations in South East Asia 3rd May, 1945 to 12th September, 1945,' *London Gazette (Supplement)*, 19 April 1951, p. 2155.

[40] Bose, *The End of the War*, p. 158.   [41] Park, 'Air Operations in South East Asia', p. 2158.

[42] Christopher Bayly and Tim Harper, *Forgotten Wars: The End of Britain's Asian Empire* (London: Allen Lane, 2007), p. 49

[43] Murfett et al., *Between Two Oceans*, p. 280.

noting that 'the sides and galleries resembled batteries of searchlights', marring 'the conduct of proceedings' by causing them to 'resemble a football match'.[44] Austere though the surrender ceremony may have been, in other words, theatricality nevertheless loomed large.

Moreover, what was played out at the level of mass spectacle was equally at work in mundane details. Bose reports that, after Mountbatten discovered he had forgotten to bring the medal ribbons for his white admiral's uniform for the ceremony the following morning from SEAC headquarters in Kandy, Sri Lanka, he had a subordinate begin to improvise a makeshift set overnight. In the event, the decorations arrived in time for the ceremony on a plane specially despatched for the task. This only reinforces the significance of relatively small-scale symbols in ensuring the legitimacy of the event as a whole.[45]

That said, these somewhat dismissive attitudes about the theatricality of the ceremony – both at the time, as illustrated by the attitude of Power, and today, as expressed by Bose – arguably overlook an additional contextualising element that heightens the stakes of the surrender and raises a further question about its representational status. As Michael Gordin points out, it is easy today to forget how unexpected Emperor Hirohito's capitulation was. While its suddenness has come to be seen as a logical reaction to the unprecedented atomic destruction visited upon Hiroshima and Nagasaki, at the time, it 'caught Washington rather off-guard, unprepared for demobilization or the economic shocks of peace'.[46] That suddenness also altered the nature of the surrender. As John Sbrega puts it, the 'unexpected end of the war had stranded millions of Japanese troops in largely intact units throughout the Far East ... Many of these units, bewildered by the Tokyo government's inexplicable capitulation to Allied demands, held positions of great strength.'[47] Mountbatten was aware of this threat and wrote to MacArthur expressing his concern that the circumstances of the capitulation would 'enable the Japanese leaders to delude their people into thinking they were defeated only by the scientists and not in battle, unless we can so humble them that the completeness of defeat is brought home

---

[44] Bose, *The End of the War*, p. 253.

[45] Recounted in a report by Richard Munby, a sergeant in the Royal Signals attached to Mountbatten's personal staff. Cited in Bose, *The End of the War*, p. 115. In a distant but resonant historical echo of this detail, the Sentosa Development Corporation reported in 1977 that '[i]mprovements were made to authenticate the uniforms of a few of the wax figures in the Surrender Chamber', including the addition of a pair of King George VI Cyphers to the epaulettes of Mountbatten's uniform. Sentosa Development Corporation, *Annual Report for the Year Ended 31 March 1977* (Singapore: Sentosa Development Corporation, 1977), p. 11.

[46] Michael D. Gordin, *Five Days in August: How World War II Became a Nuclear War* (Princeton, NJ: Princeton University Press, 2007), p. 7.

[47] J. J. Sbrega, 'The Japanese Surrender: Some Unexpected Consequences in Southeast Asia', *Asian Affairs: An American Review*, 7:1 (1979), 46.

to them'.[48] Indeed, Itagaki had delayed in agreeing to the surrender in Singapore, flying to Saigon three days after Hirohito's 15 August surrender announcement to consult with Terauchi. It was only after Prince Kan'in flew to Singapore with a copy of the Imperial Rescript on 20 August that, on 22 August, Itagaki finally ordered his officers to abide by its terms. On 12 September, the *Straits Times* briefly reported that 300 Japanese officers had committed suicide with hand grenades after drinking sake together, as had a separate platoon.[49]

Clearly, it fell to the surrender ceremony to serve a distinctive role, carrying not only symbolic significance but performative force so as to diminish the likelihood of further resistance to disarmament and demobilisation from a large and indignant Japanese Army. Indeed, so tenuous was the Allied grip on power in Singapore, one has to wonder how much the ceremony comprised a formal representation of a change in state and governance, and how much it was simply an isolated event that referred first and foremost to its own enactment. Personnel shortages meant Japanese soldiers were drafted to guard the parade route of their own surrender,[50] and Mountbatten openly included Communist guerrillas from the Malayan People's Anti-Japanese Army (MPAJA) in the event. They had fought alongside the Allies during the Japanese occupation, but had developed a powerful anti-colonial ideology, informed in part by Japanese narratives of western colonial oppression. While Mountbatten was aiming to reinitiate British control of Malaya, his early accommodation of the MPAJA would be instrumental in its seeking greater political power, ultimately leading to the so-called Malayan Emergency when its members found their plans frustrated.[51]

Meanwhile, refracting the original surrender ceremony through the waxworks throws into relief a particularly intriguing detail: the eye-witness account of the *Straits Times* makes multiple references to the 'impassive' and 'immobile' Japanese in the surrender party. With the exception of one 'who twiddles his thumbs and twitches his feet', the delegates remain 'looking straight ahead',[52] a point picked up in the STPB research document, which notes 'the expressionless faces of the Japanese representatives who were

---

[48] Ibid., p. 47.

[49] 'Mass Hara Kiri', *Straits Times*, 12 September 1945, p. 2. For other reports of *hara kiri* in Singapore at the time, see Lee Geok Boi, *The Syonan Years: Singapore under Japanese Rule 1942–1945* (Singapore: Singapore National Archives and Epigram, 2005), pp. 270–71.

[50] Murfett et al., *Between Two Oceans*, p. 282.

[51] For a detailed account of the post-surrender mishandling of the MPAJA within the context of the fallout of the war, see John Springhall, 'Mountbatten versus the Generals: British Military Rule of Singapore, 1945–46', *Journal of Contemporary History*, 36:4 (2001), 635–52.

[52] 'Japanese in Malaysia Surrender at Singapore', *Straits Times*, 13 September 1945, p. 4.

looking straight at the Allied table'.[53] Even accounting for orientalist journalistic clichés about inscrutable Asians, this behaviour strikes a distinctive note. At the very least, we can say that the Japanese officers sought to withdraw their subjectivity from the event; we might venture to say they were withholding their selves from subjugation. Writ large, we can point to a significant cultural hinterland that extolled the virtues of fortitude and composure in the face of suffering: the Imperial Rescript itself called upon Japanese subjects to '[c]ultivate the ways of rectitude' to assist in 'enduring the unendurable and suffering what is insufferable'.[54] Writ small, we might say that this behaviour anticipates the present context in an intriguing way: whether chosen by the principals or produced by the massively straitened circumstances in which they found themselves, the Japanese were already approaching the condition of wax.

Today: What the Waxworks Do

While the basic fact of the Japanese surrender provides a distinct turning point in the history of Singapore, therefore, many of the circumstances surrounding the event suggest its meanings and effects were far from clear-cut. Its composition was improvised, its meanings fragile, its relation to the situation it sought to transform tenuous, and its principles unevenly invested in its execution. It stands to reason that a similarly contingent relationship would obtain between the event that took place in 1945 and the attraction that represents it today. This becomes apparent if we analyse the document *Historical Research on the Surrender Ceremony at City Hall on 12th September 1945*, produced by the STPB in 1971. Written for those creating the exhibit, the document summarises everything its authors could discover about the surrender. Published in 1975, they believed it offered a model of 'the kind of research that is necessary in the development of certain physical tourist projects particularly of a historical nature'.[55] Aspiring to provide sufficient information to create a life-sized, three-dimensional, realistic rendering of the event, however, the document also catalogues everything that was unavailable or incompletely understood about it. This highlights the singular nature of the representation

---

[53] STPB, *Historical Research on the Surrender Ceremony at City Hall on 12th September 1945*, p. 15.

[54] Lee, *The Syonan Years*, p. 275. On the resurgence of Bushido codes of Samurai honour during the war, see O. Benesch, *Inventing the Way of the Samurai: Nationalism, Internationalism and Bushidō in Japan* (Oxford: Oxford University Press, 2014), pp. 174–213. Other cultural sources of such behaviour can be traced to the 'Imperial Rescript to Soldiers and Sailors' of 1882, and the publication of the *Senjinkun*, or *Instructions for the Battlefield*, in 1941.

[55] STPB, *Historical Research on the Surrender Ceremony at City Hall on 12th September 1945*, foreword.

that greets the visitor today and establishes a basis for appreciating its contemporary effects.

For instance, the report notes gaps in contextualising information, such as the identities of five of the seven Japanese officers. The limited number of images available meant that there are gaps in what can be seen, including expressions of the leading figures, close-ups sufficient to distinguish the faces of the Japanese, the legs of the Japanese, relevant details of participants' uniforms and decorations, the positioning of ceremonial guards, and the banners on the pillars of the room. There are no colour images, leading the authors to fret that 'it is impossible for the maker of wax figures to reproduce the colours of the uniforms, decorations, ribbons, skins, hair, etc. of the key Allied persons who took part in the Ceremony'.[56] And since all journalists were positioned in the same place, all visual documentation is from the same angle, with the viewer offered 'mostly left profiles and "three-quarter-face" views of the Japanese representatives'.[57] Overall, the expressed concerns of the report's authors point to the necessity of recreating an event in the round whose documentation was only available from one perspective, with speculation and educated guesswork required to compensate for the missing sides.

Some of this information – such as the identities of the Japanese officers – would be added later. Nevertheless, the STPB researchers' investments both in the information that could be wrung from extant documents and in the cataloguing of the gaps seem to speak of a desire for total visual knowledge that would be disappointed not only for the usual reason that such knowledge is impossible, but, more specifically, because surrenders, as Wagner-Pacifici puts it, 'have unstable representability: they are by nature suffused with deictic deferral and transformations'. This means their representations 'both entail and suppress a sense of an interregnum – a break in the narrative flow of history. And they all struggle to be competent in navigating and successfully signifying this middle ground where an end meets a beginning, where one world meets another.'[58] To encounter the waxworks today is to be presented with a discrete object whose presence and consistency lend it an authority that belies the complexities of the moment it represents. It does so because it is actually a representation *of* representations: a composite of actions and configurations that took place over the course of a ceremony that seemed already to be performing the role of theatrical representation of many other representations: a surrogate event, peopled by surrogates, archived in profile, then filled out by a combination of guesswork and the casts of other people's bodies.

Nor does this rather abstract point mark an end to the chain of stand-ins that arc back through the history of the waxworks. For we have yet to reckon with

---

[56] Ibid., p. 14.   [57] Ibid., p. 12.   [58] Wagner-Pacifici, *The Art of Surrender*, p. 28.

the bodies of the spectators who observe the exhibit, and how they experience its uncanny combination of facticity and contingency – a quality that has only intensified as the waxworks have aged. When the resort island of Sentosa was re-branded and re-launched in 2004, a *Straits Times* article noted:

Before it can be a Singapore idol, it must face the harshest panel of judges: Singaporeans themselves.

Industry insiders say it must overcome decades of prejudice among deeply unimpressed citizens, some of whom possibly still associate it with school excursions to see scary wax figures in the Surrender Chamber.[59]

With the passage of time, the waxworks have become museum pieces in their own right. Nothing in the display reflects on their historicity – the basic fact, for instance, that an ever-greater span of time has elapsed since their inauguration in 1974 than the twenty-nine years between that moment and the event they depict, or that the Mountbatten figure wears a uniform worn by Mountbatten himself, and donated, as reported in 1976, 'to help depict the reality of this historic scene'.[60] At the same time, one has the sense that the figures continue to be displayed more because longevity itself has earned them a privileged claim to unmolested perdurance than because they perform serious educational, historical, or touristic work. Eclipsed both by the 'Images of Singapore' and Madame Tussauds attractions they anticipated and by many more kinetic, immersive tourist experiences on offer today, if anything they testify to the major transformations in Singapore's tourist industry over the past several decades.

But to the curious observer, the relative obsolescence of the exhibit provides an opportunity for quiet reflection on its meanings and effects. *As* waxworks, they participate in a museological tradition of figuration associated today with celebrity, and historically with the macabre notoriety of criminals. Following on from wartime atrocities and the atomic bombs, and foreshadowing the war crimes trials in Tokyo and elsewhere in Asia, the Japanese surrender scene is glossed by the same associations: three of the Japanese depicted were subsequently executed, and in the wake of Mountbatten's assassination by the IRA in 1979, a *Straits Times* obituary would recall his visit to the surrender scene several years previously.[61] But waxworks are not only associated with death by dint of their macabre Tussaudian appeal. The texture and implicit warmth of wax as a material, and the combination of uncanny verisimilitude and absolute stillness it affords, locates the resulting figures unsettlingly between life and death. At least, that was my experience the first time I visited the waxworks in

---

[59] 'Will Extreme Makeover Fix Sentosa's Image Problem?', *Straits Times*, 19 June 2004, p. 1118.
[60] 'Mountbatten's Visit to Chamber Trip down Memory Lane', *Straits Times*, 3 October 1976, p. 9.
[61] 'A Realist Who Set Stage for Dissolution of the British Empire,' *Straits Times*, 29 August 1979.

2016 for this essay. Alone in the exhibit for an hour or so, I could subject them to a level of scrutiny they might not ordinarily be expected to support, and nor I: for to spend time in the Surrender Chamber is to find the historical elements of the scene falling rapidly away, and confronting, instead, the details of hands, eyes, or hair – theirs and your own. It is to feel quickened amongst the eerily still, mortal at a frozen moment. Surrendered.

Here, the unevenness of the STPB's original information becomes apparent: despite an overall attempt at verisimilitude, some parts of the waxworks appear in clearer focus than others. The heads of the Japanese are especially unsettling: the almost uniform buzzcut has left exposed some distinctly mis-shapen craniums. Meanwhile, their Japaneseness is in question: created in the United Kingdom in the early 1970s, one has the impression several of the officers were only tokenistically Japanised versions of western heads. One solution to this blind spot seems to have entailed *giving the Japanese hands*. In almost all extant images of the ceremony, only Itagaki's hands can be seen; those of the others remain hidden in their laps. In the waxworks, five of the seven Japanese officers have their hands on the table (Fig. 7.3). This adds character and dynamism. Indeed, the hands return subjectivity, in wax, to those who withheld it at the event itself: hands can be expressive without being

Figure 7.3 One of the five Japanese officers 'given hands' in the Japanese surrender tableau.
Photo: Paul Rae.

beholden to a distinct reference point as heads are; you can cast them from a stranger of roughly the right size, and no one should mind too much, even if some of them are suspiciously well-manicured for the occasion.

By contrast, the individuality of the Allies is minimised. The contemplative chin-holding of Admiral Arthur Power, apparent in photographs, has been replaced by a more routine table action, with both hands before him. Likewise, while Brigadier K. S. Thimayya largely clasped his hands during the ceremony, footage shows he briefly extended them before him – and it is this fleeting moment that has been captured in the display (Fig. 7.4). If the addition of Japanese hands restores subjectivity, then, the selection of Allied postures from different moments in the ceremony introduces temporality into the frozen exhibit. We are looking not at the tableau of a single moment but at a

Figure 7.4 Allied figures in the Japanese surrender tableau.
Photo: Paul Rae.

'supercut' of appropriate gestures, with poetic license on the part of the Japanese thrown in for good measure.

These are the kinds of observations I had time to make on my first visit to the waxworks. By my second visit, a year later, the exhibit had been reframed by a time-based audio-visual accompaniment. A voiceover and special effects now usher the visitor peristaltically through the separate chambers, with both the British and Japanese surrender waxworks illuminated for short periods within the larger narrative. The technology remains rudimentary: the entirety of the bombings of Hiroshima and Nagasaki is captured in a single strobe flash. Nevertheless, the reframing changes one's engagement with the exhibit. With less time for scrutiny, the representational shortcomings of the waxworks are minimised. Instead, they crystallise the preceding narrative of Japanese invasion and local wartime suffering, the upheavals of the war and the stakes in the surrenders now partially displaced from the waxwork figures into the bodies of spectators themselves. Automated lights guide viewers towards and then away from the things they are invited to look at or listen to, requiring more active, embodied participation as one variously observes, pushes interactive buttons, and bends to listen to small speakers. Dramatic music, coloured and flashing lights, and the shift from light into darkness create an immersive experience that is felt affectively as much, if not more, than processed cognitively. Uncanny when left to their and the visitor's own devices, as previously, the waxworks have now been co-opted into the narrative. There is an equalisation of the various kinds of bodies in the rooms – figures' and visitors' alike – which all take responsibility for registering the meanings and effects of the events depicted. An additional room at the end of the exhibit now rounds out the story. Exiting the chamber, visitors are invited to confess the morality of their participation in the experience by sharing their 'message of peace' on a poppy-shaped post-it note that they can then stick on the 'lest we forget' wall. The messages left during my own visits speak to the different kinds of responses the exhibit provokes:

> 'Singapore stay Peace And No TAX!!!'
> 'After 23 years I again relive the memories of Surrender Chamber'
> 'We will remember them always'
> 'Charles Osborne British Indian Army Engineers one of first into Changi Jail to relieve Japanese commander of his post in 1945'
> 'They should have dropped another bomb.'

Conclusion: The National Minimum?

In November 1981, an overnight power cut threatened both the climate-controlled wax figures and another Sentosa highlight, the 'Coralarium'.

An emergency generator saved one of the two displays. Or, as a newspaper headline put it, 'Generals escaped, fish did not.'[62] The living died, the undead endured. And endure still. The low-level persistence of this rudimentary exhibit – static, misshapen, ever so slowly oozing, barely seeing enough footfall to rise to the level of collective consciousness – remains as the faintest imprint of a moment increasingly distant in time, but whose legacy continues to be reassessed, and to invite controversy. 'In Asia the Second World War was only one intense and awful phase of a much longer conflict,' write Bayly and Harper: 'It continued after 1945 in a range of intense and bloody wars, both civil and against a revived European colonialism.'[63] For Chua Beng Huat, regional reckoning with Japanese aggression was delayed because of the necessity of propping up Japan as a bulwark in the Cold War theatre, and the sense of victimhood that prevailed in Japan as a result of the devastation wrought by the atomic bombs. As a result, '[t]he complex set of relations of this history continues to trouble the region, more than 70 years after the war.'[64] The remains of two generals depicted in the surrender exhibit, Itagaki and Lieutenant-General Heitaro Kimura, are among the fourteen Class A war criminals whose souls are periodically worshipped by Japanese officials at the Yasukuni Shrine, to Chinese and Korean chagrin.

In this chapter, I have suggested that the surrender waxworks' relative minimalism as a significant visual representation is what renders them so interesting. It enables them to hold within themselves, and throw into relief, several features of Singapore-Japan relations that a more iconic and readily reproducible representation might – paradoxically – obscure. Underpinning this is their questionable relation to both diplomacy and the Cold War period, and what this might, in turn, tell us about the nature of such representations. Part of the ambiguity lies in the event that the waxworks represent. Is not unconditional surrender the *opposite* of diplomacy, a coercive exercise of power by one party over another? Perhaps not. As Tarak Barkawi argues, 'diplomacy is central to the administration and conduct of war, and to the constitution and use of force more generally'. Contrasting war and diplomacy fails to recognise that the latter provides 'a permanent extraterritorial infra-structure crucial to military, security, and intelligence activities in other states and societies'.[65] A surrender, we might add, is a moment when such elements achieve distinctive visibility, though this is not to say the deployment of such

---

[62] 'Generals Escaped, Fish Did Not', *New Nation*, 17 November 1981, p. 4.

[63] Bayly and Harper, *Forgotten Wars*, p. xxvii.

[64] Chua Beng Huat, 'State Violence, Social Memory, and the Ethics of Remembrance and Forgiveness in East Asia', *Situations*, 10:1 (2017), 1–22.

[65] Tarak Barkawi, 'Diplomacy, War, and World Politics', in Ole J. Sending, Vincent Pouliot, and Iver B. Neumann (eds.), *Diplomacy and the Making of Modern World Politics* (Cambridge: Cambridge University Press, 2015), pp. 56 and 57.

elements is limited to the dominant party. In her 'transwar' analysis of Japanese diplomacy from 1933 to 1964, *The International Minimum*, Jessamyn Abel demonstrates a sustained Japanese commitment to meeting minimal standards of internationalism – and to the associated virtues of peace, progress, and prosperity – that 'resulted in outlandish contradictions between cooperative rhetoric and aggressive action [during the war], but also led to the development of new modes of engaging with the international community that continued to be used in the profoundly changed circumstances of the postwar period'.[66] Although the surrender exhibit represents a specific and consequential moment in the modern history of Singapore and of Southeast Asia more broadly, it is in relation to these more structural and extended frames of reference that the diplomatic 'work' it has done is best understood.

This points to the exhibit's second important feature: today, its interest lies as much in the meanings it has accrued and the uses to which it has been put, as in the event it depicts. Relatively little of this work has been diplomatic in the state-to-state sense; indeed, the only time that such relations have been explicitly in play have been when first the Japanese, and then the British missions in Singapore were reported to have declined cooperation in the creation of the representations of their respective surrenders to each other. More important was the centrality of the exhibit to the tourist industry in the 1970s and 1980s, and its role as a focal point during visits by Japanese, British, and Australian dignitaries, delegations, and individuals (including former combatants): a mode of public diplomacy performed by communicating aspects of Singapore's history and changing present to foreign visitors.

Ultimately, however, the most significant diplomatic contribution made is also the most elusive: the waxworks contributed to a kind of inverse diplomacy by offering an opportunity for Singapore to think about its own sovereignty. This is something the 2017 addition of the 'lest we forget' wall highlights: by including the voices of Singaporeans in the exhibit, we are reminded that the waxworks themselves shows us a Singapore without Singaporeans – a genuinely striking omission whose meanings have changed over time. Adapting Abel's thinking around Japan's 'international minimum', we might describe the waxworks as representing a 'national minimum': the necessary and constitutive corollary of the internationalism upon which diplomacy is predicated.[67]

Against this backdrop, a depiction of the Japanese surrendering to the Allies becomes a mechanism for Singaporeans to tell themselves something about who they were, and could become. Indeed, revisiting the end of the war in

---

[66] Jessamyn R. Abel, *The International Minimum: Creativity and Contradiction in Japan's Global Engagement, 1933–1964* (Honolulu: University of Hawai'i Press, 2015), pp. 3–4.

[67] As Abel points out, a core principle of her own argument is that internationalism and nationalism are 'interrelated, rather than mutually exclusive'. Abel, *The International Minimum*, p. 10.

1945 from the vantage of nascent nation-building in the 1970s was arguably a way of joining up two moments of relative political clarity and setting aside the long interregnum of the Emergency and the failed attempt at federation with Malaysia (1963–65), which had significantly muddied the waters of allegiance and identity. Wagner-Pacifici gestures to the psychology of such a moment: 'The witnesses of historical transformations are positioned to observe some-thing that happens in "real time" and yet must also attest to that happening by freezing time.... They are called on to bear witness to a vision of the world that is remade at the very moment when witnessing becomes relevant.'[68] If the surrender waxworks was one such freezing of time, they tell us as much about those who observe as those depicted. While the Japanese and Allied forces were long gone by 1974, the waxworks testified to the prevailing and increas-ingly self-reflective presence of Singaporeans as witnesses. Today, the desul-tory waxworks of the Surrender Chamber seem out of time as exhibits, but perhaps that is the reason they align so well with their subject matter. They depict a pivotal event combining decisiveness and contingency that fired the starting gun on the antagonisms and transformations of post-war Southeast Asia. Their creation tells the story of Singapore's changing attitudes towards Japan, and sense of itself. Their enduring, uncanny effects teach those who visit them what it means to be witness to a diplomatic act, at ever greater distance, as time pays out.

---

[68] Wagner-Pacifici, *The Art of Surrender*, p. 42.

8   Cosmic Envoy

Interkosmos and the Poetics of Late Socialist Spaceflight

Gerard Sasges

On 23 July 1980, the Vietnamese pilot Phạm Tuân became the first Asian and the first citizen of a developing nation to fly in space. Tuân's spaceflight was part of the Interkosmos program of joint crewed spaceflights between 1978 and 1988 that saw fourteen non-Soviet cosmonauts fly on missions to the Salyut and later Mir space stations.[1] The Czechoslovakian Vladimír Remek flew first in 1978, followed by comrades from Poland, the German Democratic Republic (GDR), Bulgaria, and Hungary. The year 1980 saw a turn to the developing world with flights by Phạm Tuân and Arnaldo Tamayo Méndez of Cuba. Even the first Western European to fly in space, Jean-Loup Chrétien of France, did so as part of the Soviet-led program in 1982.

The Interkosmos spaceflights were highly complex, elaborately staged, and hugely expensive exercises, and one has to ask what exactly they were meant to achieve beyond the simple resupply of Soviet orbital stations. This chapter argues that the missions were a powerful means of encoding – both symbolically and materially – the complex relationship between the Soviet Union and its international partners. The images and other texts produced to document the mission operated at multiple levels, symbolizing not only two nations' relationship with each other but also their citizens' relationship with an imagined future. In this way, the photographic record of an extraordinary event like a space mission can be read to reveal the quotidian functioning of Cold War diplomacy.

In this chapter, I explore the poetics of Vietnamese spaceflight in two types of texts: one is photographs from the archives of the Vietnam News Agency, the other is articles from the Vietnamese People's Armed Forces daily newspaper (*Quân đội nhân dân*). Together, they document Phạm Tuân's journey to the centre of the socialist world by way of the Salyut space station. These texts

---

[1] Research for this chapter was supported in part by the MOE AcRF – Tier 1 Grant Number R R-117-000-048-115. I'd like to thank Per Anders, Chris Goscha, Vu Tuong, and Liam Kelley for their invaluable input on earlier drafts of the chapter. Translations, along with any errors, are my own.

The program dates to the late 1960s with uncrewed missions.

emerge from the intersection of Soviet and Vietnamese agendas: the rituals of spaceflight may have been created by Soviet engineers and officials, but they were participated in, documented by, and reimagined for Vietnamese. The story they tell points simultaneously to an imagined socialist future and to a long history of Vietnamese engagement with powerful patrons. It is a story that allowed Vietnamese to acknowledge the immense disparities that marked the relationship yet be proud of their contributions to a shared socialist project. Above all, it is a story that transcended simple material benefit and reflected a genuine belief in the transformative power of a socialist civility defined not only in terms of science, technology, and industry but also in terms of its capacity to transform the human and the social.

New Heroes and Old Rituals

Since the beginning, manned spaceflight has mixed theatre and ritual. In the 1960s at the height of the Cold War, theatre predominated. Its plots featured heroic pioneers, risking their lives to achieve spectacular firsts and push the frontiers of human dominion – and Soviet and American competition – beyond the boundaries of the earth itself. But by the 1970s, both spaceflight and geopolitics had changed, and the theatrical had been overtaken by the ritual. The Interkosmos flights were not firsts, nor did they push boundaries in exciting new ways. Instead, they were routine and ritualized. Each followed the same script: training in Star City at the Yuri Gagarin Cosmonaut Training Center, launch from the Baikonur Cosmodrome, and a week of work aboard the Salyut or Mir space stations. At least part of cosmonauts' research would be devoted to work with material chosen to represent their nation of origin: East German optics for remote sensing, for example, or the Vietnamese water fern. Immediately upon returning, the non-Soviet national would sign the capsule that had returned them safely to earth, conduct the first of many interviews and receptions, and then slowly circle in on the centre of Soviet power by way of the Baikonur Cosmodrome, Star City, and finally the Kremlin, where they would receive the Order of the Soviet Union. Following their investiture at the Kremlin, the Interkosmos crew would then travel to the foreign cosmonaut's home country, where the Soviet medals would be reciprocated with the local equivalent. The stability of the script even when the program was expanded to include non-aligned or pro-Western nations like India, Austria, or France underlines its ritual nature.

Phạm Tuân was an ideal participant for the ritual. Benoît de Tréglodé has explored how the figures of the exemplary 'Emulation Fighters' and 'New Heroes' were deployed by the regime in Hanoi after 1945 as part of its efforts to transform and to control the new nation. The practice had its roots in the Soviet New Man and the emulation campaigns of the 1930s that created 'the outlines of a new internationalist ideal ready for export to the socialist world'.[2] According to de Tréglodé, in Vietnam the figure of the hero looked both to the past and to the future: playing on older traditions of exemplary elite leadership and of resistance to foreign aggression while at the same time serving as the human incarnation of socialist transformation.[3]

Phạm Tuân's biography suited him perfectly to the role: son of poor farmers in rural Thái Bình, he volunteered for the army at the age of eighteen and completed his training as a fighter pilot in the USSR two years later. After further training in night combat, he was credited with downing an American B-52 bomber in December 1972 and recognized as a Hero of the Vietnamese People's Armed Forces.[4] Here was the Vietnamese New Man who could simultaneously inspire his compatriots to ever greater feats of emulation, while fitting seamlessly into global socialist idioms and rituals like Interkosmos.

Interkosmos expressed international socialist cooperation and solidarity at the same time it confirmed Soviet leadership of the socialist bloc. Yet if we look beyond the science and technology, there are clear parallels with the system that for hundreds of years saw envoys from the different realms of the Sinitic cultural world – places like Japan, Korea, and Vietnam – undertake ritualized journeys to the centre of the Middle Kingdom. Highly trained scholars who were deemed to possess exemplary moral and intellectual qualities were selected as representatives. They were invested with high rank, provided with gifts and an entourage, and feasted before being sent on their journey. Over the course of their travels, these envoys would be exposed to the marvels of the Middle Kingdom and interact with other scholars and envoys in a process that would not only confirm the superiority of their shared civilization, but also promote their own moral perfection.

Like the relationship of the Soviet Union to its allies, the nature of this system has been hard to grasp for modern scholars accustomed to think of interstate relations in binaries of equality or subservience, independence or dependence. Where previous generations of scholars characterized Vietnam's relationship with China in terms of 'tribute' and 'vassalage', post-colonial scholars have tended to see envoy missions as strategic acts of submission that hid the nation's fiercely defended independence. However, the scholar of early-modern Vietnam, Liam Kelley, has used a close reading of the poetry of Vietnamese to suggest an alternate reading. Although Vietnamese envoys saw their own domain as politically separate from that of their powerful neighbour

---

[2] Benoit de Tréglodé, *Heroes and Revolution in Vietnam, 1948–1964* (Singapore: NUS Press, 2012), p. 27.

[3] Ibid., pp. 11–38.

[4] American sources dispute this claim, contending that the B-52 was brought down by surface-to-air missiles.

to the north, at the same time they saw it as one of the realms of 'manifest civility', with a basis in a shared body of texts and radiating from a centre located in the northern capital of Beijing. Like the rest of the early-modern Vietnamese elite, these high officials 'endeavoured in countless ways to ensure that their domain stay on "the same tracks" as the Middle Kingdom. They did this out of a belief in the "benefit" that participation in this larger world would bring, a benefit that was the result not of cold calculations but of a passionate and sincere belief in the transformative power of a shared civility and its texts, rituals, and language.'[5]

In many ways, these contrasting interpretations of diplomacy in the Sinitic world can be mapped onto changing understandings of the Cold War. Where once scholars emphasized Soviet or American hegemony, more recently others have found instead the agency of post-colonial actors who used superpower support to their own ends.[6] Both interpretations take an ironic stance: the former based on the knowledge that the seemingly unassailable Cold War system was about to collapse, the latter based on the recasting of superpowers as super dupes. But the relationship of the Soviet Union and its partners, like that of the Chinese to the larger Sinitic sphere, was more complex than this irony allows. And that relationship was constituted not just in terms of the military, economic, or technological forms that are the basis of conventional analyses but also in terms of culture and symbol.

Irony is certainly the dominant mode when we think about post-1975 Vietnam and its relationship to the Soviet bloc. Conditioned by what we think we know about 'renovation' and 'transition', the period is easily reducible to hardship, necessity, and the gradual building of a wave of 'reform'.[7] Vietnamese working in the Eastern bloc have little patience for socialist solidarity, but instead spend their time devising ways to evade export controls and smuggle home gold, watches, and the occasional motorcycle.[8] Ask any Vietnamese about Phạm Tuân today, and the response will almost certainly include a reference to popular sayings like the one recorded by the journalist

---

[5] Liam Kelley, *Beyond the Bronze Pillars: Envoy Poetry and the Sino-Vietnamese Relationship* (Honolulu: University of Hawaii Press, 2005), p. 197.

[6] For an account of the Cold War as a story of US and Soviet intervention in the 'Third World', see Odd Arne Westad, *The Global Cold War: Third World Interventions and the Making of Our Times* (Cambridge: Cambridge University Press, 2007). For a response from the 'Third World', see Clapperton Mavhunga, 'A Plundering Tiger with Its Deadly Cubs? The USSR and China as Weapons in the Engineering of a "Zimbabwean Nation"', in Gabrielle Hecht (ed.), *Entangled Geographies: Empire and Technopolitics in the Global Cold War* (Cambridge, MA: MIT Press, 2011).

[7] See David W. P. Elliot, *Changing Worlds: Vietnam's Transition from Cold War to Globalization* (Oxford: Oxford University Press, 2012).

[8] Alena K. Alamgir, 'The Moped Diaries: Remittances in the Czechoslovak-Vietnamese Labor Migration Scheme', in Mahua Sarkar (ed.), *Work out of Place* (Berlin: De Gruyter, 2018).

and historian Huy Đức, which roughly translated runs: 'Even though we scrimp, we must still pad the rice with sorghum; so what the hell are you going into space for, Tuân?'[9]

Yet while these examples are all true, they get us only so far. They fail, for example, to explain how the Party General Secretary and supposed market reformer Nguyễn Văn Linh might find himself in Berlin in October 1989, just weeks before the opening of the Berlin Wall, pleading with other communist leaders for a global alliance to save socialism.[10] In more cultural terms, they don't explain the strange love of Northern Vietnamese for smoked sausages and Czech-style pilsner beer. Nor do they make space for a generation of women named 'Nga', a given name with the double meaning of 'Moon' and 'Russia'. Indeed, the well-known love of Vietnamese for wordplay, so frustrating for translators, points to the sort of 'seeing in stereo' this period demands: when thinking about late socialist Vietnam and its relationship with the USSR we need to see multiple possibilities at once: satire and sincerity, realism and idealism, scepticism and faith. Above all, it demands that we take the period on its own terms, not ones predicated on the impending collapse of the Eastern bloc and the Vietnamese embrace of market reforms.

It also captures a historical moment when the Communist leadership in Hanoi, after years of negotiating a trajectory between the two poles of Beijing and Moscow, was finally entering fully into the Soviet orbit.[11] After the Sino-Soviet split intensified in the 1960s, this negotiation had grown increasingly difficult. Yet despite Vietnam's growing dependence on Soviet military aid, Soviet leaders remained unable to convince their Vietnamese allies to adopt an explicitly pro-Soviet standpoint. It was only with the end of the Second Indochina War that relations between Vietnamese and Chinese Communists finally broke down completely as Chinese leaders responded to a perceived threat of encirclement and to Vietnamese pretensions to an Indochinese sphere of interest. The Chinese suspension of aid in May 1978 saw Vietnam join the Council for Mutual Economic Assistance (COMECON) the following month; by November, Vietnam and the USSR had signed a twenty-five-year mutual defence treaty. In February 1979 China responded to Vietnam's invasion of Cambodia with its own invasion across Vietnam's northern border. While the attack did not compel the withdrawal of Vietnamese troops from Cambodia, it did make it clear to Vietnamese leaders the realities of living with a hostile

---

[9] 'Bo bo còn phải độn mì / Mi lên vũ trụ làm gì hở Tuân.' Huy Đức, *Bên Thắng Cuộc, vol. 1: Giải Phóng* (Los Angeles: OsinBook, 2012), p. 330 n. 512. My thanks to Jason Picard for this reference.

[10] Vu Tuong, *Vietnam's Communist Revolution: The Power and Limits of Ideology* (New York: Cambridge University Press, 2017), p. 261.

[11] On wartime Soviet policies toward the Democratic Republic of Vietnam, see Ilya Gaiduk, *The Soviet Union and the Vietnam War* (Chicago: Ivan R. Dee, 1996).

China and leave them little choice but to tie their fortunes to that of the Soviet-led block.

Hungarian scholar Balazs Szalontai has used the archives of the Eastern bloc foreign policy working group, Interkit, to explore the evolution of the Soviet-Vietnamese relationship between 1967 and 1985.[12] It was a complicated evolution that simultaneously reflected Soviet strategic concerns in the face of Chinese 'hegemonism', Vietnamese ambitions to consolidate political and military control over Indochina, and broader concerns to shore up an Eastern bloc in the face of the increasingly fluid geopolitical situation of the 1980s. As Szalontai's article shows, it was a relationship best described as one of complex interdependence.

This relationship, I argue, can be read not only in foreign ministry archives but also in the poetics of spaceflight. Unlike an envoy-diplomat from centuries past, Phạm Tuân was no poet. He was a soldier and a pilot, a man of action, not words. Poets were in his entourage, though. Soviet and Vietnamese photographers and filmmakers documented every step in the formation of the trainee cosmonaut. And as the spaceflight approached, the entourage was swelled by journalists who would provide coverage of the historic event in print, on radio, and on state television. Through these various media, millions of Vietnamese were able to participate virtually in Tuân's envoy mission and to experience the same encodings of a Soviet-led socialist civility expressed above all in its industrial and technological achievements. Yet while the technology and the hero may have been new, the rituals had a long history.

Spaceflight as Theatre, Spaceflight as Ritual

From the beginning, Soviet and American space programs were part of global diplomacy. Along with cultural missions, international exhibitions, and grandiose development plans, space programs were intended to demonstrate technological and ideological superiority at the same time they set out national cultural ideals embodied in the person of the cosmonaut/astronaut. As a result, administrators on both sides controlled the minutest aspects of the programs' public faces. From the careful polishing of Sputnik's aluminium-alloy shell that rendered visible its trajectory across the American night sky to the exhausting schedule of public appearances by space pioneers like Gargarin, Titov, and Tereshkova to *LIFE* magazine's exclusive contract with the Mercury astronauts and their families, enormous energies were expended to ensure the programs and their heroes projected appropriate images of the

---

[12] Balazs Szalontai, 'Solidarity within Limits: Interkit and the Evolution of the Soviet Bloc's Indochina Policy, 1967–1985', *Cold War History*, 17:4 (2017), 385–403.

nation to audiences both at home and abroad.[13] The results were sometimes less than ideal. Publishers in the United States, for example, complained that interviews were so carefully vetted that US astronauts inevitably appeared 'deodorized, plasticized, and homogenized'.[14] Yet if the performance may have lacked spontaneity, space programs were nevertheless one of the Cold War's most visible expressions of soft power, allowing the world's super-powers to perform their visions of the nation on a truly cosmic stage.

Space programs were ideally suited to promote an idealized vision of the nation that was simultaneously social and individual. On the one side, they demonstrated the technological mastery on which visions of prosperous and harmonious future societies were imagined to depend; on the other hand, cosmonauts and astronauts were held up as personal examples of the skilled, industrious, self-sacrificing men and women who would realize these futures. In the Soviet Union this vision of a utopian future found its clearest expression in the Third Party Program, adopted in 1961. The ambitious program – the first since 1917 – marked a new phase in Premier Nikita Khrushchev's policies of de-Stalinization and liberalization.[15] It contained detailed blueprints for eco-nomic, technological, and social advances that would allow the USSR to surpass the United States in production; to provide housing, consumer goods, and leisure time to the mass of Soviet citizens; and finally to realize the promise of communism, all within just twenty years. As the program's final line proclaimed, 'the current generation of Soviet people will live under communism'. Along with other achievements like the testing of the world's most powerful thermonuclear device, the gargantuan Volgograd hydroelectric plant, or the 'Khruschyovka' prefabricated apartment complexes that sprouted across the USSR in the 1960s, the Soviet space program and its impressive string of firsts seemed to confirm the capacity of Soviet science and technology to overcome social, economic, and political problems and usher in a new era of peace and prosperity.[16]

This vision of the future would be realized by the Soviet 'New Man'. The Third Party Program included a twelve-point 'Moral Code of the Builder of Communism' that highlighted such qualities as devotion to communism, commitment to labour for the good of society, mutual respect between

---

[13] The following discussion of representations of the Soviet space program and its relationship to Soviet society is indebted to the scholarship of Slava Gerovitch. See particularly Slava Gerovitch, *Soviet Space Mythologies: Public Images, Private Memories and the Making of a Cultural Identity* (Pittsburgh: University of Pittsburgh Press, 2015). See also Matthew Hersch, *Inventing the American Astronaut* (London: Palgrave, 2012).

[14] Walter Cunningham, *The All-American Boys* (New York: J Boylston, 2009), p. 192.

[15] William Taubman, *Khrushchev: The Man and His Era* (New York: W. W. Norton, 2003).

[16] Paul Josephson, 'Rockets, Reactors, and Soviet Culture', in Loren Graham (ed.), *Science and Soviet Social Order* (Cambridge, MA: Harvard University Press, 1990), pp. 169–177.

individuals, moral purity, modesty in social and private life, mutual respect in the family, and solidarity with the working people of all countries. Cosmonauts were held to embody these virtues in all aspects of their professional and private lives, from training to spaceflight to participation in household chores. 'On the one hand, the cosmonauts were portrayed as exceptional human beings, glorifying the Motherland with their heroic deeds. On the other, the media stressed that the cosmonauts were just like ordinary people – coming from a humble background, living regular family lives, and pursuing usual pastimes – and thus embodying the very spirit of the Soviet people.'[17] Where the space program served as a powerful symbol of an imminent future society, its cosmonauts symbolized the New Man, who was both exceptional and ordinary, both product and producer of this world.

These exemplars of the Soviet New Man were subjected to a gruelling program of public appearances both at home and abroad. Between 1961 and 1970, cosmonauts attended more than 6,000 public events in the Soviet Union alone. Foreign trips were an important part of projecting this new vision on a global stage. In the four months after his historic spaceflight, Gargarin visited nine different countries, some close allies such as Bulgaria or Cuba, and others core members of the Western bloc such as Canada and the United Kingdom. In an interview, Gargarin once compared the cosmonaut's burden of fame to the g-forces they endured during take-off. Yet thanks to tireless work by the first generation of cosmonauts, the public image of the USSR underwent major change. Slava Gerovitch writes how 'Gargarin's natural charisma, geniality, and openness began to shape a new image of the Soviet man abroad. The old imagery – the menacing-looking dictator Stalin, the dogmatic Party bureaucrat, and the stern Soviet soldier – was replaced by this cheerful and charming young man.'[18]

This projection of Soviet soft power extended to the Democratic Republic of Vietnam (DRV). Hanoi media chronicled the exploits of the Soviet space program, underlining how 'the successes of our Soviet brothers and sisters are also successes shared in by all socialist republics'.[19] Following Gherman Titov's multiple-orbit mission in April 1961, then-President Hồ Chí Minh was moved to pen two articles for the *People's Daily*. The articles denigrated the relative lack of success of the American space program to date and attributed

---

[17] Gerovitch, *Soviet Space Mythologies*, p. 138. See also Iina Kohonen, 'The Heroic and the Ordinary: Photographic Representations of Soviet Cosmonauts in the Early 1960s', in Eva Maurer et al. (eds.), *Soviet Space Culture: Cosmic Enthusiasm in Socialist Societies* (London: Palgrave, 2011).

[18] Gerovitch, *Soviet Space Mythologies*, p. 139.

[19] Chu Thị Ngọc Lan, 'Chủ Tịch Hồ Chí Minh với anh hùng vũ trụ G.S. Titôp', http://ditichhochiminhphuchutich.gov.vn/articledetail.aspx?articleid=556&sitepageid=556#sthash.obAJ56Tt.dpbs, accessed 7 March 2018.

Soviet achievements to the superiority of the socialist system.[20] In January 1962, Titov made an official visit to the DRV, then rapidly escalating its struggle with its southern-based rival, the Republic of Vietnam (RVN). During a visit tightly packed with appearances, Titov was awarded the Vietnamese Order of the Hero of Labour and accompanied Hồ Chí Minh on a visit to picturesque Halong Bay, where the President renamed one of the bay's islands 'Titov Island' (Đảo Ti Tốp).[21] Reflecting on the honour, Titov explained to his Vietnamese hosts that Soviet cosmonauts had accomplished their spaceflights in order 'to preserve peace, to allow every person to dream and sleep soundly, so that every morning they can awake to see the sun in the sky'.[22]

While official visits and media coverage may have been meticulously crafted, nevertheless public enthusiasm for spaceflight and its heroes was real, particularly in the early days. For much of the 1960s, a remarkable series of firsts seemed to proclaim the superiority of Soviet technology and, as Hồ Chí Minh argued, the socialist system. The historian Loren Graham, present at Gargarin's triumphal Red Square reception in April 1961, writes that the day marked 'the apogee in Soviet citizens' belief that they held the key to the future of civilization. The celebrations on the street were genuine and heartfelt. Soviet science was, they were sure, the best in the world, and Soviet rockets succeeded where American ones failed.'[23] At the same time, the fact that a few select humans had finally escaped from earth's gravity seemed to hold out the promise that others too might one day escape the grip of life's mundane realities. In his biography of Gargarin, Andrew Jenks writes that 'many Soviets believed that the launching of a man into space, like the coming of Christ, presaged the dawning of a new age – as if rockets could somehow liberate people from the constraints, cramped apartments, tedium, petty arguments, boring jobs, gritty poverty, and injustices of daily life'.[24]

If anything, Vietnamese in 1980 had at least as much reason to dream of a better world as their Soviet counterparts had a generation earlier. And while Vietnamese science and technology may have lagged behind that of the USSR, nevertheless, the recent history of victory in the Second Indochina War offered ample proof of the nation's capacity to succeed in the face of overwhelming odds, thanks to determination, sacrifice, hard work, and the indomitable will of the people. Thus, as they crafted their narratives of Vietnamese spaceflight, officials and journalists could tap into many of the same subjective yearnings as had earlier Soviet propagandists.

---

[20] 'Vượt hơn 1428 lần', *Nhân dân* 10 August 1961, and 'Hai chế độ, hai kết quả', *Nhân dân*, 16 August 1961. The president wrote under the pseudonym 'TL'.
[21] It had previously been known as Cát Nàng island.   [22] *Nhân dân*, 24 January 1962.
[23] Loren Graham, *Moscow Stories* (Bloomington: Indiana University Press, 2006), pp. 18–19.
[24] Andrew Jenks, *The Cosmonaut Who Couldn't Stop Smiling: The Life and Legend of Yuri Gagarin* (DeKalb: Northern Illinois University Press, 2012), p. 152.

At the same time, however, spaceflight had undergone important shifts in the intervening decades. One was the partial eclipse of the Soviet space program by the American. After an impressive string of firsts that included the first artificial satellite in orbit and the first man in space, by the end of the 1960s the Soviet space program had lost ground to the American program. This was symbolized most dramatically by the US moon landing in 1969 and the effective termination of the Soviet moon landing program in 1974.[25] The result was to shift resources to the development of orbital space stations. The Salyut (Russian for 'Salute' or 'Fireworks'; Vietnamese: 'Chào Mừng', or 'Welcome') program consisted of a series of four crewed scientific research orbital stations and two crewed military reconnaissance orbital stations between 1971 and 1986. Missions aboard the civilian stations included research on topics such as astronomy, biology, earth observations, and the study of the effects of spaceflight on the human body. The success of the Salyut program contrasted with that of the American Skylab station. After suffering damage during launch in May 1973, Skylab was occupied only for about twenty-four weeks and fell to earth spectacularly in 1979. Thus, the Salyut program allowed the Soviets once again to claim a leading role in space exploration at the same time as they effected a narrative shift from spaceflight as exclusively Soviet theatre to spaceflight as a ritual in which envoys from all the socialist domains might take part.

Ritual 1: Testing the New Hero

Two complete crews trained for each Interkosmos mission. The mission that left for Moscow in April 1979 was thus led by two envoys, Lieutenant Colonel Phạm Tuân and Captain Bùi Thanh Liêm. Their ranks signalled Tuân's potential primacy, yet the final selection would be made only at the last moment.[26] Each man was assigned a Soviet counterpart, went through the same training, and participated in exactly the same photo ops until the final selection just days before the launch. At least in the archives, the photographic and cinemagraphic records of Interkosmos unfold in stereo, with the two trainees appearing in eerily similar images. At events where the two appear together, neither one is given obvious priority.

Fig. 8.1 shows Tuân at 'Star City' undergoing vestibular training on a 'spin chair'. Photos of cosmonauts undergoing gruelling training and testing were a standard feature of Soviet space imagery. Complex, highly specialized pieces of equipment like this one emphasized the futuristic technologies that made

---

[25] The crewed lunar flyby 'Zond' program was cancelled in 1970; the crewed lunar landing N1/L3 program was effectively terminated in 1974 and officially cancelled in 1976. Details of the abortive Soviet lunar program were only made public after 1990.

[26] While Tuân may have outranked Liêm, the latter was better connected: his father-in-law was the famed Southern revolutionary Dương Quang Đông.

Figure 8.1 'Vietnamese Cosmonaut Practices on the Turning Disc at the Salyut Training Station'. AF.3653.
Uncredited. Copyright Vietnam News Agency. Used with permission.

space flight possible, and the stoic, confident expressions of cosmonauts confirmed them as exemplary heroes. In this image, the impression is further enhanced by a low-angle shot and dramatic lighting. Implicitly, the images were metaphors for the creation of a new kind of people and a new kind of society. As an article in the *Armed Forces Daily* put it, 'the real product of Star City is human: the socialist human'.[27]

Ritual 2: An Inclusive Socialism

In Fig. 8.2, the Vietnamese trainees flank their Soviet crewmates, Valeri Bykovsky and Viktor Gorbatko. They are walking along 'Cosmonauts Alley', in northern Moscow, a broad, tree-lined pedestrian avenue featuring stone memorials to important figures in the Soviet space program. In the background, at the far end of the avenue, is the 'Monument to the Conquerors of Space'. The 107-metre-tall, titanium-clad monument, completed in 1964, depicts a rocket soaring into space on a plume of exhaust.[28] A poem at the monument's base proclaimed that the Soviet people have 'forged these flaming wings' in order to 'overcome powerlessness and darkness' for the benefit of an entire age.

---

[27] 'Thành phố Ngôi Sao: Năm tháng con người, kỳ tích', *Quân Đội Nhân Dân*, 27 July 1980.
[28] The following year would see the completion of the Memorial Museum of Cosmonautics located at the base of the monument.

Figure 8.2 'Soviet and Vietnamese Cosmonauts Strolling on Cosmonauts Alley in the Soviet Union'. AF.3613.
Uncredited. Copyright Vietnam News Agency. Used with permission.

The visit was meant to materialize, for audiences in Vietnam as much as for the two trainees, the achievements of an earlier generation of cosmonauts who had led the way in space exploration. But it also promoted a certain vision of socialist civility. In 1980, the avenue already featured busts of the first man in space, Yuri Gargarin, and the first man to undertake extravehicular activity in space, Alexei Leonov. Thus, it is significant that the photographer posed the four men in front of the bust of Valentina Tereshkova, who in 1963 became the first woman in space. After retiring from active duty as a cosmonaut, Tereshkova became a deputy to the Supreme Soviet and served as the Soviet representative to a variety of international initiatives on the theme of women and peace, including the World Peace Council in 1966, the UN Conference for the International Women's Year in 1975, and the World Conference on Women in Copenhagen in 1980. The decision to pose the four men in front of a picture of the famous female cosmonaut and campaigner for women's rights thus encodes a vision of socialist civility in which men and women, from the developed world and the developing world alike, might participate equally.

Ritual 3: Brothers in Training

Fig. 8.3 shows Phạm Tuân and Viktor Gorbatko training in a mock-up of the Salyut space station. Tuan reaches forward to the control panel while

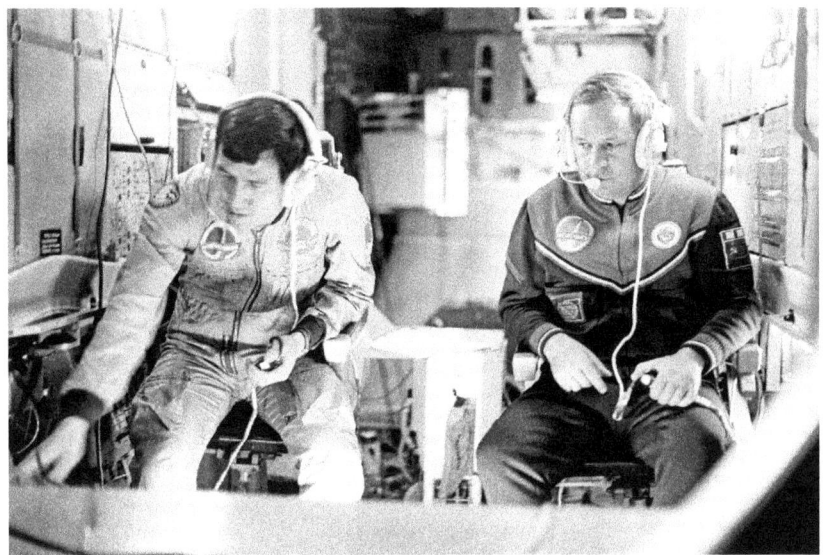

Figure 8.3 'The Team of Gorbatko and Phạm Tuân Practice in the Spacecraft at the Salyut Training Station'. AF.4295.
Credit: Tiến Dũng. Copyright Vietnam News Agency. Used with permission.

Gorbatko watches cautiously. Stock images like these underlined the dedication, hard work, and courage of cosmonauts and the difficulty of the tasks they were called upon to perform. The Interkosmos program and its practice of pairing experienced Soviet commanders with less experienced 'research cosmonauts' added another layer to the underlying narrative. In an interview, Tuân related how

Before, I was just a farmer's child, born in a thatched hut, tending the buffalos and growing rice; now I've taken on an extremely difficult and complicated mission. Victor Gorbatko told me, 'No problem at all, Tuân. I also had to start from A, B, C: together, we'll be able to do it all.' Not much later, he himself made it known that the Soviet-Vietnamese flight crew had grasped the entire program and that there were no more difficult problems.[29]

The passage conveys the two central points of the story of Vietnamese spaceflight: Phạm Tuân was an ordinary Vietnamese from the countryside, called upon to perform a difficult and daunting task. Yet thanks to the help of his older, more experienced Soviet brothers, challenges would be overcome and the mission completed. Tuân's spaceflight becomes a metaphor for post-1975 socialist development: ordinary Vietnamese in villages across the countryside were called upon to lift the nation from grinding poverty to prosperity;

[29] 'Thế giới nhiệt liệt chào mừng chuyến bay vũ trụ Việt Nam – Liên Xô', *Quân đội nhân dân*, 27 July 1980.

with the help of their Soviet brothers, the seemingly impossible task would prove easy, and in short order Vietnam would be a modern, developed nation.

Ritual 4: The Socialist Family

Fig. 8.4 shows Phạm Tuân, his wife Trần Thị Phương Tiến, and their daughter Thu receiving Viktor Gorbatko and his wife at their accommodations at Space City, outside Moscow. Pictures of the idealized domestic life of early cosmonauts like Yuri Gargarin or Gherman Titov – despite personal lives that were far from ideal – had been standard since the inception of the Soviet space program. Such images portrayed the cosmonaut as a socialist everyman, an ordinary worker with simple pleasures and household chores like any other. At the same time, they represented a sort of blueprint of sanctioned domestic consumption, implying that, someday, similar lifestyles will be available to all socialist citizens. In the picture, Tuân and Tiến, a military doctor, are both dressed casually, even fashionably. Tuân, the decorated fighter pilot, has taken off his jacket and undone his shirt collar; Tiến's turtleneck sweater is set off with a necklace of heavy chains. On the table in front of the two families sit

Figure 8.4 'Family Life of Air Force Lieutenant Colonel and Military Hero Comrade Phạm Tuân in the Soviet Union during His Time Studying Space Travel at the Salyut Training Station'. AF.3633.
Credit: Tiến Dũng. Copyright Vietnam News Agency. Used with permission.

large crystal goblets and a box of sweets, perhaps presented by the guests to their hosts.

While the image is explicitly one of socialist domestic contentment, implicitly it enmeshes its worker-heroes in a particular relationship. Where pre-Interkosmos images had represented the cosmonaut and their family alone, Interkosmos images now placed two families together. Space travel operated to make men of different nations part of a single socialist family. That family may have been hierarchical, with Gorbatko as elder brother and Tuân as younger, but it was one based on a bond that transcended alliance, partnership, or tutelage. Vietnamese propagandists formulated it in terms of 'Vietnamese-Soviet friendship forever' (tình hữu nghị Việt-Xô muôn năm). As the motto implied, it was a friendship that looked to a civil and prosperous tomorrow. Thu – the very promise of Vietnam's future – rests at ease in the warm embrace of the Soviet matron.

Ritual 5: Socialist Inspiration

As the launch date approached, Phạm Tuân and Bùi Thanh Liêm were joined by a delegation from Vietnam led by General Võ Nguyên Giáp, Central Committee Member and famous architect of the victory at Điện Biên Phủ in 1954.[30] In Fig. 8.5, Giáp, together with the two trainee cosmonauts and Vietnamese and Soviet representatives, stands in front of a full-sized mock-up of the Salyut 6 space station. The figures are dwarfed by the space station, which measured more than fifteen metres in length by five metres in diameter, and which was capable of simultaneous docking by two spacecraft as well as resupply by uncrewed Progress freighters.[31] Taken together, these technologies made the Salyut 6 the first space station effectively capable of continuous occupation, and to this day the International Space Station features a Salyut-derived module at its core. By any measure, the Salyut space station was impressive. Not only did it bring together a string of technological firsts and reconfirm Soviet leadership in one of the most challenging and unforgiving fields of science and technology, but also it symbolized the unmatched ability of the USSR to open new domains to human investigation, colonization, and exploitation.

Yet at the same time it impressed and inspired, the Salyut 6 station and the Interkosmos program it supported stood for a vision of peace, progress, and international cooperation. At least in theory, the knowledge generated by the

---

[30] The two had already been visited in Moscow by Vietnamese Communist Party General Secretary Lê Duẩn on 15 July.

[31] David S. F. Portree and NASA, *Mir Hardware Heritage* (Washington, DC: Johnson Space Center Reference Series, 1995).

Figure 8.5 'July 1980, General Võ Nguyên Giáp Visits the Gargarin Training Center in the Soviet Union'. AF.3713.
Uncredited. Copyright Vietnam News Agency. Used with permission.

colonization of space would be the result of cooperative research by cosmonauts from every socialist nation, and its benefits would be shared with the whole world. The water fern (*azolla*) that Pham Tuân brought to study under conditions of zero gravity was the source of wet rice agriculture's remarkable sustainable productivity. Understanding better its growth and nitrogen-fixing properties held out the promise of alleviating hunger on a global scale. Impressed by the material achievements of Soviet science and industry and inspired by the ideals of socialist civility, Giáp had reason to smile.

Ritual 6: Selecting the Envoy

Fig. 8.6 shows Phạm Tuân and Viktor Gorbatko at the press conference, held on 21 July 1980, announcing their selection for the mission, set to launch just two days later. The image thus marks the point where a stereographic account – with Tuân and Liêm appearing interchangeably – switches to mono. The photo, taken from the back of the room by a Vietnamese photographer, emphasizes the presence of the international press: the foreground is made up of rows of reporters and features two film crews: one filming the two cosmonauts and the other recording the audience. The picture asserts the mission as a matter of world historical import. And it offers to the world a

Figure 8.6 'Afternoon of 21 July at Baikonur City (USSR), after the Official Selection of the Crew, Lieutenant Colonel Phạm Tuân and Viktor Gorbatko Hold a Press Conference'. AF.4378.
Credit: Thế Trung. Copyright Vietnam News Agency. Used with permission.

new vision of Vietnam, one that transcends a past dominated by war and looks to a peaceful future built by confident young women and men like Tuân.

War, however, remained present. Above the two cosmonauts is a banner with headings in Vietnamese above and Russian below: 'Ready to successfully complete the assigned task.' In Vietnamese, the slogan has echoes of the wartime 'three readies': ready to fight and die, ready to enlist or re-enlist, and ready to serve anywhere. Such themes were woven into accounts of Tuân's downing of an American B-52. According to an article in the *Armed Forces Daily*, the young pilot had told his comrades, 'We're not foolhardy men, but if required we can use our planes as missiles,' that is, as part of a suicidal attempt to down American bombers. The article explained how 'by making this determination, Tuan brought peace to his spirit. This is how he was able to sleep soundly. And this is how he had the strength of mind, the sense of calm, and the fearlessness to engage the enemy.'[32]

By highlighting Tuan's wartime record and his determination to complete his mission no matter the cost, the article did more than confirm his status as an

---

[32] 'Từ trận thắng ở "Thung Lũng Míc" Ấy!', *Quân đội nhân dân*, 27 July 1980.

exemplary hero and morally suitable envoy. It also reminded audiences of the sacrifices Vietnamese had made during the long years of war and their readiness to make the ultimate sacrifice for the fatherland. While Viktor Gorbatko may have been the older, more experienced pilot, Tuân and millions of Vietnamese had been the vanguard of the struggle against US-led imperialism in ways few Soviet citizens ever would. It was a powerful means of asserting a kind of equality, and even leadership, within the socialist community.

Ritual 7: Appropriating Interkosmos

In Fig. 8.7, Phạm Tuân, still in his Sokol spacesuit, signs his name to the Soyuz space capsule that returned him and Gorbatko safely to earth on the night of 31 July 1980. Behind him, men shine spotlights, while around them photographers dutifully record the scene. Despite the ritual nature of a scene that was first enacted five flights before, Tuân beams with obvious joy and probably more than a little relief.

His signature is one half of an act of mutual appropriation: at the same time he was integrated within a Soviet-led program of space exploration and a Soviet-led socialist bloc, Tuân in turn took possession of material components

Figure 8.7 'Phạm Tuân Signs His Name to the Soyuz 37 Re-entry Capsule'. AF.4750.
Credit: Quang Thành. Copyright Vietnam News Agency. Used with permission.

of both projects for Vietnam. This act extended beyond scrawling his name on the capsule's heat shield. When Tuan returned to Vietnam, he would take with him both his spacesuit and the Soyuz capsule. They are still displayed today in the Vietnam People's Air Force Museum, artefacts in titanium, aluminium, and plastic composite of the nation's participation in space exploration and its historic role in a larger socialist project.

Ritual 8: The Meanings of Communion

Fig. 8.8 shows Phạm Tuân and Viktor Gorbatko after they both received the Hero of Labour and the Hồ Chí Minh awards. With them are the leading figures of the Vietnamese Communist Party, including General Secretary Lê Duẩn, President Nguyễn Hữu Thọ, Prime Minister Phạm Văn Đồng, and National Assembly President Trường Chinh. The ceremony took place two days after a similar one at the Kremlin, where the cosmonauts had been awarded the Hero of the Soviet Union and the Lenin awards by the General Secretary of the Communist Party of the USSR, Leonid Brezhnev. The formal reciprocity of the diplomatic ceremonies symbolized the equality of the two nations, and confirmed capitals like Hanoi as nodes from which socialist

Figure 8.8 'On the Afternoon of 28 July 1980, at Our Nation's Presidential Palace, Was Organized a Solemn Ceremony to Confer the Awards of Hero of Labor and Hồ Chí Minh on Comrades V. V. Gorbatko and Phạm Tuân'. AF.5336.
Credit: Kim Hùng. Copyright Vietnam News Agency. Used with permission.

civility and progress would spread to the rest of the world. The ceremonies were the final act in a kind of communion, a ritual confirmation of membership in the socialist community. Yet membership had many meanings.

Brezhnev's speech at the award ceremony stressed regularity, normalcy, and the multilateral nature of the Interkosmos program. For him,

the visits to the USSR's orbital station by the research cosmonauts of the Socialist nations have already become a regular occurrence. The representatives of Czechoslovakia, Poland, the German People's Republic, Bulgaria, Hungary have all worked productively in orbit together with Soviet cosmonauts. All of us are now especially pleased to know that now they have been joined by a representative from Vietnam.[33]

Two days later, some of Brezhnev's sentiments were echoed by Trường Chinh. The president of the National Assembly explained how the mission 'illustrates once again the preeminent character of the socialist system, the mighty power of the Soviet economy and its advanced science and technology, the cornerstone of the world revolutionary movement'.[34] Yet it was also proof of a special bilateral relationship with crucial strategic consequences. For him, the mission symbolized the

battle-tested solidarity of the two parties, the two states, the two peoples of the two nations of Vietnam and the Soviet Union forever united whether on the earth or in space, always arm-in-arm in the task of building socialism and communism, in the battle against American-led Imperialism and the battle against the gang of Chinese expansionists and hegemonists along with all the other reactionary forces, in order to safeguard the global socialist system and peace and friendship among all peoples.

This bilateral relationship would not only safeguard Vietnam's position on the frontline of a global struggle, but also be the source of Vietnam's socialist transformation. The mission was 'an eloquent expression of the great and effective assistance in the spirit of international proletarianism of the Soviet Union for Vietnam in the task of building socialism'. For Brezhnev, Interkosmos was an act of confirmation; for Trường Chinh, it was a promise of transformation. For the former, Interkosmos occurred in the Soviet Union's present tense; for the latter, it unfolded into Vietnam's future.

Ritual 9: A Cosmic Future

Following the award ceremony in Hanoi, the two cosmonauts embarked on a tour of the nation's south, culminating with a parade in Ho Chi Minh City.

---

[33] 'Liên Xô tặng huân chuông cho đội bay vũ trụ quốc tế Liên Xô – Việt Nam', *Quân đội nhân dân*, 27 August 1980.

[34] 'Phát biểu của đồng chí Trường Chinh tại buổi lễ trao tặng huân chuông', *Quân đội nhân dân*, 29 August 1980.

Figure 8.9 'Comrade Phạm Tuân and Comrade Gorbatko Wave to the
Citizens of Ho Chi Minh City'. AF.5400.
Credit: Hữu Hiền. Copyright Vietnam News Agency. Used with permission.

In Fig. 8.9, the two pass before the former Presidential Palace of the Republic
of Vietnam, since 1975 transformed into 'Independence Palace'. The façade of
the building is decorated with the Soyuz mission emblem and festooned with
banners proclaiming, 'Cheers for Victor Gorbatko!', 'Cheers for Phạm Tuân!',
and 'Vietnam – USSR friendship forever!' The mission over, the photographic
record has switched back to stereo, and mission alternate Bùi Thanh Liêm has
been allowed to march in the parade behind his comrades.

For many, the parade must have represented a welcome distraction. In the
summer of 1980, the nation faced diplomatic isolation, an increasingly dire
economic situation, low-level hostilities on the northern border, and a grinding
war in Cambodia. And yet Phạm Tuân's exploits seemed to confirm the power
of Vietnamese to overcome any difficulty and to rise above the gravitational
pull of division, war, poverty, and underdevelopment to create a unified,
peaceful, prosperous, and modern socialist republic. The two youths dressed
in improvised space suits flanking the cosmonauts are clearly meant to sym-
bolize this imagined future, where a new generation of Vietnamese and Soviet
hero-workers would continue to build socialism on earth as in space. But the
expressions of the different figures hint that not everyone had the same degree
of faith. While Phạm Tuân and his young companions smile and look ahead to

the future, Gorbatko and Liêm seem circumspect, attuned less to an imagined future than to the complex reality around them.

The Poetics of Spaceflight and the Legacy of Cold War Imagery

The way Interkosmos could support multiple readings was the source of its power. Much like the diplomatic missions of Vietnamese envoys hundreds of years before, Phạm Tuân's journey served for both Soviets and Vietnamese as a confirmation of membership in a community based on shared texts, language, and ideals. All could refer to mutually intelligible vocabularies of exemplary heroes and New Men, and aspire to similar visions of peaceful, inclusive, egalitarian societies underpinned by the might of Soviet science, technology, and industry. Brezhnev clearly saw this as ordinary, and Phạm Tuân as an envoy little different from the Hungarian Bertalan Farkas before him or the Cuban Arnaldo Tamayo Méndez, who would fly two months later. But for Trường Chinh, Interkosmos was not just about recognizing Vietnam's place in a global community but also about the special relationship between two leading members of that community. This special relationship would be the source of multiple transformations: on the level of the individual and the society, of the regional and the geopolitical, of culture and economy.

At first, recasting Tuân's exploits in the terms of an eighteenth-century envoy to the imperial capital in Beijing may seem little more than a conceit. And yet Vietnamese envoys to the imperial capital in Beijing saw themselves as engaged in a similarly transformative enterprise, one that would bring peace, prosperity, and civility to the individual, the society, and the region in equal measure. And the ease with which his journey can be transposed – Beijing becomes Moscow, Confucius and Mencius yield to Marx and Lenin, poetry becomes technology, 'manifest civility' shades into 'manifest socialism', and elephant tusks become water fern – reminds us there can be surprising continuities in diplomatic forms and symbols. Whether in the eighteenth century or the twentieth, large and small polities need rituals that draw from shared vocabularies and yet support different readings, ones that can encode independence and dependence simultaneously, and that can be told in both the present and the future tenses, depending on the teller. Whether they were Vietnamese and Korean in the eighteenth century or Vietnamese and Hungarian in the twentieth, such envoy missions perform similar work in similar ways.

Moreover, Tuân wasn't the only envoy to make the journey. The year 1980 and Interkosmos coincided with the massive expansion in the number of Vietnamese living, studying, and working in the Eastern bloc. Where earlier Vietnamese had travelled primarily for training and higher education, now large numbers went for work. In part, their labour went to repay Vietnam's debts to its COMECON partners, primarily the USSR, GDR, and Czechoslovakia. But whatever the equity of the arrangement, it also gave hundreds of thousands of Vietnamese an opportunity to experience socialist civility first-hand, to be individually transformed by the experience, and to act as agents of technological, social, and economic transformation upon their return. One can discern the effects to this day, from my bicycle mechanic Hùng who worked as a machinist in Dresden to the nation's first billionaire, Phạm Nhật Vượng, who studied at the Moscow Geological Prospecting Institute. It may not have been exactly the one its architects had intended, but it was a transformation nonetheless.

One can also discern the effects in a certain nostalgia for the command economy period. This might take the more critical form of a hugely popular exhibit at the national Museum of Ethnography in 2006 and 2007, or the more commercial forms of the Cộng café chain of coffeehouses and the resurgence in sales of Thăng Long cigarettes, apparently just as rough and cancer-causing as ever. Part of this nostalgia is ironic, a longing for an authentic past in reaction to an increasingly unreal present, particularly among those too young to have experienced the 1970s or 1980s. But even those who did can express a longing for a simpler, slower, and more egalitarian world where hardships were shared more or less equally, workers participated in their own management, education was free, and a brighter future was just one more emulation campaign away. Images like the ones explored above encoded Cold War diplomacy at the same time as they helped build forms of sentiment and affect that persist to this day. Thus, attention to the poetics of Vietnamese space flight reveals continuities not only in how greater and lesser powers enact their relationship but also in our longings for a better future – even one imagined in Vietnam's late socialist past.

A Diplomatic Image and Its Afterlife
       Bangkok 1967 and ASEAN's Creation Myth

Deepak Nair

Bangkok 1967: A Photograph and a Painting

The unveiling of the ASEAN mural was set to be a stirring moment in an otherwise placid ceremony to commemorate the fiftieth anniversary of the founding of the Association of Southeast Asian Nations (ASEAN). As chair of ASEAN for 2017, the Philippines' Foreign Secretary Alan Peter Cayetano delivered a welcome speech to an audience of diplomats packed in the front rows of the Leandro Locsin–designed Philippines International Convention Centre in Manila. With the speech over, Cayetano was joined by Le Luong Minh – ASEAN's first Vietnamese Secretary General– with each taking opposite ends of a movable board veiled under a curtain of red velvet. An emcee with an Americanized accent cued the significance of the impending act: 'Ladies and gentlemen, we are pleased to present to you the painting depicting *the exact moment when ASEAN was born*, the signing of the ASEAN Declaration on August 8, 1967 in Bangkok, Thailand' (emphasis added).

As they unveiled the painting (Fig. 9.1), an operatic 'ASEAN anthem' filled the hall and spotlights swept from the corners of the stage to the centre, momentarily flooding the painting in light. Cayetano and Minh clapped from the corners, and the audience joined in too.[1] And so a painting was unveiled that depicted the birth of ASEAN in 1967 in Bangkok – at a time when ASEAN was viewed not with triumph but uncertainty as *yet another* initiative in a region littered with failed diplomatic experiments. But returning to the dramatized diplomatic stage in Manila, there was – perhaps unbeknown and unacknowledged – something odd, even perplexing, about the act that had just unfolded.

For one, there was the quirky gendered quality of the creation act: of men giving birth to a painting about 'founding fathers' who were in turn giving birth to ASEAN. Two, there was the odd thing about the painting itself – it was almost entirely based on a black and white photograph taken on the day of the

---

[1] Video footage of this moment can be viewed at '50th ASEAN Foreign Ministers' Meeting (AMM) – Opening Ceremony and Group Photo 8/5/2017', YouTube, www.youtube.com/watch?v=FCfVLtEtbYQ (accessed 23 June 2020).

Figure 9.1 The Philippines' Foreign Secretary Alan Peter Cayetano (R) and
ASEAN Secretary-General Le Luong Minh unveil a painting of the 'founding
fathers' of ASEAN during the opening ceremony of the fiftieth ASEAN
Regional Forum meeting in Manila, 5 August 2017.
MOHD RASFAN/AFP via Getty Images.

1967 signing ceremony in Bangkok (Fig. 9.2). This is a photo of five signatories from newly independent Southeast Asian states seated along a rectangular table, captured in the act of putting their signatures to ASEAN's founding document, called the ASEAN Declaration or Bangkok Declaration. The photographer behind this image is unknown, and the image has been attributed to multiple sources over the years.[2] Indeed, the painter – the Filipino artist Peter Paul Blanco – expressly used the black and white photo as the basis for his commemorative painting. Approaching it as a 'historical painting', Blanco conducted research for nearly a year to accurately represent this photograph on canvas and in colour.[3]

---

[2] It is unlikely this was a 'hand-out image', and more likely taken by one of the Thai journalists assembled at the event. Over the years the image has been attributed to the *Bangkok Post*, the ASEAN Secretariat, the Agence France-Presse (AFP), CFP Foto (an Italian agency), the Ministry of Information and the Arts (MITI) in Singapore, and the Singapore *Straits Times*, among others.

[3] Interview with Peter Paul Blanco, 26 May 2020. Blanco was selected in a competitive process by the Philippines Department of Foreign Affairs in 2016.

Figure 9.2 The iconic photograph of the signing of the Bangkok Declaration, 8 August 1967.
Reproduced with the permission of the Ministry of Foreign Affairs, Thailand.

The painting, then, is a stylized reproduction of the photograph. It is a reproduction in that it *shares* with the photograph the same side-angle perspective on the unfolding moment, the same protagonists in the exact order of seating, the same dramatic act (of signing), and the material props of the stage (tables, clothes, microphones). It is *stylized* in that it renders the historical moment in colour – in fact, the painter Peter Paul Blanco interviewed retired ASEAN diplomats for information on the colour of business suits worn that day. It also differs from the photograph in its calculated effort to expunge the banality and everydayness that lurked in the corners of the diplomatic moment in Bangkok in 1967. The four male diplomats standing dutifully in the background of the photograph disappear from the painting; the unruly and overlapping country flags in the photograph are disciplined under the painter's gaze with their national symbols abutting in no uncertain terms; and the painter heightens the 'seriousness' – as he puts it – of the moment by directing the viewer's gaze to the foreground where the protagonists shine in the painter's glow while the background recedes in monochrome darkness.

This takes me to a third aspect of the painting, which was not just odd but also perplexing: with its birth in a secular ritual (an unveiling ceremony) the commissioned *painting* entered into an ambivalent relationship with the *photograph* on which it was based. Which is the original? Which is authentic? Which is the authoritative representation of the diplomatic moment of 1967? (As the emcee declared, the painting 'depicts the exact moment ASEAN was born'.) Let me explain.

In his 1935 essay 'The Work of Art in the Age of Mechanical Reproduction', the Marxist cultural theorist Walter Benjamin observed that the mechanical reproduction of traditional art (photographic reproductions of famous paintings, for instance) could reproduce the content of an original artwork but not its *aura*.[4] The aura denotes the singular uniqueness of the original, a quality that emerges from its presence in time and space as a witness to history (bearing deteriorating physical conditions, changes in ownership, societal upheavals), and what John Berger notes as its embodiment of the 'silence and stillness [that] permeate the actual material, the paint, in which one follows the traces of the painter's immediate gestures'.[5] The aura, then, *is that which cannot be copied*. While a chemically produced (now digitally disseminated) black and white photograph of ASEAN's 1967 birth may have appeared first in chronological time, to speak of this as the 'original' and 'authentic' is meaningless. As Benjamin observed – 'from a photographic negative, for example, one can make any number of prints; to ask for the "authentic" print makes no sense'.[6] Unsurprisingly, this is also why there is no preserved, framed, and memorialized physical copy of an 'original' photograph of the signing of the Bangkok Declaration. Instead, what we have is a circulation of chemical and digital copies capturing a diplomatic moment, mostly uncredited or credited to multiple sources, and raising the intractable, somewhat absurd question: Which among *these copies* is the original?

But the painting pulls a fast one. Even though it is a *copy* of a photographic image, it is being gradually endowed with the aura of the *original* and authentic. Indeed, this new commissioned painting promises to steer Benjamin's early twentieth-century thesis in reverse. If the revolution of mechanical reproduction by photographs made images 'ephemeral, ubiquitous, insubstantial, available, valueless, free',[7] then this painting appears to *rein in*

---

[4] See Walter Benjamin's 'The Work of Art in the Age of Mechanical Reproduction', in Hannah Arendt's *Illuminations* (New York: Schocken Books, 1935/1968), pp. 217–52. Also see Nick Piem, 'Walter Benjamin in the Age of Digital Reproduction: Aura in Education: A Rereading of "The Work of Art in the Age of Mechanical Reproduction"', *Journal of Philosophy of Education*, 41 (2007), and Jillian M. Rickly-Boyd, 'Authenticity & Aura: A Benjaminian Approach to Tourism', *Annals of Tourism Research*, 39 (2012), 269–89.

[5] John Berger, *Ways of Seeing* (London: Penguin, 1972/2008), p. 31.

[6] Benjamin, 'The Work of Art in the Age of Mechanical Reproduction', p. 222.

[7] Berger, *Ways of Seeing*, p. 32.

the restlessness of the photographic reproduction and fix it within its gilded frame. Similarly, if the revolutionary quality of the photograph was to detach artwork (like paintings and sculpture) from the realm of religious or secular ritual, then the painting's unveiling is the *first act* of anchoring this *photographic image* in secular ritual and tradition – from an opening ceremony where it was unveiled by high representatives of the state (Figure 9.1), and its subsequent display in the lobby of the Philippines Department of Foreign Affairs on Roxas Avenue in Manila,[8] to its final installation with an official reception at the 'ASEAN Gallery' of the ASEAN Secretariat in Jakarta. Note the making of tradition: a painting originally unveiled to commemorate a diplomatic event (ASEAN's fiftieth anniversary in Manila) now secured a celebratory reception *of its own*.

Only time will tell how this ambivalence is resolved. But the winds are blowing favourably for the painting. While the ASEAN Secretariat's official Twitter (now X) handle posted the black and white *photograph* to publicize ASEAN's founding-day celebrations in 2015, the same official Twitter handle posted a digitized image of the colour *painting* to observe 'ASEAN Day' a few years later in 2019. Similarly, the painting and the painter have come to attract some celebratory attention and commentary: the Philippines Mission to ASEAN in Jakarta produced a special video chronicling the painting and the painter titled 'Peter Paul Blanco and His Tribute to ASEAN's Founding Fathers'.[9] Beyond this, if the painting emerges as a fecund artefact for ASEAN's secular rituals and tradition (visits by state dignitaries to view the painting at the 'ASEAN Gallery' inside the Secretariat; prints and postcards sold at the 'ASEAN gift shop'), then one should not be surprised if the painting acquires the aura of 'original' and 'authentic', eclipsing the photograph it sought to reproduce.

Notwithstanding this, the unveiling of the commissioned painting in Manila is testament to the remarkable afterlife of the black and white diplomatic photograph that memorialized ASEAN's birth. Despite plenty of subsequent stock photos of ASEAN – of the (in)famous ASEAN Way handshake of plaited, interlaced hands; of playing golf; and singing karaoke – it is this particular image of signing the Bangkok Declaration that has enjoyed a thriving afterlife and has emerged as a pre-eminent visual symbol to convey the 'ASEAN story' to a new generation of audiences in Southeast Asia and beyond.

---

[8] Interview with Peter Paul Blanco, 26 May 2020.
[9] 'Peter Paul Blanco and His Tribute to ASEAN's Founding Fathers', YouTube, 20 April 2018, www.youtube.com/watch?v=w3Nr4TbNbQ4 (accessed 7 November 2022).

It is possible to suggest this image as the closest[10] ASEAN has to an image that is 'iconic'.[11] The image has also become a 'primary marker' insofar as 'an event is recognized publicly not by its political content but by its photographic representation'.[12] Moreover, like other iconic images, this image is elevated, detached from context, transposable, and movable.[13] The image can signify the specific episode of the birth of ASEAN but can also just stand in for 'ASEAN' (hence its easy dissemination).

Importantly – and like other iconic images – this image is serviceable for multiple agendas and raison d'état. This is where this chapter intervenes. While it traces the busy afterlife of this diplomatic image, it also examines the narratives attached to its reproduction and dissemination. It isolates one trope accompanying the image's dissemination which, in particular, has emerged as salient and influential in representations of ASEAN. This is a trope that packages ASEAN's birth (and ASEAN writ large) as an *act of heroic reconciliation* among Southeast Asian actors *in the face of astounding cultural diversity*. I take issue with this narrative and demonstrate how this diplomatic image of ASEAN's birth – memorialized first in the photograph and now in the commissioned painting – contains within it the seeds of an alternative reading that defies this creation myth. I argue that rather than embodying exceptional and heroic diversity, the image tells us what was profoundly (and problematic- ally) *similar* among these diplomatic performers. The diplomatic image enables a critique of ASEAN's creation myth and opens a door to reconsider ASEAN's founding story.

I proceed in three steps. First, 'reading' the image, I discuss the (inter- national) politics of the moment captured and represented in both the photo and painting. Second, I examine the afterlife of this image and the meanings that have accompanied its thriving reproduction over the decades. Third, I will return to the image to recover an alternative reading of ASEAN and its origins.

---

[10] Note the caveat 'closest'. Robert Hariman and John Lucaites suggest that iconic photographic images represent 'historically significant events, activate strong emotional identification or response, and are reproduced across a range of media, genres, or topics'. Taking this definition as a yardstick one can see how the Bangkok image approximates but also falls short of each criterion. This image is recognized and remembered (but not widely); it represents a historically significant event (not globally but in Southeast Asian political history); activates an emotional response ('seriousness', albeit more successfully with the message of rousing anthems and voiceovers); and it is reproduced in multiple kinds of media. See Robert Hariman and John Lucaites, 'Icons', in Roland Bleiker (ed.), *Visual Global Politics* (London: Taylor and Francis, 2018).

[11] Lene Hansen, 'How Images Make World Politics: International Icons and the Case of Abu Ghraib', *Review of International Studies*, 41 (2015), 263–88.

[12] Bleiker (ed.), *Visual Global Politics*, p. 8.

[13] Rebecca Adler-Nissen, Katrine Emile Andersen, and Lene Hansen, 'Images, Emotions, and International Politics: The Death of Alan Kurdi', *Review of International Studies*, 46:1 (2020), 75–95.

The Image in Context

To understand why this image remains popular, serviceable, and (as I suggest later) disruptive for the thriving discourse on ASEAN, some forensic work on the image and the moment it captures is essential. Who are the subjects? Why are they here? And what are they doing?

A Diplomatic Gathering to Mediate Estrangement

The thickset table-top microphones and sprawling cables in the image instantly take one to an older era of diplomacy in post-war and Cold War Southeast Asia. The broader – but not so distant – backdrop to this gathering of foreign ministers in 1967 was the low-level military conflict between states in Island Southeast Asia known as Confrontation (1963–66). Britain's plan to exit colonial administration in Southeast Asia by cobbling together a federation of its territories including Malaya, Singapore, and parts of Borneo was viewed with suspicion by Sukarno's Indonesia. 'Malaysia' was seen as a neo-colonial plan that would secure British interests in the region despite formal decolonization. While Sukarno and his Foreign Minister Subandrio initially went along with the Malaysia plan, differences remained over procedure and timing. The premature declaration of Malaysia's creation by Tunku Abdul Rahman in September 1963 – without consultation and feelers to Sukarno – antagonized Jakarta and Manila, and escalated Indonesia's policy of Confrontation against Malaysia.

'Confrontation' was a campaign of coercive diplomacy against Malaysia that fell short of a full-fledged war.[14] It was ultimately unsuccessful – partly because the Malaysians were backed by the still formidable British and – more fatefully– because of regime change in Indonesia. Following an abortive coup on 30 September 1965, the Indonesian army led by Major-General Suharto staged a counter coup that gradually displaced Sukarno from power. With this takeover, elements in the military hastened an ongoing process of secret diplomacy with the Malaysians to end Confrontation. The outreach was secret because even though Sukarno was marginalized, the army leadership had to proceed without undermining the Sukarnoist discourse of anti-colonialism and

---

[14] For a more complete account on the lead up to and the end of Confrontation, see Harold Crouch, *The Army and Politics in Indonesia* (Ithaca, NY: Cornell University Press, 1979), and Michael Leifer (ed.), *Indonesia's Foreign Policy* (London: Royal Institute of International Affairs, 1983). On how the end of Confrontation served as a backdrop to the formation of ASEAN, see Dewi Fortuna Anwar (ed.), *Indonesia in ASEAN: Foreign Policy and Regionalism* (New York: St. Martin's Press, 1995), and Deepak Nair, 'Spooks, Goons, "Intellectuals": The Military-Catholic Network in the Cold War Diplomacy of Suharto's Indonesia', *History and Anthropology* 33:3 (2021), 372–90.

national independence shared among elements within the military and public. With a mix of secret and quiet diplomacy, Indonesia and Malaysia formally ended Confrontation in 1966 with peace accords signed in Bangkok and Jakarta.

This brings us closer to the proximate backdrop of the diplomatic image. It was at the sidelines of meetings to negotiate the end of Confrontation in 1966 that the idea for a new regional organization was mooted. The venue for these talks was Bangkok, with a key mediating role played by Thai Foreign Minister Dr Thanat Khoman. Several biographical and scholarly accounts suggest that it was during these talks that Thanat Khoman suggested the idea of a regional association to the Indonesian representative Adam Malik. Malik is said to have responded positively to the idea but asked for time to first stabilize relations with Malaysia. This set into motion a series of consultations that lasted a year, leading to the Bangkok meeting where ASEAN was established in 1967.

There was also an alternative idea circulating at this stage. Favoured by the Tunku Abdul Rahman of Malaysia, this plan was to revive the Association of Southeast Asia (ASA) and to incorporate Indonesia. However, with the Tunku seen as champion, ASA was not going to be Indonesia's vehicle of choice to re-enter regional diplomacy. For Indonesia, ASA was tainted by its proximity with Western bloc agendas, while Maphilindo – yet another experiment in regional diplomacy, this time organized around racial lines – was tainted by its association with the domestic Indonesian Left and figures of the Guided Democracy (Maphilindo was a brainchild of the now incarcerated left-wing Foreign Minister Dr Subandrio).[15]

A new diplomatic platform had to be created. This is why dignitaries arrived in Bangkok in August 1967 to discuss a Thai- and Indonesian-drafted proposal to create a 'Southeast Asian Association for Regional Cooperation' (SEAARC). Thailand was the natural venue for this gathering. Thanat Khoman enjoyed a reputation for mediation given his role in hosting the talks that ended Confrontation. Thailand was also the only state not embroiled in fractious bilateral disputes with other invitees. This was no small consideration. At this point, Malaysia-Indonesia relations were just turning the corner from the diplomatic vilification and military campaigns of the Confrontation; Malaysia-Philippine relations were strained by the Sabah dispute; Singapore had fractiously broken off from Malaysia in 1965; while Singapore-Indonesia

---

[15] That said, it is worth noting the significance of the ASA as an existing diplomatic arrangement in this intervening period immediately after the Confrontation. The ASA provided a platform for players like Thanat Khoman to activate consultations on regional diplomacy suspended during the Confrontation and offered a blueprint of what this regional diplomacy could look like in discursive and institutional terms. Its contribution, then, was to keep the notion of regional diplomacy alive.

relations were clouded by Singapore's decision to convict two Indonesian marines for acts of terror committed during the Confrontation (they would be hanged in 1968).

Ministers and their delegations arrived in Thailand on 3 and 4 August. The first to arrive was Sinnathamby Rajaratnam, the foreign minister of Singapore. Archival video footage shows Rajaratnam received in person by Thanat Khoman at the Bangkok airport.[16] Rajaratnam was subsequently led to a waiting lounge where he spoke with assembled officials with a cigar in his hands. He is then seen relaxing in a lounge chair, speaking to journalists huddled around him. The next to arrive was Narciso Ramos, the foreign secretary of the Philippines, who was similarly welcomed, garlanded, and ushered in by Thanat Khoman. Arriving the following day were the Indonesian Foreign Minister Adam Malik and Deputy Prime Minister of Malaysia Tun Abdul Razak (for the Tunku was both prime minister and foreign minister). Underscoring the significance of these two delegations for the fate of the gathering is an image of Thanat Khoman clasping the hands of the Malaysian and Indonesian representatives by his side upon their arrival in Bangkok.

After the welcome, these representatives and their delegations were driven a hundred kilometres southeast to the beach town of Bangsaen, a popular tourist destination facing the Gulf of Thailand. The sprawling former residence of the military dictator Field Marshal Plaek Phibunsongkhram at Laem Thaen was the venue for the talks. As they interacted over nearly four days, the ministers played golf in the mornings, and carried this golf camaraderie to the bungalow in Lam Thaen, where they held discussions in the afternoon. The airy sea-facing villa was furnished in the latest fashions of the space-age 1960s: tables, sofas, and lounge chairs with sharp geometric edges and pencil legs. With its large halls, rooms, and balconies, this villa provided the five delegations ample space to hold collective plenary discussions and to break out into smaller groups when required. During these discussions, representatives insisted on informality and quiet diplomacy – from their casual clothing to one-to-one chats without their aides. In short, they were giving form to the practices that would become the core stock of the so-called ASEAN way of doing diplomacy. This style is

---

[16] The footage can be viewed in a Thai-produced video titled 'The Birth of ASEAN'. This video has exceptional archival material on the first ASEAN gatherings in Bangsaen and Bangkok. The fifty-four-minute long video, alongside available primary and secondary writings, are the main sources for the reconstruction of these meetings presented here. The video states that it was produced by a certain Dr Tommy Sungkum, the 'Director of Foreign Relations and ASEAN and Project Manager of NOE Plaza'. While the voiceover is by a male speaking in an oddly American accent, the video includes long interviews with Thai officials, including an older Thanat Khoman and the seasoned Thai diplomat Tej Bunnag. See Trakoonsak Singk, 'The Birth of ASEAN,' YouTube, www.youtube.com/watch?v=BzeL0ToM2WA&t=2530s, 15 September 2012 (accessed 7 November 2022).

also recounted in first-hand recollections of the event. Writing on ASEAN's twentieth anniversary, Thanat Khoman recalled,

After a brief official welcome, we moved to Bangsaen, a small seaside resort on the Gulf of Thailand, to work out the Charter for the new regional body. After a few days of discussions over the draft prepared by the Thai Foreign Office, interspersed by tasty repasts and a few games of golf which unfailingly produced beneficial effects, agreement was reached.[17]

Similarly, the former ASEAN Secretary General Rodolfo Severino – then a junior diplomat in the Philippine Foreign Services – writes,

On the golf course in Bangsaen and tie-less on easy chairs, the five men engaged in the convivial banter, the jocular repartee and the warm give-and-take that have characterized multilateral diplomacy in Southeast Asia ever since. As Thanat Khoman described it almost 37 years later, they played golf in the morning, had meetings in the afternoon and gathered for informal dinner in the evening.[18]

The conviviality of these interactions lubricated some difficult discussions. The most serious disagreement was over the Indonesian insistence that the new body convey a corporate position towards the status of foreign bases in Southeast Asia. On the Indonesian side, the newly consolidating military regime was under domestic pressure to retain the Sukarnoist accent on non-alignment and a free and independent foreign policy. This raised challenges in achieving reconciliation with neighbours who until recently had been viewed as instruments of neo-colonial influence owing to their security relationships with external powers – Thailand and the Philippines were formal treaty allies of the United States, while Singapore and Malaysia retained military ties with Britain, Australia, and New Zealand under the Anglo-Malayan Defence Arrangement (reformulated as the Five Power Defence Arrangements [FPDA] in 1971). Indonesia's position regarding foreign bases caused disquiet among others, especially Singapore and the Philippines. The issue was resolved by way of tempered wording in the draft declaration that embodied the spirt of Indonesia's proposal but did not cause any practical disadvantage to others. Indeed, the wording on foreign bases drew on a previous formulation in the Sukarno-era Maphilindo agreement, and had three elements: that 'foreign bases were temporary', would remain only with the 'expressed concurrence of the countries concerned', and would 'not be used directly or indirectly to subvert the national independence and freedom of states in the area'.[19]

---

[17] Thanat Khoman, 'Reminiscences', *Contemporary Southeast Asia*, 10 (1988), 211–17.

[18] Rodolfo Severino (ed.), *Southeast Asia in Search of an ASEAN Community: Insights from the Former ASEAN Secretary-General* (Singapore: ISEAS, 2006), p. 2.

[19] ASEAN, 1967, Bangkok Declaration/ASEAN Declaration, Centre for International Law Database, National University of Singapore, https://cil.nus.edu.sg/databasecil/1967-asean-dec laration/ (accessed 25 June 2020).

Signing ASEAN into Existence

After nearly four days of what local newspapers called 'family talks' in the sea-side town of Bangsaen,[20] the delegations left for Bangkok on 7 August for a final meeting at the Thai foreign ministry to iron out sticking points. It was here that Adam Malik came up with 'Association of Southeast Asian Nations', or 'ASEAN', as the name for this new body. This allayed concerns aired by the Philippines that the earlier acronym 'SEAARC' sounded like the word 'shark', which the *Bangkok Post* observed 'may have an unhappy connotation'.[21] The same night, delegates attended a dinner function at the invitation of the Thai prime minister and military dictator Field Marshal Thanom Kittikachorn. Toasts were raised to the ministers and the new regional project.

The next day, 8 August, the five representatives convened once again at the Thai Foreign Ministry for the official signing ceremony of the two-page 'ASEAN Declaration', also called the Bangkok Declaration. The informality of the preceding days now turned to ceremony. The golf course made way for the stately gilded rooms of the Saranrom Palace (home to the Thai Foreign Ministry); sleeveless shirts and golf attire gave way to lounge suits; and the secluded interactions at the beach resort now gave way to the glare of an audience of international press and diplomats.

Visual footage shows the material and symbolic organization of the stage for this signing ceremony.[22] At the centre of this stage was a long, rectangular table with place cards indicating the names of the five participating countries. The table was not on an elevated platform but was casually placed at the same level as the audience. The order of seating was not by alphabetical order (as would become the ASEAN protocol from this moment onwards) but was arranged in a way that placed the host country, Thailand (and Thanat Khoman), at the centre. Radiating from this centre, as it were, were the seats for Indonesia and Malaysia, and at the outer flanks of this table were the seats for the Philippines and Singapore (it is not difficult to infer the hierarchy informing this order of seating). Besides the country place cards on the table, the identity of states was symbolically presented by the flags planted behind each chair.

The climactic moment came late morning (around 11:30 am). The video shows the reception hall in Saranrom Palace packed with journalists and diplomats waiting for the impending act, with the five signatories standing to the side of the table. Signalling the start of the ceremony, Thanat Khoman extends an arm courteously in the direction of the table and asks the ministers to take their place. Narciso Ramos and Adam Malik file past him and take their

[20] Theh Chongkhadikij, 'New Grouping Named "ASEAN": Delegates to Sign Declaration Today', *Bangkok Post*, 8 August 1967.
[21] Ibid.   [22] See 'The Birth of ASEAN', 42:08–43:30.

seats. Thanat Khoman is next, followed by Tun Razak and S. Rajaratnam. They momentarily stand in file as a photographer darts to the side to take a picture. Tun Razak nearly sits down, as does Rajaratnam by his side, but they retract immediately, seeing that the others are still standing. With a smile, Thanat Khoman motions them to sit down. Soon, they are grappling with the printed textual artefact before them – the two-page declaration bound in hard copy. The signing is brief, perhaps a few minutes at most, and it is at some point here that the famous photograph is taken.

Archival video adds texture to the image frozen in the photograph. While the photograph captures our ministers gazing intently at the document and adding their signatures imperturbably, with singular focus – an intensity that is further heightened in the painting – the video reveals the kinetic quality of this moment. In quick and brief moves spanning a few seconds, we find the delegates eyeing the document, uncapping pens placed next to them, donning glasses, glancing quickly at their neighbours to see how they were going about this business (at one point, Thanat Khoman leans into Adam Malik to say where to sign the document), and finally gripping the document with their left hand and bringing pen to paper with the right hand (they were all right-handed).

The signing protocol in play here is different from other such ceremonies of their time. Rather than signatories taking turns to sign one document (as with the SEATO treaty) the assembled five delegates sign *five* copies of the Declaration, with each delegation presumably taking a copy back to their capitals. Upon signing a copy before them, they pass the hard-bound folder to whoever is seated to their left. Junior male diplomats in the background (who are cropped out in the painting) circulate the copy from one end of the table to the other. With this brief performative act, ASEAN is signed into existence, and the signing ceremony is followed by a reception where the delegates are photographed standing before their country flags and, later, huddled affably in conversation. These other images are also part of the visual archive of this moment.

An Image and Its Afterlife

An Image Forgotten and Revived

Images from the Saranrom Palace of the five figures chatting, standing, and signing the Declaration made it to the next day's English-language newspapers in the region.[23] Thereafter, the image faded into the background for nearly

---

[23] Besides the *Bangkok Post*, whose reporter Theh Chongkhadikij covered the story closely, the news and image appeared in 'The ASEAN Aims: First 7-Point Accord Signed', *Straits Times*, 9 August 1967, and 'A Joint Action Call to Block Alien Meddling', *Straits Times*, 9 August 1967.

three decades. There is a simple reason for this. In contrast to the contemporary lionizing account of ASEAN's creation in 1967, actors in their time had little reason to have monumental expectations from this new organization. As noted earlier, Southeast Asia was littered with such experiments, and three recent projects (with their now forgotten signing ceremonies) had run aground in the tide of turbulent regional relations and schisms of the Cold War (SEATO, ASA, and Maphilindo).

The image bided its time, as it were, waiting for ASEAN as a body to consolidate over several decades. And consolidate it did. ASEAN emerged as a key diplomatic platform for capitalist Southeast Asian states to cohere against communist victories in Indochina in 1975.[24] Subsequently, it served as *the* vehicle to mount a diplomatic offensive against Vietnam during the Third Indochina conflict.[25]

In the span of three decades (1967–97), ASEAN came to be viewed as a foreign policy 'cornerstone' in its member states and was widely recognized in international diplomatic circles. Indeed, it was now talked about as the most successful regional project outside Europe.[26] With its Cold War successes and post–Cold War expansion (with erstwhile foes lining up to join the association, starting with Vietnam in 1995), the time was right for ASEAN's policy elites to fashion an ASEAN story for international and domestic audiences. The time was also right for scholarly appraisals of the Association's diplomacy. It was in this post–Cold War narrativizing and evaluating that the image became a handy visual marker. In the 1990s, the image was featured in a blown-up poster cast in a gilded frame at the entrance of the ASEAN Secretariat library in Jakarta. It featured in celebratory memoirs on ASEAN, such as the *Know Your ASEAN* booklet and an 'ASEAN for Dummies' account of the association.[27] It also appeared on the front cover of serious scholarly explorations of this diplomacy, notably, the cover of Jurgen Haacke's 2003 book on the organization.[28]

---

[24] Michael Leifer (ed.), *ASEAN and the Security of Southeast Asia* (London: Routledge 1989).

[25] For an appraisal of this success, see Yuen Foong Khong, 'The Elusiveness of Regional Order: Leifer, the English School and Southeast Asia', *The Pacific Review*, 18 (2005), 23–41. For a critique, see Lee Jones (ed.), *ASEAN, Sovereignty and Intervention in Southeast Asia* (Basingstoke: Palgrave Macmillan, 2012), pp. 79–91.

[26] Kishore Mahbubani and Jeffrey Sng (eds.), *The ASEAN Miracle: A Catalyst for Peace* (Singapore: National University of Singapore Press, 2017), p. 6; Barry Desker, 'The 1976 Bali Summit: ASEAN Shifts Gears', in T. Koh, S. L. Seah, and L. L. Chang (eds.), *50 Years of ASEAN and Singapore* (Singapore: World Scientific, 2017), p. 33; Amitav Acharya (ed.), *Constructing a Security Community in Southeast Asia: ASEAN and the Problem of Regional Order* (New York: Routledge, 2000), p. 208.

[27] ISEAS (ed.), *Know Your ASEAN* (Singapore: Institute of Southeast Asian Studies, 2010), p. 53.

[28] Jurgen Haacke (ed.), *ASEAN's Diplomatic and Security Culture: Origins, Development and Prospects* (London: RoutledgeCurzon), 2003.

However, the image truly took off in the era of social media and online digital reproduction where it emerged as *the* stock photo for ASEAN. By the time of ASEAN's fiftieth anniversary in 2017, the image was being actively reproduced across multiple media platforms to commemorate ASEAN's birth and to showcase the association's 'founding fathers' – those five signatories who had golfed and confabulated back in Bangsaen and Bangkok in 1967.[29]

An overview of some of these reproductions from ASEAN's fiftieth anniversary commemoration is in order. The image appeared in several op-eds and commemorative stories published on the online websites of leading regional media (*Straits Times*, *Bangkok Post*, etc.).[30] It featured in the historical timeline of a fiftieth-anniversary commemorative book on Singapore-ASEAN relations.[31] The image and the signing ceremony from 1967 were featured in various social media platforms. On Facebook, the ASEAN Foundation headquartered in Jakarta produced an e-poster with thumbnail images of the five signatories under the banner 'Founding Fathers of ASEAN'. The Philippines' Department of Foreign Affairs (as ASEAN chair for 2017) produced five digital posters, each carrying a black and white image of ASEAN's 'founding fathers' accompanied with quotes from their remarks made right after the signing ceremony.[32] In one poster we find Thanat Khoman looking into the distance, with the adjoining text, 'What we have decided today is only a small beginning ... of accomplishments.' In another, a smiling Tun Razak is seen alongside his words: 'The idea and desire for regional cooperation ... a happy augury for the future'. S. Rajaratnam is seen saying, 'We have approached ASEAN as standing for something, not against anything.' These posters were shared by the Philippines Department of Foreign Affairs on their Facebook and Twitter accounts and subsequently shared by other ASEAN agencies on their online platforms.

[29] Katerina Francesco, 'Who Are ASEAN's Five Founding Fathers?', Rappler.com (Philippines), www.rappler.com/newsbreak/iq/177220-asean-founding-fathers; Termsak Chalermpalanupap and Tang Siew Mun, 'The Spirit of ASEAN's Founding Fathers Lives On', *Today Online* (Singapore), 11 March 2016; '1967: ASEAN Berdiri', *Media Indonesia*, 8 August 2017, https://mediaindonesia.com/read/detail/116535-1967-asean-berdiri-1; Khairy Jamaluddin, 'Continue to Build on the Dreams of ASEANs Founding Fathers', *Straits Times*, 8 August 2017, www.straitstimes.com/opinion/continue-to-build-on-the-dreams-of-aseans-founding-fathers; 'In Honor of the Last of ASEAN's Founding Fathers', *Bangkok Post*, 7 March 2016, www.bangkokpost.com/opinion/opinion/888672/in-honour-of-the-last-of-asean-founding-fathers.
[30] Roberto F. de Ocampo, 'Time for an Asian-ASEAN Century', *Straits Times*, 8 August 2017, www.straitstimes.com/asia/se-asia/time-for-an-asian-asean-century; Mahathir bin Mohammad, 'ASEAN Is More than It May Seem', *Nikkei Asian Review*, 8 August 2017, https://asia.nikkei.com/Features/ASEAN-AT-50/ASEAN-is-more-than-it-may-seem; Francesco, 'Who Are ASEAN's Five Founding Fathers?'.
[31] Koh et al. (eds.), *50 Years of ASEAN and Singapore*.
[32] These can be viewed on Twitter at https://twitter.com/dfaphl/status/892173192038690816 and also on Facebook: www.facebook.com/dfaphl/photos/a.858261067662062/858720147616154/?type=1&theater (accessed 7 November 2022).

Also in 2017, the ASEAN Secretariat in Jakarta produced a video titled 'Tribute to the Founding Fathers,' which begins with images from Saranrom palace in 1967 – an image of signatories standing against country flags, which segues to the image of them seated and signing the Bangkok Declaration.[33] A male voiceover narrates (perhaps with some exaggeration) that 'fifty years ago, five visionaries came together to sign the Bangkok Declaration, an agreement that would change the course of history'. The speaker asks in falsetto, 'Who were they?' After listing the names of the five signatories, the video introduces us to the children, grandchildren, and nephews of the (now deceased) signatories, each of whom shares their memories of these 'founding fathers' and speculates what their ancestors would have thought of ASEAN had they been alive.

Besides op-eds, digital posters, and videos, in 2017, Singapore's postal service Singpost issued a stamp commemorating the fiftieth anniversary of ASEAN. The stamp is set against a collector's sheet depicting 'ASEAN's five founding fathers'. This sheet is a watercolour rendition of the five signatories huddled convivially in conversation at Saranrom Palace right after they had signed the Bangkok Declaration.[34] The climax of these commemorative events on ASEAN's fiftieth anniversary was the painting of the five 'founding fathers' (Fig. 9.1) signing ASEAN into existence, which I recounted in the opening of this chapter.

In short, the otherwise unexceptional image of the signing ceremony at Saranrom Palace in 1967 has enjoyed a remarkable afterlife. While other images from this diplomatic moment have also shared the spotlight, it is this image that has emerged as the single most recognizable visual signifier for ASEAN.

Image and Discourse: Weaving an Origin Myth

Images don't merely *depict* a moment, as the emcee at the signing ceremony asserted in an American accent. They also carry meanings and narratives – often partial and partisan – that advance a particular interpretation of the moment being remembered. Such is the case with this image. As it was being hurriedly reproduced across online articles, op-eds, Twitter, and Facebook, we were being told something about ASEAN's creation and the ASEAN story in general. This story – a creation myth no less – portrays the association's birth as a heroic moment of reconciliation in the context of astounding cultural diversity and difference. Perhaps the clearest distillation of this creation myth

---

[33] ASEAN Secretariat, 'Tribute to Founding Fathers Full', YouTube, 23 August 2017, www .youtube.com/watch?v=l3EU3cw-CkU (accessed 7 November 2022).

[34] Collectors Sheet CSK17CS. The stamp and sheet can be viewed at the Singapore Post website: www.singpost.com/shop/stamp-collectibles/50th-anniversary-asean-collectors%E2%80%99- sheet (accessed 7 November 2022).

comes in the writings of the veteran Singapore diplomat and writer Kishore Mahbubani. In an opinion piece in the *Straits Times* featuring the black and white Bangkok photo, Mahbubani reflects on how ASEAN can serve as a model to the European and American intelligentsia for managing societal difference and inter-state peace. He writes that

[T]he story of Asean can bring some hope to our troubled times. The five brave men who came together to sign the founding Asean declaration on 8 August 1967 were a Buddhist Thai, a Christian Filipino, two Muslims and a lapsed Hindu. They *could not have come from more diverse cultural universes* [emphasis mine]. If one had to put together a cast of characters to launch the second-most successful regional organisation in the world, one would not have started with this cast of five characters from five countries.... *Yet the political divisions among the five founding fathers of Asean were equally great, if not greater* [emphasis mine]. If we remember the organisation's 1967 starting point, Asean's achievements are nothing less than spectacular.[35]

Indeed, Mahbubani suggests that ASEAN deserves no less than a Noble Peace Prize for embodying this heroic bridging of 'vastly different cultural universes', a suggestion declared unambiguously in the title of the piece. Mahbubani is not alone in this view of ASEAN's creation story. Writing on the fiftieth anniversary in an op-ed flanked with the same black and white photo, the former Malaysian Prime Minister Mahathir Mohamad observes, 'The countries of Southeast Asia may be close to each other geographically. But they have very different backgrounds, particularly in terms of their divergent experiences in the colonial era.'[36] This trope of ASEAN's creation, despite astounding cultural differences, political divisions, colonial histories, and so on, finds purchase in the memoirs of diplomats too. The former secretary general of ASEAN, Rodolfo Severino, underscores the 'arduous' nature of the Bangsaen and Bangkok talks as they unfolded in the backdrop of great diversity among its member states. He writes,

Southeast Asia was, and is, indeed, extremely diverse, much more than is Europe – diverse in race and ethnicity, diverse in the role of religion in political as well as social life, diverse in legal and political systems and modes of governance, diverse in levels of economic development and in approaches to development, diverse in values as well as historical experiences, culture, the practice of religion, and strategic outlook.[37]

---

[35] Kishore Mahbubani, 'Why ASEAN Deserves a Nobel Peace Prize', *Straits Times*, 26 March 2017, www.straitstimes.com/opinion/why-asean-deserves-a-nobel-peace-prize.
[36] Mahathir Bin Mohammad, 'ASEAN Is More than It May Seem'. To be sure, Mahathir rightly points to the diversity of colonial experiences, but as I suggest below, ASEAN effectively excluded this register of political diversity with its band of accommodationist independent regimes.
[37] Rodolfo Severino (ed.), *Southeast Asia in Search of an ASEAN Community: Insights from the Former ASEAN Secretary-General* (Singapore: ISEAS, 2006), p. 8.

Similarly, the former Indonesian Foreign Minister Marty Natalagawa writes of ASEAN's formation in the context of 'rich diversity', which lay not only in the histories and political systems of its member states but also in their foreign policy orientations given the split between pro-west and non-aligned states (such as Indonesia).[38]

This trope of near-insuperable diversity is buttressed by scholarly accounts of ASEAN's creation. In a book-length appraisal of ASEAN's history, Donald Weatherbee writes of the 'great political and cultural diversity among the five [founding] countries' as he proceeds to outline these differences in the familiar registers of religion (Islam, Christianity, Buddhism), ethnicity (Chinese, Malay, etc.), and political regimes (constitutional monarchy, parliamentary democracy, military dictatorship, etc.).[39] Amitav Acharya argues that unlike countries in the trans-Atlantic area, with the shared political culture of liberal democracy, 'ASEAN lacked such background conditions at the time of its inception and continues to lack them today.'[40] He adds that 'the sheer diversity among the ASEAN members in terms of size, populations, cultural and linguistic differences, and political systems predisposes Southeast Asia against a viable form of regionalism'. Writing on the limited levels of trust among Southeast Asian elites, Ralf Emmers observes that 'historical animosities – combined with diversity in the cultural, ethnic, religious, and economic spheres – continues to affect regional relations'.[41] Similarly, Alice Ba explains ASEAN's dialogue-driven process as starting from an acknowledgement of its diversity: 'if there is one point that most observers of Southeast Asia ... would seem to agree on, it is Southeast Asia's diversity'.[42]

The Origin Myth Revisited

I suggest that the humble black and white photo contains within it the seeds for an alternative reading of ASEAN's creation. The assertions regarding 'different cultural universes' and remarkable diversity sit somewhat uncomfortably with the striking uniformity captured in this diplomatic image. The five

---

[38] Marty Natalegawa, *Does ASEAN Matter? A View from Within* (Singapore: ISEAS-Yusof Ishak Institute, 2019), pp. 59, 71. Also see the collection of essays on ASEAN by practitioners and think-tankers in Y. Lee (ed.), *ASEAN Matters: Reflecting on the Association of Southeast Asian Nations* (Singapore: Institute of Policy Studies, 2011).

[39] Donald Weatherbee (ed.), *ASEAN's Half Century: A Political History of the Association of Southeast Asian Nations* (Lanham, MD: Rowman & Littlefield, 2019), p. 12.

[40] Acharya (ed.), *Constructing a Security Community*, p. 254.

[41] Ralf Emmers, *ASEAN and the Institutionalization of East Asia* (Abingdon: Routledge, 2012), p. 17.

[42] Alice. D. Ba (ed.), *Renegotiating East and Southeast Asia: Region, Regionalism, and the Association of Southeast Asian Nations* (Stanford, CA: Standard University Press, 2009), p. 5.

signatories are bespectacled old men, although this deeply gendered dimension to post-war diplomacy should be unsurprising. They are seen wearing western business suits with ties and pocket squares. While this choice of western formal wear should also be unsurprising given the European aristocratic and bourgeois heritage of diplomacy, what makes this surprising is how this (ASEAN) diplomatic encounter differed from the sartorial choices of the Bandung conference a decade earlier, where western business clothing mingled with deliberate and assertive displays of national clothing to register a new postcolonial moment in international diplomacy.

The photograph also suppresses differences in what Erving Goffman would call the 'fixed' aspects of their personal front – in this case, the racial features of the participants.[43] Awash in the blinding flash of cameras, the five signatories in the photograph appear uniformly fair-skinned, despite the considerable diversity in racial tone between the Sino-Thai Thanat Khoman on the one end and S. Rajaratnam of ethnic Tamil ancestry on the other end. Indeed, this suppression of racial diversity carries onwards into the painting where all figures appear uniformly in ochre-yellow shades. This was deliberate. The painter explains that 'we are really brothers here in Asia so ... in a way I would like to have an idea of "we are all the same" regardless of the complexion of the skin, the physical features'.[44]

The similarities that appear in this diplomatic image are not merely accidental, individual, or biographical. They point to a story that is patterned and structural. The *maleness* of this formative diplomatic moment prefigured the deep male homosociality that would be fostered over golf courses and meeting rooms and would lubricate the formula for conflict avoidance in ASEAN.[45] The western clothing (business suits) was less an instance of 'masking difference'[46] than representing the newfound valorization of western cultural capital among these sociologically similar Anglophone elites. These apparent similarities captured in the image also direct our attention to perhaps the most important axis of convergence that definitively belies ASEAN's diversity trope: the extraordinary likeness of social and political orders among the five signatories on that table in Bangkok. As I discuss in detail elsewhere, ASEAN's creation epitomized and indeed was made possible by the triumph

---

[43] Erving Goffman, *The Presentation of Self in Everyday Life* (London: Penguin, 1959), p. 34.

[44] Interview with Peter Paul Blanco, 26 May 2020.

[45] Deepak Nair, 'Sociability in International Politics: Golf and ASEAN's Cold War Diplomacy', *International Political Sociology*, 14 (2020), 196–214.

[46] A functionalist reading of diplomatic dressing would suggest that participants wear similar clothing to a diplomatic encounter precisely to mask and suppress their differences. This may well hold in some instances but, I would suggest, not here. I thank Naoko Shimazu for this point.

of counter-revolutionary political forces in Cold War Southeast Asia.[47] The
five signatories in Bangkok represented regimes that were politically conservative, were to the right of the political spectrum, were staunchly anti-
communist, had sided with the western camp of the Cold War, and had
embarked on projects of authoritarian state-building at home. The five signatories also represented conservative political social groups that had triumphed
during domestic struggles for decolonization.

These individuals were bearers of this convergent political complexion in
more ways than one. The Philippines Foreign Secretary Narciso Ramos was
the father of Fidel Ramos – the future president of the Philippines – who at that
time was deployed in the Vietnam War. The Thai Foreign Minister Thanat
Khoman led the Foreign Ministry during two US-backed military dictatorships
in Thailand. S. Rajaratnam had been a key figure of the British-backed
Anglophone faction of the People's Action Party (PAP), led by Lee Kuan
Yew, which had politically defeated and marginalized a more left-wing, anti-
colonial, and Sinophone faction that split from the PAP and became the
Barisan Socialis. Tun Razak hailed from the upper echelons of the same
Malay nobility that had collaborated with the British during decolonization
and would become the architect of a new era of one-party dominance in
Malaysia after the 1969 race riots. And Adam Malik was the civilian face of
a new right-wing military regime in Indonesia, which was consolidating its
power on the back of the destruction of the Indonesian communist party and
the mass killings of nearly a million suspected communists. It is essential to
underscore that ASEAN's birth was possible only because Indonesia – the
region's largest and most populous member – had politically fallen in line with
the other conservative pro-west and anti-communist regimes of
Southeast Asia.

To be sure, Southeast Asia *is astoundingly diverse*. In his sociology of
knowledge of 'Southeast Asia' as a representation for the region, Donald
Emmerson argues that it was precisely the diversity in linguistic, ecological,
topographical, religious, and cultural terms that historically complicated efforts
to demarcate a neat region.[48] So, while Southeast Asia was and remains
remarkably diverse, ASEAN's diplomatic project is not. The conformity in
the black and white image is mirrored (indeed, was made possible) by the
wider structural convergence among five deeply anti-communist and increasingly authoritarian regimes that sought to collectively bolster regime security.

---

[47] Deepak Nair, 'Saving Face in Diplomacy: A Political Sociology of Face-to-Face Interactions in
the Association of Southeast Asian Nations', *European Journal of International Relations*, 25
(2019), 672–97.

[48] Donald K. Emmerson, 'Southeast Asia: What's in a Name', *Journal of Southeast Asian Studies*,
15 (1984), 1–21.

Conclusion

I have been guided by two aims in this chapter. The first is to account for a diplomatic image from Cold War Southeast Asia that is unexceptional compared with other striking and evocative images featured in this edited volume but is exceptional in its thriving afterlife. Second, I have demonstrated how diplomatic images are not mere visual archives of past encounters, but are complicit in how the past is framed, memorialized, and reproduced in the service of contemporary raison d'état. As the editors note in the Introduction, diplomatic historians and scholars of international relations have traditionally used images for illustrative purposes, as visual markers for a lineal recounting of the past. But images encourage – even insist upon – a raft of interpretations. Unsurprising, then, that this image from Bangkok 1967 is reproduced not merely to illustrate ASEAN's birth, but also to tell a story about ASEAN, a story that involves a selective interpretation of the wider Cold War (geo) political moment the image captures. I have shown how this very humble and somewhat boring image allows us to recover a different story of ASEAN's origins. This alternative reading helps us destabilize the creation myth of ASEAN's founding as an act of heroic reconciliation in the context of great Southeast Asian diversity. Instead, the image points to what was deeply (and problematically) similar about these regimes and political orders embodied by the five signatories assembled in Bangkok.

The image and the myth promise to thrive if ASEAN endures and expands. There is a wry parallel here. Just as the painting discussed at the start of this chapter promises to obscure and displace the black and white photographic image as the 'original' and 'authentic' depiction of ASEAN's founding moment, the ASEAN creation myth too quietly obscures the striking (and problematic) uniformity that accompanied the Association's birth in 1967. The image is a quiet witness to these acts of suppression and displacement but – as I have suggested – it remains a resource for recovering counter-narratives and thinking of alternative political possibilities. In these effects and opportunities – actualized and exploited, unrealized and latent – we are reminded again of the power of images.

10   Picturing Power
A Photographer's View

Tom White

[Editors' note: Tom White is a photographer whose area of specialisation includes diplomatic events. As a practitioner, his involvement from the start of our interdisciplinary collaboration was critical in deepening our understanding of the process of image creation in global diplomacy. White offers here an experiential point of view as a diplomatic photographer covering some of the recent high-profile events in Singapore, ending with his view on an iconic image from the Cold War.]

Photographing the Funeral of Lee Kuan Yew: A Few Thoughts on Being a Photographer of Political Spectacle

In 2015, Lee Kuan Yew, the founding father of Singapore, passed away. I was working as a stringer (a freelancer) for the European Pressphoto Agency (EPA) and on the day of the funeral procession was situated overlooking the Padang – an open field in the city centre dating from colonial times – a choice that was expected to give me the opportunity to take a variety of shots of the gathered crowds, the twenty-one-gun salute, and the passage of the procession. As I waited with other assembled members of the media, the rain that had been mostly persistent all morning began to come down heavier. 'I'm in the wrong place,' I thought to myself, watching the crowd's futile attempts to keep dry with umbrellas and flimsy plastic ponchos. I'm supposed to be telling 'The Story', and the story was down there among the people and their grief and fascination, and here I was removed from that. A front of dark clouds was rolling over the Singapore skyline, swallowing the pinnacles of the financial district's skyscrapers. I took a photograph with my phone's camera and sent it to the EPA editorial team via a WhatsApp chat group, with the despondent comment that this was my current view. The enthusiastic reply from the picture desk was to send a 'proper' photograph of this vista, by which they meant one taken with my dedicated camera, and not my phone. I dutifully obliged (Fig. 10.1). The resultant photograph was published online in the *New York Times*, and also on the front page of the following day's edition of *MyPaper*, the newspaper

Figure 10.1 The funeral procession of Lee Kuan Yew, Singapore 2015.
Photograph by Tom White for the European Pressphoto Agency.

that was for a time handed out for free at MRT stations and various locations around Singapore.[1]

To my surprise, the grey, overcast landscape of the Padang had struck a chord. I even saw the image shared on Facebook with comments stating how the picture reflected the mood of the day. Yet, at the moment of it being taken, I was lamenting the fact that I was not down among the crowds sharing in their expressions, that my own feet were already soaking wet in my shoes, and the day had not even yet properly begun. Another image I made from that same position, this time with a telephoto lens, of the casket being driven past the sodden crowds, through rain falling so thick it created a sheen of interference that seemed to fragment the image, was also used by the *New York Times* and published on the front page of the Malaysian newspaper *The Star*.

I later saw many photographs made by Singaporean photographers that I wish I had made, including ones from in amongst that rain-drenched crowd. These were collected in the book *Thank You Mr Lee*,[2] to which I also

---

[1] Sonia Kolesnikov-Jessop, 'Singaporeans and World Leaders Gather for Final Farewell to Lee Kuan Yew', *New York Times*, 29 March 2015, https://nyti.ms/1I928cM. The article's header image was later replaced with another of my photographs from the day, of the cortege, which also appeared on the front page of the Malaysian daily *The Star*.

[2] Platform, *Thank You Mr Lee* (Singapore: Basheer Graphic Books, 2015).

contributed. However, I look back on those two front pages with a sense of humility. If one role of the photojournalist is to be a witness to history, then it is often the scene to be photographed in front of me that is important, and not just the photographs I might wish to make. The members of the crowd could not at that moment see themselves as I saw them, from a position reserved for the media. As a photojournalist documenting a historic occasion, the photographs I took that day were not necessarily for me, and despite my effort on occasion to infuse some of them with as much of my own opinion as I could bring to bear, ultimately their use-value in the networked infrastructure of representation was as objective documents. At another location on the same day, Lee Kuan Yew's casket was transferred along a street relatively empty of the spectators who had lined the roadside in the morning, and I saw an elderly gentlemen hold up an outdated phone and quickly take a photograph as the vehicle passed. I managed to catch a glimpse of his screen where the speed of his action and the poor quality of his older phone's camera resulted in a pixelated blur of an image. Yet the way he cradled the device and gazed at that blur was for a moment a confirmation for him that he was there; it was evidence that he had witnessed some part of an event that was dominating the national news, and being reported on in the international media. I was not happy with much of what I had photographed that day, but I later came to realise that the significance of that single wide-angle image taken over the Padang, that different perspective on the event, was perhaps more valuable to Singaporeans as an addendum to their own memories of the experience than the images I had not been able to make from within the crowds vying for a glimpse of history. We all have different roles at different times, and sometimes where you are is exactly where you are supposed to be.

The Trump-Kim Summit: Chasing a Non-event

As I stepped up to the reception desk of the hotel, the concierge looked up and tried to hide the scepticism in his expression. I didn't look like I was about to check in. He almost sighed when I asked him if the hotel had a guest by the name of Dennis Rodman, formerly of the Chicago Bulls, National Basketball Association (NBA) championship winner, actor, wrestler, and unlikely associate of both US President Donald J. Trump and North Korean dictator Kim Jong-Un.

I was working as a stringer for the European Pressphoto Agency and was part of a media team covering the much-hyped June 2018 summit between President Trump and Supreme Leader Marshal of the Republic Kim Jong-Un. I myself had sighed audibly when I heard the summit would be held in Singapore, where I lived. This admittedly historic meeting between the leaders of the United States and North Korea would be a media circus, and my personal opinions of the personalities of the two leaders did not lead me to hold out much hope for a meeting of intellectual and diplomatic heft to match the propagandising swirling around the announcement.

With the full-time photographers of the agency covering – or attempting to cover – the main events, I was a roving reporter looking to add some extra context and colour to the coverage of the summit. Thus it was that I found myself enquiring after Dennis Rodman in the lobby of a luxury hotel. Of course, it was denied that this was where he was staying. A good concierge is not about to divulge information about guests to just anyone, even if they do have press credentials. However, I'd been given a tip-off that this was where he was staying, and the presence of others in the lobby sporting cameras, microphones, and lanyards told me I was not the only one with this information, nor was I the first to make this enquiry at the reception desk. So I did something that is a large part of being a news photographer: I waited for something to happen.

It was the second time that day I had waited patiently. At 5 a.m. I was standing outside another hotel, surrounded by TV crews who looked like they had already been there for days, peering through a small gap between a security screen and some trees that was the only line of sight to the hotel entrance where Kim Jong-Un was staying. He was due to leave the hotel at some point in the morning, and my editors had requested I photograph his limousine, if possible flanked by bodyguards who had been previously seen jogging alongside Kim's limo. I placed myself in an empty spot further down the road, and waited for the expected image to materialise.

When the car did eventually leave the hotel, the jogging bodyguards were nowhere to be seen. I later found myself appearing in a photograph of the day's events in an online gallery with the caption describing 'Journalists from around the world' (Fig. 10.2). Of the four photojournalists prominent in the image, two are Singaporean – Amrita Chandradas and Grace Baey – and a third, myself, lived in the country. As the stretch limousine drove past and swiftly disappeared down the road, we filed our images of its tinted windows, obscuring the occupants within, and moved on, in search of the day's next photograph.

In the hotel lobby, I did not have to wait long before Rodman appeared, flanked by a small entourage. He was immediately swamped by the media, surrounded by a swarm of video cameras with blinking red lights, microphones thrust forward, voices clamouring with questions, and bright LED panels shining through Rodman's sunglasses to illuminate his half-closed eyes under the red 'Make America Great Again' cap worn by Trump supporters. As a photographer in this situation, I don't need to ask questions or get a soundbite; I just need to make a compelling image. In this instance I had two clear intentions, to make an image of Rodman isolated, a portrait of sorts, and

Journalists from around the world have gathered along Tanglin Road, across The St Regis Singapore, in hopes of catching a glimpse of North Korean leader Kim Jong Un leaving for the summit. BT PHOTO: SEOW BEIYI

Figure 10.2 Screenshot of a photograph by Seow Bei Yi in which the author appears as one of the 'journalists from around the world'. Published online by the *Business Times*.[3]

another to show the context of what was occurring, the media spectacle. Jostling with maybe fifteen to twenty others in the tightly compressed pack around Rodman, I managed to get both of these images, and retreated to let the spectacle play out.

The question of what Rodman was doing in Singapore, on the fringes of a high-level diplomatic summit, is an interesting case in itself. Several years previously he had made a visit to North Korea on a basketball-related trip and struck up an acquaintance with Kim Jong-Un. While the extent of this friendship has been hyped by both the media and Rodman himself, the reality seems to be much more transactional and superficial, essentially limited to Kim using Rodman to bring NBA players over to North Korea to perform. Nevertheless, Rodman has carved out a role for himself as a proponent of what the US media has termed, with typical hyperbole, 'basketball diplomacy'. Rodman began

---

[3] While the image and slideshow no longer appear online, the original article was published in the *Business Times*, 12 June 2018, www.businesstimes.com.sg/government-economy/trump-kim-singapore-summit-talks-off-to-positive-start-after-one-on-one-meeting.

speaking out on political matters and encouraging dialogue between Presidents Obama and Trump and the North Korean leader. On one 2017 visit he presented North Korean officials with copies of Donald Trump's book *The Art of the Deal*, having publicly endorsed Trump for president in 2016. Rodman's tumultuous relationship with Trump involves Rodman appearing on, and being fired twice from Trump's reality game show about business skills *Celebrity Apprentice*, while Trump was seemingly happy to use Rodman's celebrity to boost his own brand, something the reality TV star and president does not have a monopoly on by any means. Rodman tellingly arrived in Singapore sporting a T-shirt with the slogan 'Peace Starts in Singapore' and bearing the logo of the sponsors of his trip, a cryptocurrency group for marijuana merchants in the United States.

It seems Rodman never did meet Trump or Kim in Singapore, or act as the peace broker he had offered himself to be. Instead, the story dissolved into another case of a public figure feeding a media eager for anything beyond the mundane. As bizarre as this sideshow to the summit may seem, it had the desired effect of those behind the stunt. Rodman's celebrity, and his surreal connection to the diplomatic narrative of the United States and North Korea, was too tempting to ignore. Media outlets around the world ran articles on Rodman's Singapore visit; the pictures I made played well; and my editors were happy. In this way Rodman is here part of a continuum where politics, celebrity, and entertainment collide.

The absurdity of what became known as the Trump-Kim summit was not confined to Dennis Rodman's appearance. Around 2,500 journalists from around the world descended on Singapore. The host country took its role as host of the summit as an opportunity to promote the Singapore brand. Upon arrival and registration, journalists were handed a press pack full of information on the host country, with discounts for many local attractions. Singapore was engaging in a charm offensive to promote the city-state,[4] and not only with the journalists who were being encouraged to write positively about the country.

One evening during the summit I had hung up my camera and was at home when I saw a notification that Kim Jong-Un would be touring Marina Bay with Singapore's Foreign Affairs Minister Vivian Balakrishnan and Education Minister Ong Ye Kung. I messaged members of the agency team who were in the area, and they abandoned their dinner to rush over to photograph this rare glimpse of a North Korean leader being given what essentially amounted to a sightseeing tour.

---

[4] Yuen-C Tham, Yi Seow Bei, and Ng Jun Sen, 'Trump-Kim Summit: The Making of a last-Minute Meeting in Singapore', *Straits Times*, 17 June 2018, www.straitstimes.com/politics/the-making-of-a-last-minute-meeting.

One can only speculate, but this was likely a response to a request from the North Korean delegation to see Singapore's overexposed skyline as a model for future developments in North Korea and a propaganda opportunity for the North Korean state media, which swiftly published documentation of the event, a novelty for the country.[5] This was also a chance for Singapore to pitch to the North Korean leader for any opening-up of the country to include opportunities for Singaporean investment. In the absence of any access or chance to question the participants, we are left with images taken by state media, social media posts by ministers, and empty articles revealing next to nothing of real substance.[6]

Throughout the summit, access to the two leaders was severely restricted, with only a handful of photographers and reporters allowed at the main events. As the leaders met, only a privileged few were granted access, as can be seen in an image (Fig. 10.3) posted to Twitter by *Los Angeles Times* White House correspondent Noah Bierman.[7]

Compare this with another historic meeting hosted by Singapore in 2015, when President Xi Jinping of China and President Ma Ying-jeou of Taiwan walked out in front of a horde of cameras to shake hands in an equally choreographed display of performative diplomacy – an occasion I missed as I was out of the country at the time. In pictures and footage of the assembled media, one thing I noted is that the front row of seated photographers includes many Singapore-based staff photographers of the main news organisations and agencies. Local connections can guarantee a prime position.

With little access, then, writers, television news crews, and photographers were limited to staking out hotel entrances from behind significant security barriers, roving the city looking for some 'colour' to add to their reports, or even interviewing and reporting on other journalists in the media centre.[8] Here, comfort was in abundance, with long desks set up under an array of TV screens, broadcasting the official stream of events for journalists to follow

---

[5] Matt Stiles, 'Swift North Korean Coverage of Kim Jong Un's Trip a Departure for Nation's Typically Delayed Media', *LA Times*, 12 June 2018, www.latimes.com/world/la-fg-trump-kim-north-korea-summit-updates-htmlstory.html#swift-north-korean-coverage-of-kim-jong-uns-trip-a-departure-for-nations-typically-delayed-media.

[6] Lee Yi Ying, 'Kim Jong Un Explores Singapore's Gardens by the Bay, Marina Bay Sands on Night before Summit', Channel News Asia, 11 June 2018. Archived at https://web.archive.org/web/20180612161752/https://www.channelnewsasia.com/news/singapore/kim-jong-un-explores-singapore-gardens-by-the-bay-before-summit-10421126 and originally published at www.channelnewsasia.com/news/singapore/kim-jong-un-explores-singapore-gardens-by-the-bay-before-summit-10421126.

[7] Noah Bierman, Twitter post on 12 June 2018, https://twitter.com/Noahbierman/status/1006332609532776454?s=20.

[8] Cheow Sue-Ann, 'Excitement among Reporters Covering Trump-Kim Summit', *New Paper*, 13 June 2018, www.tnp.sg/news/singapore/excitement-among-reporters-covering-trump-kim-summit.

Noah Bierman ✓
@Noahbierman

This is where Trump and Kim will shake hands. Some in the press pool are up on an observation deck, separated by a moat.

8:29 AM · Jun 12, 2018 · Twitter for iPhone

Figure 10.3 Screenshot from the Twitter feed of White House correspondent Noah Bierman.

while partaking of the lavish catering. I even saw TV crews reporting on the food provided for the media.[9] The irony and absurdity of 2,500 journalists travelling from around the globe to sit in an air-conditioned room, a few kilometres short of the summit's location, with coverage via TV screens

---

[9] Mandy How, 'Journalists Fed Copious Amounts of Free Good Food at F1 Pit Building Trump-Kim Summit Media Centre', *Mothership*, 12 June 2018, https://mothership.sg/2018/06/trump-kim-summit-food-media-centre/.

Figure 10.4 A reporter delivers an address to the camera in the press centre during the summit between US President Donald J. Trump and North Korean leader Kim Jong-Un in Singapore, 12 June 2018.
Photograph by Tom White for the European Pressphoto Agency.

(Fig. 10.4), of event they were prohibited from accessing directly was not lost on many of us.[10]

For photographers this is particularly frustrating. The limited access meant that news outlets would have to rely on 'handout' images from state media or from the handful of correspondents who had been granted privileged access. Singapore's local broadsheet, the *Straits Times*, benefitted particularly here, with photojournalist Kevin Lim among those whose images were then syndicated to media around the globe.[11] One anecdotal image of Lim's is revealing. Photographs from the summit of the two leaders strolling through the grounds of the Capella Resort Hotel seem to indicate an impromptu, casual, and genial relationship between them, yet one of Lim's images shows President Trump pointing to the side of the path, where the caption reveals that a remote camera

[10] Suki Kim, 'Covering the North Korea Summit While Trapped in a Warehouse in Singapore', *New Yorker*, 13 June 2018, www.newyorker.com/news/dispatch/covering-the-north-korea-summit-while-trapped-in-a-warehouse-in-singapore.
[11] Low De Wei, 'ST Photojournalist Kevin Lim's Trump-Kim Shots Make Media Splash', *Straits Times*, 20 June 2018, www.straitstimes.com/singapore/st-photojournalists-trump-kim-shots-make-media-splash.

is being pointed out.[12] Several of these remote cameras seem to have been set up, with the *New York Times* publishing images made from this low angle under the headline 'Unscripted Moments Steal the Show at Trump-Kim Singapore Summit'.[13]

We as viewers might assume – especially given the headline – that these are 'fly-on-the-wall' photographs, when in fact they are of a stage-managed nature. The setting up of remote cameras operated from a removed position, revealed by Lim's images from an overlooking vantage point, and the choreographed stroll along a prescribed route point to an exercise in public relations that the press duly complied with. While the *New York Times* photojournalist Doug Mills is not the headline writer, and in placing the cameras and recording these images is simply carrying out his assigned task of documenting the event within the constraints imposed upon the press, the anecdotal image by Lim of Trump's gesture of acknowledgement is important in revealing the façade. A video later published on the *Straits Times* website further reveals Trump and Kim walking toward a group of journalists, who have been placed at the end of the path to witness this supposedly casual stroll. Perhaps not so unscripted after all.

The closest many of us got to the two leaders was through yet another publicity stunt. Lookalikes of both Trump and Kim had arrived in Singapore and were seen out and about in tourist hotspots, posing for photographs. One tech start-up that claims to 'connect influencers to their fans in a unique way' hired the duo to spend the weekend in a shopping mall, where people could pose with the impersonators at the cost of ten Singapore dollars for one, or fifteen for both – payment in advance via the company's app. Of course, with no access to the main event, I dutifully photographed this, mildly amused at the number of people willing to be parted from their cash in this manner.

One of the reasons cited for choosing Singapore as the host of the summit was the safety and security offered by the country, which has a reputation for not tolerating or allowing dissent of any kind. Despite some robust commentary being published and widely accessible, and fierce exchanges online, displays of public protest are rare, and in most cases permits are required for public assembly. During the summit, a 'Peace Gathering' was held at 'Speaker's Corner', a section of Hong Lim Park in the city centre designated as a 'free speech area'. I photographed a handful of attendees at this gathering laying out lights in the shape of the Campaign for Nuclear Disarmament peace symbol, and a few of the handwritten placards. This quiet and poignant event,

---

[12] 'In Pictures: US President Donald Trump and North Korean Leader Kim Jong Un Meet for Historic Summit', *Straits Times*, 12 June 2018, www.straitstimes.com/multimedia/photos/in-pictures-us-president-donald-trump-and-north-korean-leader-kim-jong-un-meet-for.

[13] Motoko Rich, 'Unscripted Moments Steal the Show at the Trump-Kim Singapore Summit', *New York Times*, 12 June 2018, www.nytimes.com/2018/06/12/world/asia/trump-kim-summit-theatrics.html.

attended by fewer people than were paying to pose with impersonators, and virtually ignored by the media, both international and local, was to me more significant in its sincerity than anything else I witnessed during the summit.

The Trump-Kim summit, an event of extraordinary political grandstanding and narcissism, is perhaps an extreme example of the superficial nature of much diplomatic theatre, with this one being particularly hollow. The shell of a grand event was there, yet beneath the surface, the substance was conspicuously absent. With regard to relations between the United States and Korea, and the situation across the Korean peninsula, it was little more than a reiteration of past diplomatic occasions. Despite the alternating rhetoric of friendship and antagonism that preceded the meeting, there was none of the volatility of either leader on display, and both seemed happy to play their part as well-intentioned international statesmen. What this achieved beyond satisfying the ego is difficult to ascertain. With Singapore keen to promote its brand to the world through its role as host, and with celebrities and start-ups rushing to capitalise, the real beneficiaries of the event can perhaps be discerned by this quote from the CEO of the Capella Hotels & Resorts group, host of the summit, when asked if they had picked up any business from the event:

It's hard to say precisely. Singapore is seen as an ideal venue to begin with. It's a well-oiled machine. Bloomberg did its conference here a few months after the summit. It was going to be in China, and they moved it. I'm not sure the reasons, but it was last minute, the request came after the Trump-Kim Summit, and we were able to accommodate it, and it was very profitable. Chanel bought the hotel out recently for their best customers in the world. Again, I can't say for sure, but there is a halo.[14]

World leaders and dignitaries can perhaps be forgiven for going to great lengths to engage in perception management. As magnets of scrutiny, and often the focus of divided opinion, it is of little surprise that throughout history those in a position of authority and power have wrapped themselves in such pageantry and performance. Even a simple meeting or speech can become the object of much attention, and the opportunity for spectacle is rarely missed. As the critic and writer John Berger has noted: 'the photographed image of the event, when shown as a photograph, is also part of a cultural construction. It belongs to a specific social situation, the life of the photographer, an argument, an experiment, a way of explaining the world, a book, a newspaper, an exhibition'.[15] Today we can add to this the meme, the social media ad, and the viral post, all inhabiting a distributed and fragmented media landscape.

---

[14] Doug Gollan, 'The Trump-Kim Singapore Summit Yields Unexpected Benefits', *Forbes*, 19 December 2019, www.forbes.com/sites/douggollan/2019/12/16/the-trump-kim-singapore-summit-yields-unexpected-benefits/#287829d07a25.

[15] John Berger, *Appearances in Understanding a Photograph* (London: Penguin Classics, 2013), p. 67.

This is not without its problems. The largest corporate social media platforms struggle to find the will and the means to control viral outbreaks of misinformation and deliberate efforts to manipulate public opinion, often playing directly into the hands of those with power and influence, with little regard for the veracity of their claims. A tendency toward polarisation ensues, often at the expense of nuanced debate over the complexities of an issue.

The Aura of an Icon

In 2013, Daw Aung San Suu Kyi visited Singapore for the first time. 'The Lady', as she is known, was the chairperson and general secretary of Myanmar's National League for Democracy (NLD), then the opposition party in a country under military control, and an icon of resilience and human rights, a role she both embraced and rejected. Her tumultuous entry into politics, her years of house arrest, and the legacy of her father's assassination are well documented and discussed, and in 2013 the aura surrounding her and the torch of hope she bore was still bright.[16] This would come to be radically diminished in the years following her eventual electoral victory of 2015 and subsequent handling of the persecution of the Rohingya. In 2017, the Myanmar Armed Forces launched attacks on Rohingya villages, resulting in over 6000 deaths and forcing more than 750,000 to flee into Bangladesh. In 2019, the Gambia instigated a case at the International Court of Justice (ICJ) accusing Myanmar of abetting genocide over the crisis, prompting Aung San Suu Kyi to travel to the Hague to defend the actions of the army.[17]

In 2020, an NLD electoral victory prompted a coup d'état in early 2021 by the Myanmar Armed Forces – the Tatmadaw.[18] Peaceful protests against the military resulted in violent suppression as Suu Kyi was again arrested, along with other NLD politicians and supporters. She has since been subjected to a series of guilty charges by a military court, with each one increasing the length of her prison sentence.[19] As the country descended into chaos,[20] the less than

---

[16] See the somewhat sympathetic article on Daw Aung San Suu Kyi's position by former deputy national security advisor to President Obama: Ben Rhodes, 'What Happened to Aung San Suu Kyi?', *The Atlantic*, 26 September 2019, www.theatlantic.com/magazine/archive/2019/09/what-happened-to-aung-san-suu-kyi/594781/.

[17] See the April 2018 filing at the ICC, which quotes and links to statements by the UN High Commissioner for Human Rights, and the Special Rapporteur on the situation of human rights in Myanmar: www.icc-cpi.int/CourtRecords/CR2018_02057.PDF.

[18] Richard C. Paddock, 'Myanmar's Coup and Its Aftermath, Explained', *New York Times*, 9 December 2022, www.nytimes.com/article/myanmar-news-protests-coup.html.

[19] Sui-Lee Wee, 'Myanmar Gives More Prison Time to Its Best-Known Convict', *New York Times*, 2 September 2022, www.nytimes.com/2022/09/02/world/asia/myanmar-coup-trial-guilty.html.

[20] 'Myanmar Spiralling "from Bad to Worse, to Horrific", Human Rights Council Hears', *UN News*, 21 September 2022, https://news.un.org/en/story/2022/09/1127361.

authoritative diplomatic efforts of ASEAN have struggled to reign in the brutal actions of the military junta.

In 2013, however, this international crisis was yet to develop and Suu Kyi still inspired awe. Her trip to Singapore would involve several events, and as a photojournalist the opportunity to photograph a person of such fame and historical importance was not only a duty but one I personally was looking forward to. As part of this, there was of course the official visit to meet Singapore's Prime Minister Lee and President Tan at the Istana (presidential palace), to which members of the press were duly invited.

The process here is the same for every visiting dignitary: media wishing to attend apply directly to the Ministry of Communications and Information in advance, who will then make the decision on who can attend. If permission is granted, then on the day you arrive prior to the meeting, you go through security checks at the Istana and are shepherded to a large, open hallway or adjacent meeting room in which the prime minister or president will receive the visiting dignitary, pose for photographs, perform a handshake, and maybe give a few brief remarks before retiring to discuss matters, away from the cameras and microphones of the press. It is a well-rehearsed performance in which we all dutifully play our part, and results in images that are consistent in their banality, with only the context surrounding the dignitaries or the signifi-cance of their meeting perhaps lending anything of interest to the photographs. The opportunity for capturing moments of candour or diplomatic tension is dampened and controlled.

In such situations I always look for the moments before and after, the brief time when the actors are on stage but not quite in the spotlight, or waiting to deliver their lines. Most politicians are practiced at the display of niceties and will not reveal anything other than patient regard for their counterparts. As such, it is difficult to make images that point to the wider context of a meeting or the particular politics at play. They are often the visual translation of the platitudes invariably uttered from behind the podium. In fact, more often than not, it is only the wider political context of the meeting that gives such images any meaning at all.

Such was the case with Aung San Suu Kyi, and I knew that only an opportunity to view her for longer than the duration of a handshake would provide an occasion to make an image into which I might be able to pour the context surrounding her position. Aside from her official Istana visit, I had heard she would be addressing the Myanmar Club, but I did not know exactly where or when this would take place. Phone numbers listed for the club rang unanswered and emails received no reply. I was about to head down to their office in person when a photographer working for another agency messaged me to let me know that the address by Suu Kyi would happen at the Resorts World Sentosa ballroom the next day.

I headed down with my government-issued press pass, and not having prior permission granted, had to plead with security and club officials to allow me to enter. A press pass does not always guarantee access. Thankfully, the gatekeepers acquiesced and I watched, awestruck, as 'The Lady' spoke to an adoring crowd of hundreds in a vast conference hall. This was prior to her visit to the Istana and my first time in her presence. I was, frankly, charmed by her poise and her charisma, and the atmosphere of intense anticipation in the hall. Although she spoke in Burmese for the most part, which I do not understand, I, like many others there, hung on her every word. She was relaxed and obviously comfortable. I made several images that showed her in the role of dignified politician addressing a supportive crowd. Then, at one point, she paused and looked directly into the long lens of my camera. I was a small figure in the crowd to her, but the telephoto lens brought my eye right to her gaze and I saw through the dignity and charisma – which was not lost – to a weariness, almost a sadness in her expression. The mask, for the briefest of instants, was dropped, and everything I knew about what she had endured and the choices she had made seemed to be revealed to me. This was, I thought, an honest picture (Fig. 10.5).

Figure 10.5 Daw Aung San Suu Kyi addresses a gathering of the Myanmar Club at Resorts World Sentosa, Singapore, 22 September 2013.
Photograph by Tom White for the European Pressphoto Agency.

After the Istana visit, I attended one more event, a press conference in a small room in the Shangri-La hotel. As we waited in the room for her to arrive, I prepared myself. I knew that once she was seated in front of the media she would be performing her role. Would there be any chance for a candid moment? I positioned myself opposite the door to the room, at an angle so that I could see a short way into the corridor outside. In such moments, you can sense the imminent arrival of someone important: their presence moves before them and you listen for small shifts in the atmosphere, changes in the pressure if you like. I raised my camera in anticipation, and, as the security detail appeared in the doorway, I made a small number of images, freezing Suu Kyi's stride as she entered the room.

She settled into her seat behind a microphone, made a few short remarks, and took questions from members of the media, many of which were innocuous, related to democracy in Myanmar and economic development issues, and none too probing.[21] The events surrounding the persecution of the Rohingya were of little concern to the international media at this time. She was eloquent and diplomatic in her answers, and I remember a mild annoyance in her voice as she answered questions on what Myanmar could learn from Singapore. In this small, almost intimate setting there was little of the aura of the grand stage, and I saw here an intelligent woman who was bearing not only a burden of her own lived experience, but the weight of history and the expectation of many millions of people. She was navigating a line of immense complexity.

As I looked through my images later and made my selection to send to the agency, the images of Suu Kyi arriving struck me. Here again I saw the weariness and sadness: even as her head was held high, her posture already displaying the composure of one who knows she is being observed, I could see the expression was not quite at rest. I had deliberately kept the composition wide, as I wanted to include the framing of the doorway itself, and allow for some degree of chance in who and what appeared in the frame alongside Suu Kyi. The gesture of the security official, glancing back over her shoulder, is one I could not have planned, but leads us to follow the gaze to Suu Kyi herself. This is what I call the unexpected image. The one you know is a possibility, without being able to pre-visualise exactly what it will look like (Fig. 10.6).

There are the images we expect to see of our politicians, of statecraft and diplomacy: the handshake, the warm smile, the serious expression of equanimity or of listening intently and speaking with sincerity – or at least with the

---

[21] See 'Aung San Suu Kyi Press Conference, Shangri-La Hotel, September 23, 2013', *Today Online*, YouTube, 23 September 2013, www.youtube.com/watch?v=Y1xhGbv3VhY.

Figure 10.6 Daw Aung San Suu Kyi arrives at a press conference held in the Shangri-La hotel, Singapore, 23 September 2013.
Photograph by Tom White.

pretence of such. Characters like Trump or Kim Jong-Un carry a degree of unpredictability in their manner, and as such the spectacle is always poised to erupt around them, even if it does not materialise. Many carefully contrive their public persona, performing versions of themselves. Rarely do we see the candid, the relaxed, the raw and real, so when we see even a glimpse of this, it is utterly compelling. Over the years, Suu Kyi has been subject to much criticism, with many feeling that her handling of the issue of the Rohingya has been a betrayal of her own principled stance on human rights. This is not the place to discuss these criticisms or the wider crisis in Myanmar, but in those moments, as I watched her through the lens of my camera, it was clear that this was someone in a difficult position, aware that the aura of idealism and hope was already coming into conflict with the practicalities of realpolitik and compromise.

Of the pictures I made of her during her visit, the one I am most proud of is that strange image of her, half obscured, mid-stride as she entered the room for the press conference. It is not a flattering image, but to me it is a very raw moment. The agency I submitted these images to never included it in their archive, and while several of my images of Suu Kyi in Singapore made their way into the pages of the press, this particular one has never been previously published.

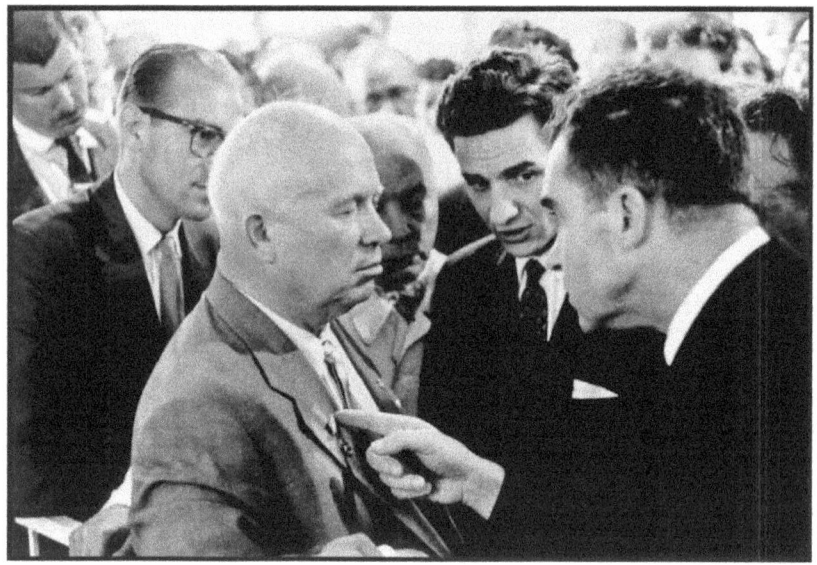

Figure 10.7 Elliot Erwitt, 'Nikita Khrushchev and Richard Nixon, USSR, Moscow, 1959'.
Image Reference NYC13628 (ERE1959038W00010/57). © Elliott Erwitt/Magnum Photos.

The Kitchen Debate: A Cold War Fallacy

In his ethnographic study of the photojournalism industry, *Image Brokers*, Zeynep Devrim Gursel explores the 'infrastructures of representation' that go into the creation, selection, and transmission of news images and examines how decisions are made based upon multiple factors that may have little to do with the scene being photographed. Gursel refers to news images as 'formative fictions', constructed representations that reflect current events yet simultaneously shape ways of imagining the world and political possibilities within it.[22] These observations help contextualise my own experiences, and help illuminate how images are created more generally. Take the example of an iconic image from the height of the Cold War, shown in Fig. 10.7.

It is Moscow in 1959, and the vice president of the United States, Richard Nixon, jabs his finger aggressively into the chest of Soviet Premier Nikita Khrushchev, leaning into the gesture, his distinctive features recognisable

---

[22] Zeynep Devrim Gursel, *Image Brokers: Visualising World News in the Age of Digital Circulation* (Berkeley: University of California Press, 2016), p. 11.

despite being hidden in profile. Khrushchev, almost passive, his expression
stoic, rests one arm casually on a metal barrier. Their two translators crowd the
scene, wearing earnest expressions of concentration as the two high-ranking
politicians engage each other.

The moment of high drama was documented by photographer Elliot Erwitt
at the site of the American Exhibition in Moscow's Sokolniki Park. Funded by
the US government, the exhibition showcased the latest trappings of American
capitalism. As the vice president gave the Soviet premier a tour, the merits of
US ideology and industry set against Soviet communism became the topic of a
lively debate. As the two dignitaries paused in front of a model kitchen, Erwitt
brought up his camera and seized the opportunity to close in and photograph
this exchange. The resultant image (Fig. 10.7), which has come down to us
across time, is one of Nixon as a hard-nosed politician, asserting his – and by
extension his country's – dominance.

When viewing the contact sheet representing the thirty-five frames made by
Erwitt, we can see a more nuanced, jovial scene unfolding, with smiles and
laughter on display (Fig. 10.8) even as Nixon and Khrushchev punctuate their

Figure 10.8 Elliot Erwitt, 'USSR, Russia, Moscow, 1959'.
Image Reference NYC33664 (ERE1959038W00010). © Elliott Erwitt/Magnum
Photos.

statements with equally assertive gestures. At a televised appearance from the event, Nixon and Khrushchev continued to thrust and parry as they appeared in front of broadcast cameras on a stage set. Watching the footage, one can see the two men locked into a verbal power play, each one keen to demonstrate their authority over the conversation with assertive language and bumbling attempts at humour: less intellectual rigour and more populist rhetoric. While tense, the televised appearance is a relatively good-natured exchange and contains an air of cautious optimism – much unlike the confrontational image of Erwitt's photograph.[23]

According to the transcript of the conversation that carried over into the television studio, Nixon does indeed strike a conciliatory tone at several points, while Khrushchev for his part acknowledges American economic strength, and he requests that his comments be broadcast with English translation to an American audience.[24]

Despite the bravado, the debate ends on a pacificatory note with both representatives of the nuclear superpowers warmly shaking hands and agreeing to broadcast the debate in full for the benefit of citizens of both countries.

While an undoubtedly heated exchange – which certainly included some tense moments – the broader context is revealing. How accurately can the temporal slice of a single photograph represent a particular moment? What is the photographer's role in this, and how does such an image come about? As Nixon and Khrushchev paused in front of the model American kitchen that lent its name to the incident later known as the 'Kitchen Debate', Erwitt made his move, recalling later:

By sheer luck, I guessed correctly where they would turn up next: which was at a display of a modern kitchen behind a barrier. I rushed to it to have an unobstructed view as they approached the rail. Luck was with me. With a direct view and no one to push and shove, I circumnavigated Nixon and Khrushchev, finding my best range. From then on, it was like shooting fish in a barrel.…
But how pictures can lie. The illusion is one of Nixon standing up to the Soviets, where the reality is an argument about cabbage soup versus red meat.[25]

---

[23] See the Associated Press video 'US-USSR Kitchen Debate – 1959 | Today in History | 24 July 16', AP Archive, YouTube, 24 July 2016, www.youtube.com/watch?v= 1JVXaEnDGDg, and CBS News report, 'Khrushchev vs Nixon: The Kitchen Debate (1959 Moscow)', Npatou, YouTube, 17 July 2017, www.youtube.com/watch?v=lN9ENvzSPfw.

[24] The transcript can be found in the CIA archives, www.cia.gov/library/readingroom/docs/1959-07-24.pdf, and in David Krugler (ed.), 'The Kitchen Debate by Nikita Khrushchev and Richard Nixon, 25 July 1959', Teaching American History.org, https://teachingamericanhistory.org/document/the-kitchen-debate/.

[25] Elliot Erwitt, as quoted in Christian Storm, 'How an Iconic Photo of Richard Nixon in Russia Was Taken by Sheer Luck', *Business Insider*, 30 July 2014, www.businessinsider.com/elliott-erwitt-richard-nixon-kitchen-debate-photo-2014-7?IR=T. The quote is attributed to the documentary that Mario Paloschi and Gianluigi Attore produced and directed: *Contact: Magnum*

Interestingly, this exact phrasing in the dialogue occurs nowhere in the official transcript. Is Erwitt's memory reliable? Are his photographs? Is the transcript? It becomes plain that even when we cross-reference primary sources, we still may be no closer to uncovering the exact truth of the matter.

Given this, what then can we make of the selection, prominently and clearly marked on the contact sheet, of an image of antagonistic conflict, one in which the US vice president appears to be asserting his authority over the Soviet premier? How did this image come to such prominence in the historical record?

An initial report of the 'Kitchen Debate' in the *New York Times* was illustrated not with the now famous image by Erwitt, but with a much less dramatic photograph made by a corporate press agent, William Safire, who later became a speechwriter for Nixon and columnist for the *New York Times*.[26] Distributed by the Associated Press, this image presents Nixon and Khrushchev as more relaxed, bored even, as they carry out their official public relations duties. The bold headline reads 'Nixon and Khrushchev Argue in Public as U.S. Exhibit Opens; Accuse Each Other of Threats', while the subheading notes 'No Tempers Lost'. The photograph itself carries the much more sedate caption, 'Vice President Richard M. Nixon describes operation of an automatic washing machine at the U.S. fair in Moscow to Premier Nikita S. Khrushchev of the Soviet Union. Mr. Nixon acted as host during the tour of the fair.'

The mundane revelations of the photograph and its caption are subordinate to the provocative headline in large lettering. The headline is sensational at best, unrepresentative at worst. Headlines are there to grab and hold attention, and to impart a message of information, but also contain an ideologically inflected editorial point of view. The overtly sensational tabloid press use large bold type and images across their front page for this very reason, while the supposedly more sober broadsheets carry a similar – though tempered – design ethos 'above the fold' in the upper half of their front pages.

If the aim is to attract attention, then how did this relatively unremarkable photograph end up on the front page of the *New York Times*, rather than the more dynamic photograph that Erwitt made? Given the headline, Erwitt's image would seem a better fit to illustrate the sentiment. According to a 1984 interview with Safire, the official Associated Press photographer was unable to get into a good position to photograph the exchange and passed

Photos (a Ballandi Arts Production, in conjunction with Magnum Photos for SKY ARTE Italy, SBS, MediaCorp, AVRO, YLE, NKS, and AMP).

[26] Harrison E. Salisbury, 'Nixon and Khrushchev Argue in Public as U.S. Exhibit Opens', *New York Times*, 25 July 1959. The front page as published in print can be viewed in the *New York Times* archive: https://timesmachine.nytimes.com/timesmachine/1959/07/25/110086326.html?pageNumber=1.

Safire his camera.[27] Safire made a few images and passed it back, recalling that he noticed Erwitt making his images at the same time. Erwitt was himself on a commercial assignment – for Westinghouse refrigerators – and the images of Nixon and Khrushchev were on his 'personal camera'.[28] Erwitt had been a member of the Magnum photographic cooperative since 1954, and these photographs from Russia would have been added to Magnum's archive, where they can be found today. As Erwitt was not on a news assignment, it is possible his images were not added to the archive immediately or distributed to the press at the time.

The Associated Press, as a 'wire' agency, would have been under pressure to quickly provide images of such a newsworthy event to their subscribers, including the *New York Times*. Hence the AP photographer's desperation to get an image, handing his camera over to Safire, just to get the shot. The film would have been processed, an image selected and printed, and then scanned and 'wired' over telephone lines to newsrooms in time for publication the following day.[29]

However, this was still a slow and expensive process, with single images taking several minutes to transmit.[30] Photographers and editors might choose only one image from an event to transmit. On occasion, photographers on tight deadlines would give their film to a courier to be taken to the office with accompanying notes, and indications of potential frames on the roll that should command the attention of editors. Wire service photographers working under such time pressures would sometimes not even see the images they had made until they appeared in the pages of the press. This was true as well for photographers working on longer news assignments where the technology was not readily accessible and film had to be shipped back to offices in large cities or to newsrooms in London, Paris, or New York. This workflow was standard practice until the prevalence of digital cameras and internet connections took over in the early to mid 2000s. In today's digital world, the pressure is even more intense, with wire service photographers and freelancers transmitting images minutes or even seconds after the photograph has been taken, sometimes even directly from the camera. With the proliferation of internet-enabled smartphones, social media, self-publishing, and live streaming, the

---

[27] William Safire, 'A Picture Story', *New York Times*, 24 July 1984, www.nytimes.com/1984/07/27/opinion/essay-a-picture-story.html.

[28] Kristen Lubben, *Magnum Contact Sheets* (London: Thames & Hudson, 2011), p. 101.

[29] The technology to transmit electronically had been patented in 1843 by Scotsman Alexander Bain, given for his 'electric printing telegraph'. The use of wire transfers expanded greatly from in the 1920s, with AP making use of this method for transmitting photographs from 1935, after purchasing the technology to do so from AT&T in 1933.

[30] The process is explained in the 1937 dramatised documentary film *Spot News* by Jam Handy: https://archive.org/details/SpotNews1937.

competition for 'first published' is fierce. In a fast-paced news context, the choice of frame to represent an event is often made very quickly.

Given the full context of the exchange, we could take the AP photograph by William Safire to be the less elegant, but more accurate depiction of the event. Certainly, it follows that its circulation by AP guarantees its prominence in the newspaper reports of the day. Gursel refers to this as the 'fast photo versus the good photo', elaborating that wire service photos were not necessarily 'bad' but 'were perceived as less complex images'.[31] Both are depictions of the same event yet bring to us perceptibly different constructions.

It seems that Erwitt's now iconic photographs were never part of the news reporting at the time. They appear to enter into public consciousness when they were used by the campaign to elect Nixon to the office of president in 1960. In fact, Erwitt later stated that the author of the AP image, Safire, was 'instrumental in tracking down my picture which was used for a 1960 campaign poster'.[32] Erwitt claimed that he gave the image free of charge to the campaign PR office as a courtesy, though not with any notion of endorsing Nixon.[33] The image's fame then comes originally not from its use as a documentary news image, but in relation to its propaganda value, which was readily seized upon by Safire.

In this instance, postcards and brochures were produced with Erwitt's image alongside captions such as 'And Mr. Khrushchev, *your* grandchildren will live under *freedom!*', 'Nixon Speaks with Authority He Stands with Courage', and 'Dick Nixon – the One Man to Deal with Khrushchev'. These quotations and slogans serve to anchor the image in a particular interpretative context based upon certain historicised, socialised perceptions of how a US president should act.

The image of a tough-talking Nixon, standing up to a cowed yet defiant Khrushchev, has become myth: a story told in a single image that plays into the Cold War narrative from an American perspective, and reduces both the personalities of the two men depicted and the situation to one of caricature and stereotype. Propaganda relies on the power of persuasion and leverages the documentary image to achieve this. Complicit in this is the role of the media in shaping ideas about the nation-state.[34] Despite the constant appeal to the oft-stated ideals of journalistic integrity – balance, neutrality, and objectivity – journalism is often in thrall to the spectacle. What we find is that the

[31] Gursel, *Image Brokers*, pp. 56–57.   [32] Lubben, *Magnum Contact Sheets*, p. 101.

[33] Paloschi and Attore, *Contact: Magnum Photos.*

[34] For a discussion on how propaganda, publicity images, and objectivity relate to photojournalism, and the larger role of the media with regard to nation-building, see David Levi Strauss, 'Photography and Propaganda', in *Between the Eyes: Essays on Photography and Politics* (New York: Aperture, 2005).

photograph has a particular potentiality to it, which is activated once it becomes situated within a discursive framework.

In an alternative reading of the actual event, a narrative of conviviality between Nixon and Khrushchev may have been a useful angle to bring to bear in defusing the threat of nuclear confrontation, but this is not the narrative chosen to promote Nixon's bid for the presidency or the meaning that has attached itself to this image. The ideological framing of the image has in turn impacted the perception of the 'Kitchen Debate' itself.

This has implications for how we interpret historical images: Whose story is being told, by whom, and for whom? What role does the media play, for example, in the construction of a Cold War dichotomy? How does this inform the choice of image, the selection by an editor, the moment the photographer decides to release the shutter? What are the personal politics of the photographer, in this case Erwitt, born in France to Russian parents? What personal agendas are at play? Had Safire, recognising that Erwitt was in a prime position to make images of the debate, remembered this and then used it to his advantage a short while later to further his career? Is this particular view of Nixon's character a construct, built around the equally constructed notion that a confrontational US response to the 'Red Terror' is the correct course of action? To what use and purpose are images being put, and what meanings are being imposed upon or drawn out of the frame?

Is this perhaps one of the strengths of Erwitt's image, an intimate observation of a candid moment within a carefully choreographed event becoming somehow akin to the diaristic? For myself, as a photographer I would agree that this is a compelling argument as to its affective power. As someone who is often in the position of an accredited representative of the media, herded and corralled into participating in the fabrication of a particular kind of image one might easily refer to as propaganda, I take it as part of my duty to find that unscripted moment to photograph, revealing the spectacle as a way to impart an honest, as well as accurate, representation of an event.

I often question how aware we photographers are of these processes, and how this informs the manner in which we make images. Do we reflect enough on the uses of photography and our role within the culture industry in which we participate? Today there is an important conversation surrounding the uses of photography being taken up by many professional practitioners, and elucidated by scholars, notably with Ariella Azoulay's ideas around a 'civil contract' of photography[35] and Robert Hariman and John Louis Lucaites' proposal

---

[35] See Ariella Azoulay, *The Civil Contract of Photography* (New York: Zone Books, 2008), and Ariella Azoulay, *Civil Imagination: A Political Ontology of Photography* (London: Verso, 2015).

to reframe the documentary image as 'public art'.[36] Among photojournalism's advocates of the efficacy of the image to affect social change are those who testify to the power of the traditional role of the photographer to bear objective witness, while others take up the argument that advocacy, inclusion, and representation are more important than a 'homogenizing struggle with repetitive visual tropes'.[37]

Debates on photography's relationship to the discourses on representation are not confined to scholarship, but can be found at the heart of organisations such as the venerable and perennially controversial World Press Photo.[38] However, it is still a relatively small percentage engaged publicly in these conversations. Despite the increase in photography as a means of communication between citizens, a corresponding increase in the visual literacy required to parse contextual meaning from these images seems yet to materialise. For many people, both in the professional world and outside it, the seductive power of the appearance of the photographic image means that much appreciation of photography remains a matter of superficial aesthetics. It is often also the case that as they ply their trade, professional photographers have to navigate the pitfalls of the culture industry, of propaganda, of the 'formative fictions' that are very much part of the landscape of image-making today.

---

[36] Robert Hariman and John Louis Lucaites, *The Public Image: Photography & Civic Spectatorship* (Chicago: University of Chicago Press, 2016), p. 1.

[37] Documentary photographer Nina Berman, quoted by Kainaz Amaria in an article looking at the problems of the 'toxic culture' within photojournalism and a media industry 'responsible for visually representing the world and its most vulnerable people'. Kainaz Amaria, 'Photojournalism Needs to Face Its #MeToo Moment', *Vox*, 7 September 2018, www.vox .com/2018/9/7/17761458/me-too-photojournalism-sexual-harassment-vii.

[38] See 'Investigating Important Issues', World Press Photo, www.worldpressphoto.org/programs/ explore/debate-and-research/28565 and 'Witness' at WorldPressPhoto.org, https://witness .worldpressphoto.org, for research and articles on various topics on photojournalism's past, present, and future.

Index

www.ingramcontent.com/pod-product-compliance
Ingram Content Group UK Ltd.
Pitfield, Milton Keynes, MK11 3LW, UK
UKHW022323310125
454380UK00006BA/27